Kickstart MySQL Fundamentals

Build Real-World Databases, Query with Confidence, and Optimize Data Using Advanced MySQL and SQL Skills

Amit Diwan

www.orangeava.com

First Published: August 2025

Published By: Orange Education Pvt Ltd, AVA®

Address: 9, Daryaganj, Delhi, 110002, India

275 New North Road Islington Suite 1314 London,

N1 7AA, United Kingdom

ISBN (PBK): 978-93-49888-64-7

ISBN (E-BOOK): 978-93-49888-82-1

Scan the QR code to explore our entire catalogue

www.orangeava.com

Dedicated To

My Family,

And

My Love for Teaching and Cricket

About the Author

Amit Diwan is the founder of **Studyopedia.com** and the creator of the tech YouTube channel **"Amit Thinks"**, which has **over 255k+ subscribers.** The channel receives 2.2 million organic views per month and serves more than 1.3 million unique visitors monthly.

Amit's interest in educational projects grew after completing his basic schooling. He completed a BCA and then an MCA from GGSIPU. In his final MCA year, faced with career choices, he preferred freelancing and took on his first Python project at age 22. After graduation, he received an offer from Accenture but spent the three-month waiting period working at IIT Delhi—an opportunity he valued highly. As a result, he decided not to join Accenture. From the beginning, Amit aimed to start his own IT company, so he focused on his role at IIT (under RDI) while continuing freelancing assignments on the side.

Amit's freelancing clients included top e-learning sites like Tutorialspoint and Sitepoint. He has created content across 40+ technologies, producing over 60,000 articles, code snippets, and videos. He also developed e-learning courses for students and professionals.

Amit launched his YouTube channel, *Amit Thinks*, along with his website, *Studyopedia.com*, to offer courses in Programming, AI, Web Development, and Databases for students, engineers, and professionals. By May 2025, his channel had amassed over 80 million views, 1.3 million unique monthly visitors, more than 2.6 million hours of watch time, 400 million impressions, and over 255,000 subscribers.

In August 2024, Amit launched Studyopedia Certifications, offering QR code-verified, ATS-compatible certificates for students, engineers, and professionals upon course completion. These certificates can be easily shared on LinkedIn with a unique verification ID. He has also launched over 40 courses in programming, AI, web development, and databases, with more than 70,000 enrollments across top EdTech platforms like Tutorialspoint, Skillshare, Packt, Eduonix, and others. Recognizing the value of quality education, Amit remains committed to sharing his knowledge and inspiring others—particularly through this book, focused on mastering MySQL databases.

About the Technical Reviewer

Tejbeer is a Senior Software Developer with deep expertise in building scalable, end-to-end applications using modern technologies. She specializes in both front-end and back-end development, with a focus on microservices architecture, enterprise application design, and user-centric web interfaces. Over the years, she has contributed to high-impact B2B and B2C projects across various industries, including e-commerce, telecom, insurance, and fintech.

Tejbeer is proficient in a wide range of technologies, including Java, Spring Boot, Angular, Hibernate, JavaScript, as well as mobile development tools such as Ionic and Android SDK. She also has extensive hands-on experience with both relational and NoSQL databases such as MySQL, Cassandra, and MongoDB, providing her a comprehensive view of data handling in distributed systems.

A passionate problem-solver and lifelong learner, Tejbeer thrives on building innovative solutions that make a meaningful impact. She is driven by curiosity, collaboration, and a constant desire to grow, both personally and professionally, in the ever-evolving world of technology!

Acknowledgements

I am deeply grateful to the many individuals who supported me throughout the writing of this book. First and foremost, I would like to express my sincere thanks to my family for their unwavering encouragement and belief in my abilities. Their support has been invaluable in helping me complete this project.

I am also indebted to the team at Orange Education Pvt Ltd for their exceptional support and guidance. Their patience and understanding allowed me to dedicate the necessary time to complete this book. Their valuable suggestions and insights were instrumental in ensuring the quality and accuracy of the content.

I am truly grateful for the contributions of everyone who has been a part of in this journey. Their support has been indispensable to the successful completion and publication of this book.

Preface

This book is a definitive guide to mastering MySQL, the world's most popular open-source relational database. So whether you are a beginner or an experienced developer, you will gain hands-on expertise in designing, querying, and optimizing databases efficiently. From foundational concepts such as constraints and operators to advanced techniques such as joins and indexing, each chapter builds your skills for real-world data management.

You will also explore MySQL's core functionalities, including built-in functions, statements, and user management, through practical examples that bridge theory and application. Learn how to write efficient SQL queries, design scalable databases, and enhance performance—essential skills for developers, analysts, and IT professionals.

The book covers critical optimization strategies, ensuring your databases are fast, secure, and reliable. By the end, you will be equipped to confidently handle complex data tasks, from troubleshooting queries to managing multi-user environments.

Structured into 12 focused chapters, this book balances depth and clarity, offering step-by-step guidance for every skill level. With clear explanations and actionable exercises, you can also unlock MySQL's full potential and elevate your database expertise. The detailed outline is as follows:

Chapter 1 introduces MySQL, a powerful open-source Relational Database Management System (RDBMS) widely used for web applications and data-driven solutions. Readers will explore the fundamentals of RDBMS, the history and evolution of MySQL, its key features, advantages, and limitations. The chapter also compares SQL and NoSQL databases, helping learners choose the right approach for their projects.

The lesson concludes with a practical guide to setting up the MySQL environment, including installation and an introduction to MySQL Workbench—a popular GUI tool for database management. By the end, readers will understand MySQL's role in modern data storage and be ready to start working with databases.

Chapter 2 dives into hands-on MySQL operations, teaching readers how to create databases and tables, insert records, and write basic queries. The key topics include the SELECT statement for data retrieval, filtering results with WHERE and DISTINCT, and using data types to define table structures. The chapter also introduces vital clauses such as LIMIT and AUTO_INCREMENT for efficient data handling.

The book contains practical examples that demonstrate how to add comments and column aliases, ensuring clarity in SQL scripts. By the end, learners will be comfortable executing foundational MySQL commands, and managing simple datasets.

Chapter 3 explores database integrity through constraints which enforce rules on table data. Readers will learn about primary keys (for unique identification), foreign keys (for table relationships), and constraints such as UNIQUE, NOT NULL, CHECK, and DEFAULT. These concepts ensure data accuracy and consistency.

The chapter also covers modifying the existing tables by adding or dropping constraints dynamically. Thus, by mastering these techniques, learners can design robust databases that prevent invalid data entries.

Chapter 4 focuses on MySQL operators necessary for filtering and manipulating query results. Logical operators (AND, OR, NOT), comparison operators (IN, BETWEEN), and pattern-matching with LIKE are explained with real-world examples. These tools enable precise data extraction.

Readers will practice combining operators to create complex conditions, enhancing their ability to query databases efficiently. The chapter also emphasizes practical use cases such as searching for ranges or partial matches in datasets.

Chapter 5 introduces MySQL's built-in functions for string, numeric, date, and aggregate operations. Readers will learn to format text, perform calculations, manipulate dates, and summarize data, using functions such as COUNT(), SUM(), and AVG().

These functions streamline data processing, eliminating the need for manual coding. By the end of this chapter, learners will be adept at optimizing queries with built-in functionality.

Chapter 6 covers essential SQL statements for data modification and structure management. The key commands include UPDATE (editing records), DELETE (removing data), and DROP (deleting tables/databases). The ORDER BY and CASE statements are also explored for sorting and conditional logic.

Practical examples demonstrate how to restructure databases, and refine query outputs, equipping learners with skills for dynamic data manipulation.

Chapter 7 explains joins that combine data from multiple tables. Readers will master INNER, LEFT, RIGHT, CROSS, and FULL joins, along with performance optimization techniques. Joins are critical for relational database workflows.

The book also includes real-world scenarios that illustrate how joins resolve complex queries such as merging customer orders with product details. By the end of this chapter, learners can efficiently query interconnected tables.

Chapter 8 delves into indexes which improve query speed by optimizing data retrieval. Topics include creating, displaying, and dropping indexes, with specialized types such as UNIQUE and clustered indexes.

Readers will learn to balance performance gains with storage overhead, ensuring efficient database design for large datasets.

Chapter 9 addresses user management and security in MySQL. Readers will create/drop users, reset passwords, and assign privileges (GRANT, REVOKE). Best practices for securing database access are also emphasized.

This chapter ensures that learners can administer multi-user environments while preventing unauthorized access.

Chapter 10 explores advanced features such as triggers, views, transactions, and stored procedures. Full-text search and partitioning are also covered, enabling sophisticated data operations.

These tools empower readers to automate tasks, maintain data integrity, and handle complex queries efficiently.

Chapter 11 ties together miscellaneous but vital topics such as GROUP BY, HAVING, table alterations, backups, and performance tips. Error handling and future trends round out the discussion.

By the end of this chapter, learners will gain a holistic understanding of database maintenance, and optimization strategies.

Chapter 12 guides readers through building a University Management System, applying all prior lessons. From database creation to advanced features, such as triggers and stored procedures, the project reinforces practical skills.

By completing this capstone project, learners will confidently design, query, and manage real-world MySQL databases.

Get a Free eBook

We hope you are enjoying your recently purchased book! Your feedback is incredibly valuable to us, and to all other readers looking for great books.

If you found this book helpful or enjoyable, we would truly appreciate it, if you could take a moment to leave a short review with a 5 star rating on Amazon. It helps us grow, and lets other readers discover our books.

As a thank you, we would love to send you a free digital copy of this book, and a **30%** discount code on your next cart value on our official websites:

www.orangeava.com

www.orangeava.in (For Indian Subcontinent)

☑ **Here's how:**

Leave a review for the book on Amazon.

Take a screenshot of your review, and send an email to **info@orangeava.com** (it can be just the confirmation screen).

Once, we receive your screenshot, we will send you the digital file, within 24 hours.

Thank you so much for your support – it means a lot to us!

Colored Images

Please follow the links or scan the QR codes to download the ***Images*** of the book:

You can find code bundles of our books on our official Github Repository. Go to the following link to and QR code to explore the further:

https://github.com/orgs/ava-orange-education/repositories

Please follow the link to download the Colored Images of the book:
https://rebrand.ly/2da460

In case there's an update to the code, it will be updated on the existing GitHub repository.

Errata

We take immense pride in our work at **Orange Education Pvt Ltd,** and follow best practices to ensure the accuracy of our content to provide an indulging reading experience to our subscribers. Our readers are our mirrors, and we use their inputs to reflect and improve upon human errors, if any, that may have occurred during the publishing processes involved. To let us maintain the quality and help us reach out to any readers who might be having difficulties due to any unforeseen errors, please write to us at :

errata@orangeava.com

Your support, suggestions, and feedback are highly appreciated.

DID YOU KNOW

Did you know that Orange Education Pvt Ltd offers eBook versions of every book published, with PDF and ePub files available? You can upgrade to the eBook version at **www.orangeava.com** and as a print book customer, you are entitled to a discount on the eBook copy. Get in touch with us at: **info@orangeava.com** for more details.

At **www.orangeava.com**, you can also read a collection of free technical articles, sign up for a range of free newsletters, and receive exclusive discounts and offers on Print Books and eBooks.

PIRACY

If you come across any illegal copies of our works in any form on the internet, we would be grateful if you would provide us with the location address or website name. Please contact us at **info@orangeava.com** with a link to the material.

ARE YOU INTERESTED IN AUTHORING WITH US?

If there is a topic that you have expertise in, and you are interested in either writing or contributing to a book, please write to us at **business@orangeava.com**. We are on a journey to help developers and tech professionals to gain insights on the present technological advancements and innovations happening across the globe and build a community that believes Knowledge is best acquired by sharing and learning with others. Please reach out to us to learn what our audience demands and how you can be part of this educational reform. We also welcome ideas from tech experts and help them build learning and development content for their domains.

REVIEWS

Please leave a review. Once you have read and used this book, why not leave a review on the site that you purchased it from? Potential readers can then see and use your unbiased opinion to make purchase decisions. We at Orange Education would love to know what you think about our products, and our authors can learn from your feedback. Thank you!

For more information about Orange Education, please visit **www.orangeava.com**.

Table of Contents

CHAPTER 1
Introduction to MySQL

Introduction

This chapter covers what RDBMS is and how MySQL is related to it. MySQL will also be introduced, along with its setup and examples. We will cover the current version of MySQL and how to set it up. This will be a benchmark for us in the upcoming chapters.

After completing this chapter, the readers will be able to understand RDBMS, MySQL, SQL, and so on. They will also be able to set up MySQL on their local system.

Structure

In this chapter, we will discuss the following topics:

- Introduction to RDBMS
- Overview of MySQL
- History of MySQL
- Features of MySQL
- Advantages of MySQL
- Disadvantages of MySQL
- MySQL Editions
- SQL vs NoSQL
- Setting Up MySQL Environment
- MySQL Workbench

Introduction to RDBMS

Relational Database Management System (RDBMS) is a type of database management system that stores data in a structured format, using rows and columns. It is based on the relational model, which was introduced by E.F. Codd in 1970. In an RDBMS, data is stored in tables, and relationships between tables are established using keys.

The most common language used to interact with RDBMS is SQL (Structured Query Language).

Features of RDBMS

RDBMS features include:

- **Structured Data Storage:** Data is stored in tables with predefined schemas, ensuring consistency and integrity.
- **SQL (Structured Query Language):** Used to query, manipulate, and manage data (for example, SELECT, INSERT, UPDATE, DELETE).
- **ACID Compliance:** Ensures reliable transactions with Atomicity, Consistency, Isolation, and Durability.
- **Relationships:** Supports relationships between tables using primary keys, foreign keys, and joins.
- **Scalability:** It handles small to large datasets, though scaling can be complex.
- **Data Integrity:** Enforces constraints (for example, unique, not null) to maintain accuracy.
- **Security:** Provides user authentication, authorization, and encryption.

Popular RDBMS include **MySQL**, **PostgreSQL**, **Oracle**, **SQL Server**, and **SQLite**. In this book, we will cover MySQL and its concepts. Let us begin with an overview of MySQL.

Overview of MySQL

MySQL is one of the most popular open-source relational database management systems. It was originally developed by MySQL AB, which was later acquired by Oracle Corporation. MySQL is widely used for web applications and is a key component of the LAMP (Linux, Apache, MySQL, PHP/Python/Perl) stack.

History of MySQL

MySQL is an open-source Relational Database Management System (RDBMS) that has become a popular choice for web applications.

Here is a brief history of MySQL:

Early Beginnings (1979-1995)

- MySQL's roots date back to 1979 when Michael Widenius, a Finnish software developer, began working on a database system called Unireg.

- In the 1980s, Widenius and his colleague, David Axmark, developed a new database system called MySQL, which was first released in 1995.

Open-Source and Growth (1995-2008)

- MySQL was initially released as an open-source project, allowing developers to freely use, modify, and distribute the software.
- In 2001, MySQL AB, a Swedish company, was founded by Widenius, Axmark, and Allan Larsson to oversee the development and commercialization of MySQL.
- MySQL gained popularity as a fast, reliable, and scalable database solution, especially for web applications built using PHP.

Acquisition by Sun Microsystems and Oracle (2008-2010)

- In 2008, Sun Microsystems acquired MySQL AB for $1 billion (approximately).
- In 2010, Oracle Corporation acquired Sun Microsystems, including MySQL, for $7.4 billion (approximately).

Continued Development and Community Support (2010-Present)

- Despite concerns about Oracle's ownership, MySQL continues to be actively developed and maintained by Oracle and the open-source community.
- MySQL remains a widely used database solution with a large community of developers and users contributing to its growth and improvement.

Today, MySQL is used by many high-traffic websites, including Facebook, Twitter, and YouTube, and is a popular choice for web applications, big data analytics, and cloud computing.

Features of MySQL

The following are the features of MySQL:

- **Open Source**: MySQL is freely available under the GNU General Public License (GPL).
- **Scalability**: It handles large datasets and high traffic efficiently.
- **High Performance**: Optimized for fast read/write operations.
- **Security**: Provides robust data security with features such as SSL support, password encryption, and user authentication.

- **Cross-Platform Support**: It runs on various operating systems, including Windows, Linux, and macOS.
- **Replication and Clustering**: Supports master-slave replication and clustering for high availability and fault tolerance.
- **Stored Procedures and Triggers**: Allows the creation of stored procedures, functions, and triggers for complex business logic.
- **Full-Text Search**: Supports full-text indexing and searching.
- **ACID Compliance**: Ensures data integrity with ACID properties.

Advantages of MySQL

The following are the advantages of MySQL:

- **Open Source and Free:** MySQL is open-source, with a free community version, making it cost-effective for many users.
- **Ease of Use:** Simple to install, configure, and manage, with a user-friendly interface and extensive documentation.
- **High Performance:** Optimized for fast data retrieval and processing, even with large datasets.
- **Scalability:** It handles small to large-scale applications efficiently, supporting vertical and horizontal scaling.
- **Cross-Platform Compatibility:** Works on multiple operating systems, including Linux, Windows, and macOS.
- **Strong Community Support:** A Large, active community provides resources, tutorials, and troubleshooting assistance.
- **Security:** It offers robust security features such as encryption, user authentication, and access control.
- **ACID Compliance:** Ensures data integrity with support for transactions (via InnoDB).
- **Integration:** Seamlessly integrates with popular programming languages (for example, PHP, Python, Java) and frameworks.
- **Flexibility:** Supports multiple storage engines (for example, InnoDB, MyISAM) for different use cases.

Disadvantages of MySQL

The following are the disadvantages of MySQL:

- **Scalability Limitations:** While scalable, it may struggle with extremely large datasets or high-concurrency environments compared to NoSQL databases.

- **Transactional Support:** Only InnoDB supports full ACID transactions; other storage engines such as MyISAM do not.
- **Complex Queries:** Performance can degrade with highly complex queries or large joins.
- **Proprietary Extensions:** Some advanced features are only available in the paid Enterprise version.
- **Limited Customizability:** It is less flexible than other databases in terms of customization and extensibility.
- **Concurrency Issues:** Under heavy load, performance may suffer due to table-level locking in certain storage engines.
- **No Built-in NoSQL Support:** Unlike some modern databases, MySQL does not natively support NoSQL features.

Applications of MySQL

MySQL is one of the most popular open-source Relational Database Management Systems (RDBMS). It is widely used across various industries and applications due to its reliability, performance, and ease of use. Here are some key applications of MySQL:

- **Web Applications**
  - **Content Management Systems (CMS):**

    MySQL is the backend database for many CMS platforms such as **WordPress, Drupal, and Joomla**.
  - **E-commerce Platforms:**

    Used by **Magento, WooCommerce, Shopify (via APIs), and PrestaShop** to store product catalogs, customer data, and transactions.
  - **Social Media and Forums:**

    Powers databases for platforms such as **Facebook (historically), Twitter (partially), and phpBB**.
- **Enterprise Applications**
  - **Customer Relationship Management (CRM):**

    Used in systems such as **SugarCRM and SuiteCRM** to manage customer interactions.
  - **Enterprise Resource Planning (ERP):**

    Supports databases for **Odoo, ERPNext, and Dolibarr**.

  - **Human Resource Management (HRM):**

    Helps store employee records, payroll, and attendance data.

- **Data Warehousing and Business Intelligence**
  - **Reporting and Analytics:**

    MySQL works with BI tools such as **Tableau, Power BI, and Metabase** for data analysis.

  - **Log and Transaction Storage:**

    Used to store logs, user activity, and financial transactions for auditing.

- **Cloud and SaaS Applications**
  - **Cloud Databases:**

    Offered as a managed service in **Amazon RDS, Google Cloud SQL, and Azure Database for MySQL.**

  - **Software as a Service (SaaS):**

    Many SaaS providers use MySQL for multi-tenant architectures.

- **Embedded Systems and IoT**
  - **IoT Data Storage:**

    Stores sensor data, device logs, and telemetry in IoT applications.

  - **Industrial Automation:**

    Used in SCADA systems for managing equipment data.

- **Mobile and Gaming Applications**
  - **Mobile Backend Databases:**

    Used with backend frameworks such as **Node.js, Django, and Laravel** for mobile apps.

  - **Online Gaming:**

    Stores player profiles, leaderboards, and in-game transactions.

- **Financial and Banking Systems**
  - **Payment Processing:**

    Used by fintech apps to store transaction records securely.

  - **Fraud Detection:**

    Helps analyze transaction patterns for suspicious activity.

- **Education and Research**
    - **Learning Management Systems (LMS):**

      Supports platforms such as **Moodle and Blackboard**.
    - **Scientific Data Management:**

      Stores research data in academic and scientific projects.
- **Government and Healthcare**
    - **Healthcare Records:**

      Manages patient data in **hospital management systems** (with proper security compliance).
    - **Public Sector Databases:**

      Used for citizen records, taxation, and administrative data.
- **High-Performance Applications**
    - **Scalable Web Services:**

      Used by companies such as **YouTube, Uber, and Airbnb** (in some parts of their infrastructure).
    - **Caching and Session Storage:**

      Works with **Redis or Memcached** for faster data retrieval.

Its ease of use, strong community support, and integration with popular programming languages make it a preferred choice for developers worldwide.

MySQL Editions

MySQL offers several editions to cater to different needs and use cases. Here are the main MySQL editions:

- **MySQL Community Server**
    - **Free and Open-Source**: Available under the GPL license.
    - **Community-Driven**: Developed and maintained by the open-source community.
    - **Features**: Includes most of the standard MySQL features, such as support for InnoDB, MyISAM, and other storage engines.
- **MySQL Enterprise Edition**
    - **Commercial License**: Requires a paid subscription.

- **Additional Features**: Includes advanced features such as Oracle Enterprise Manager integration, MySQL Enterprise Backup, and MySQL Enterprise Firewall.
- **Support**: It offers 24/7 support, including phone, email, and online support.

- **MySQL Cluster Carrier Grade Edition**
  - **High-Availability**: Designed for high availability and scalability in carrier-grade environments.
  - **Real-Time Performance**: Optimized for real-time performance and low latency.
  - **Additional Features**: Includes features such as MySQL Cluster Manager and MySQL Cluster Backup.
- **MySQL Embedded (OEM/ISV)**
  - **Original Equipment Manufacturer (OEM) and Independent Software Vendor (ISV)**: Designed for OEMs and ISVs who want to embed MySQL into their products.
  - **Customizable**: Allows for customization and rebranding.
  - **Support**: Offers support and training for OEM/ISV partners.
- **MySQL Classic Edition**
  - **Legacy Support**: Designed for legacy systems and applications that require older versions of MySQL.
  - **Maintenance and Support**: It offers maintenance and support for older versions.

Each MySQL edition is tailored to specific use cases and requirements. The choice edition depends on factors such as the level of support needed, the required features, and the intended use case.

Note: *In this book, we will cover the MySQL Community Edition, which is free and open-source.*

SQL vs. NoSQL

SQL is often compared with NoSQL databases. Let us see the differences between SQL and NoSQL:

Basis	SQL (Relational Databases)	NoSQL (Non-Relational Databases)
Data Model	Structured, table-based (rows and columns).	Flexible, document-based, key-value, graph, or wide-column.
Schema	Fixed schema (predefined structure).	Dynamic schema (schema-less).

Scalability	Vertical scaling (adding more resources to a single server).	Horizontal scaling (adding more servers).
ACID Compliance	Fully ACID-compliant.	May not fully support ACID (often BASE: Basically Available, Soft state, Eventual consistency).
Use Cases	Complex queries, transactions, and structured data.	Unstructured data, real-time applications, big data.
Examples	MySQL, PostgreSQL, Oracle, SQL Server.	MongoDB, Cassandra, Redis, Couchbase.
Performance	Optimized for complex queries and joins.	Optimized for high-speed read/write operations.
Relationships	Supports relationships (foreign keys, joins).	Relationships are not natively supported (handled in application logic).

Table 1.1: *Differences between SQL and NoSQL*

Setting Up MySQL Environment

Let us see the steps to set up MySQL on Windows 11. We will install the current version, i.e., **MySQL 8.0.41**:

Step 1: Download MySQL

Go to the official website of MySQL, i.e., **`mysql.com`**

Figure 1.1: *The official MySQL website*

We clicked the **`DOWNLOADS`** menu to reach the downloads section, as shown in *Figure 1.2:*

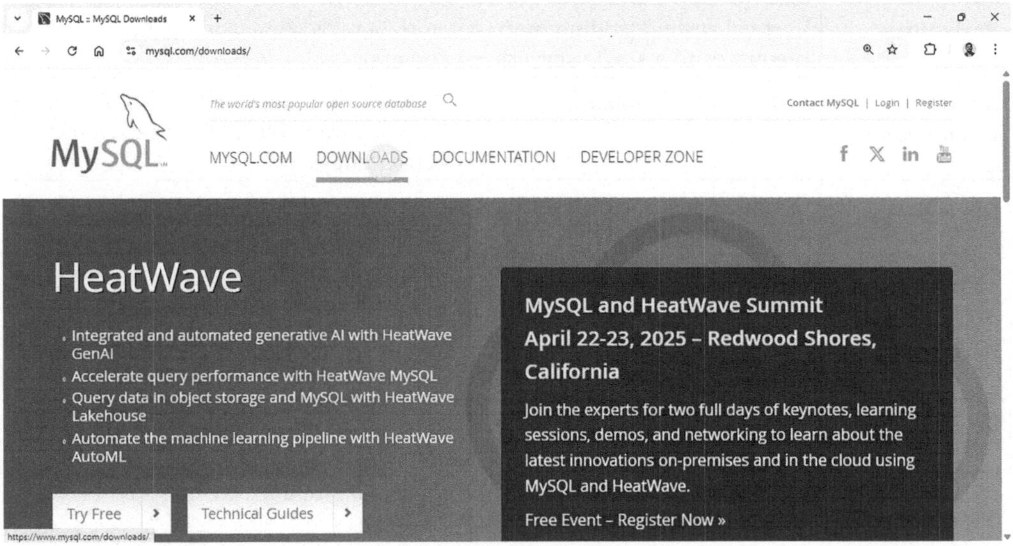

Figure 1.2: *Click the DOWNLOADS menu*

Then, click **`MySQL Community (GPL) Downloads`**:

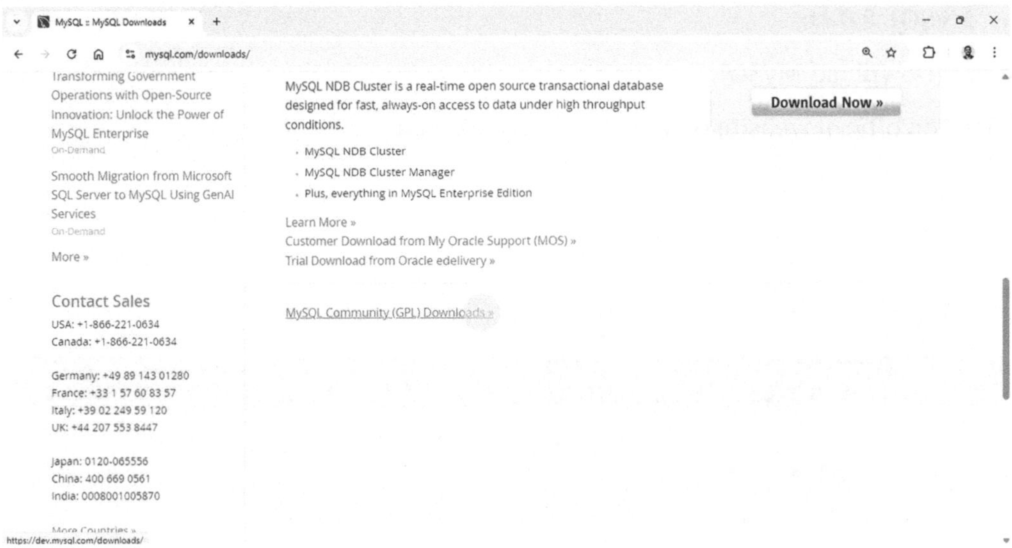

Figure 1.3: *Click MySQL Community Downloads*

Now, you will reach the **`MySQL Community Downloads`** section. Click **`MySQL Installer for Windows`**:

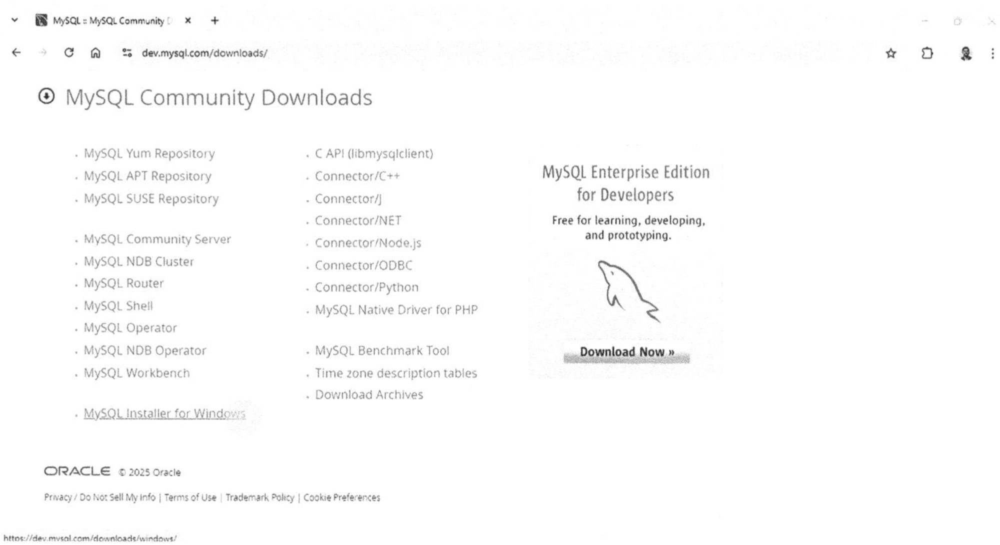

Figure 1.4: *Click MySQL Installer for Windows*

The current version of MySQL is visible. Two versions of MySQL are provided for download. We will download the 2nd version, as shown in the screenshot in *Figure 1.5*.

This version works for both 32-bit and 64-bit Windows systems. Click the **`Download`** button for the 2nd version.

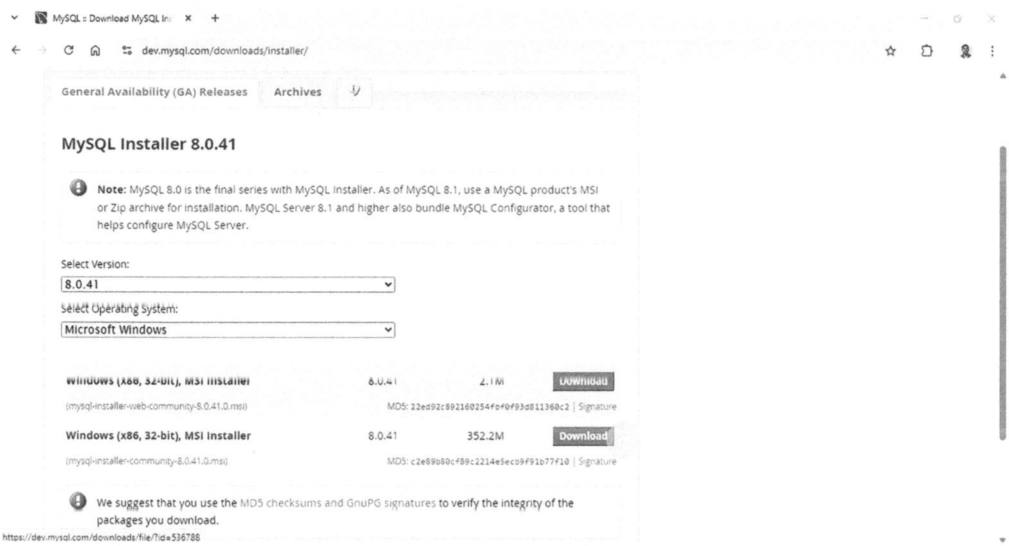

Figure 1.5: *Click the Download button*

Now, select, **`No thanks, just start my download`**:

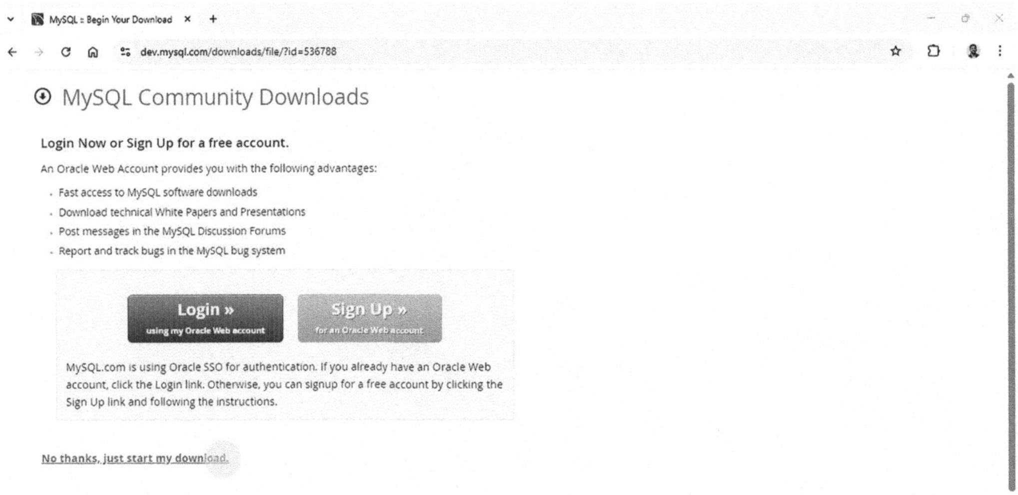

Figure 1.6: *Click no thanks, just start by download link*

The download started and was completed. Double-click the **`.msi`** executable file to begin the installation:

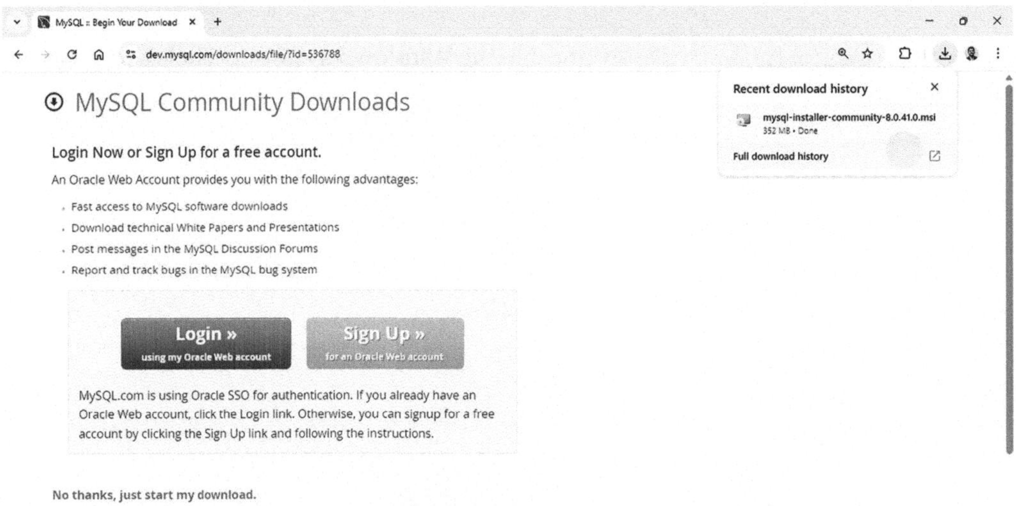

Figure 1.7: *MySQL executable file downloading*

Step 2: Choose a Setup Type

The installation started. Select the setup type. Click **`Custom`** and click **`Next`**:

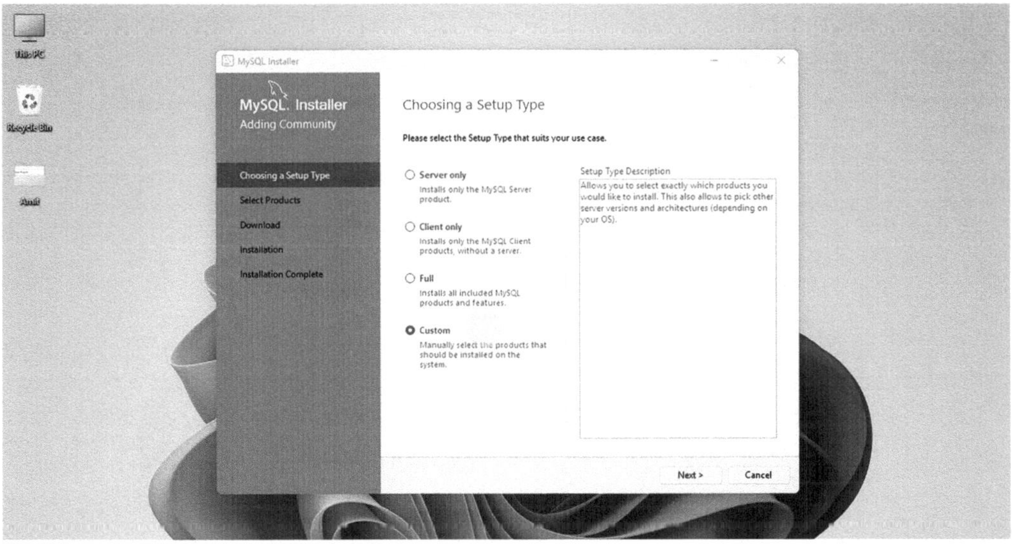

Figure 1.8: *Select Custom Setup Type*

Step 3: Select and install MySQL products

Now, select the products. We will move the **`MySQL Server`**, **`MySQL Shell`**, and **`MySQL Workbench`** from **`Available Products`** to the right so that we can install them. After that, click **`Next`**:

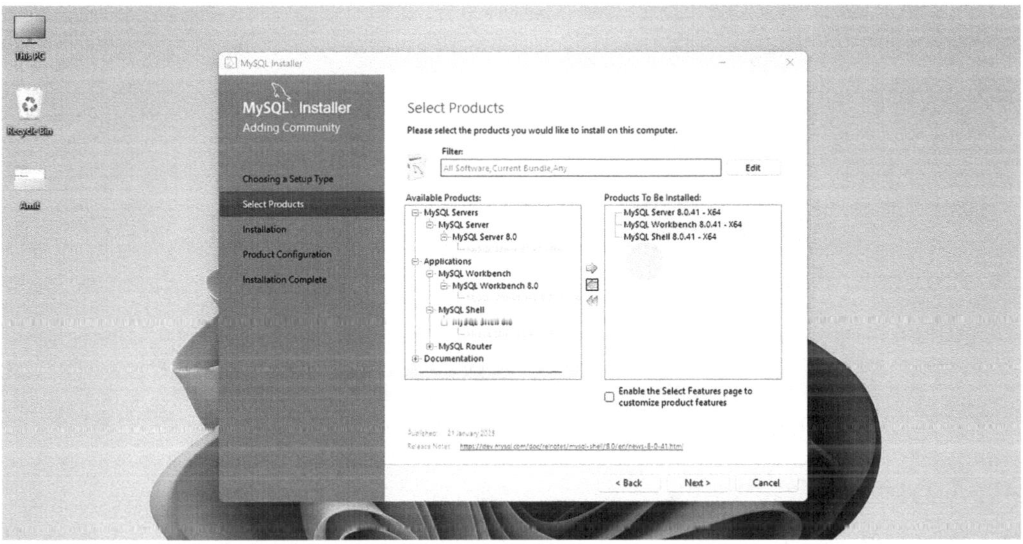

Figure 1.9: *Move the products to be installed*

After clicking **`Next`**, click **`Execute`**, and all three products will be installed one by one. For all the products, the status should be **`Complete`** so that we can proceed:

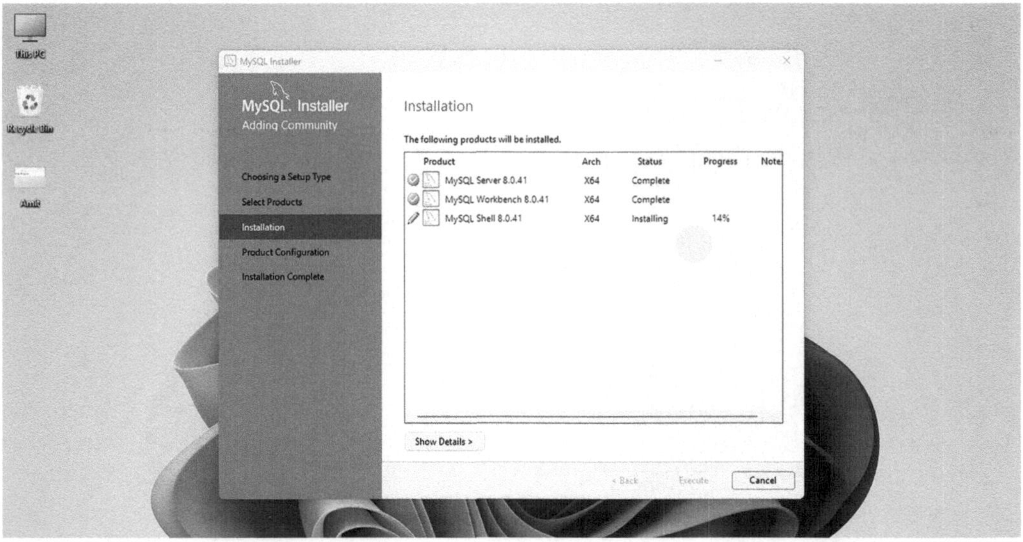

Figure 1.10: MySQL Server, Shell, and Workbench installing

The status is **Complete** for all three products. Now, click **Next**:

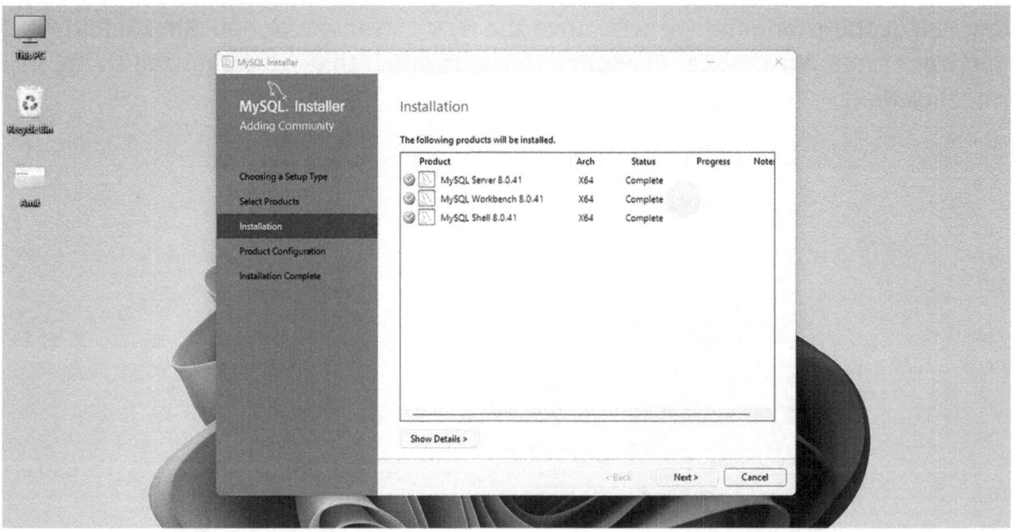

Figure 1.11: MySQL Server, Workbench, and Shell installed

Step 4: Type and Networking

The Type and Networking section is visible. The port number is 3306. Keep it as it is and click **Next**:

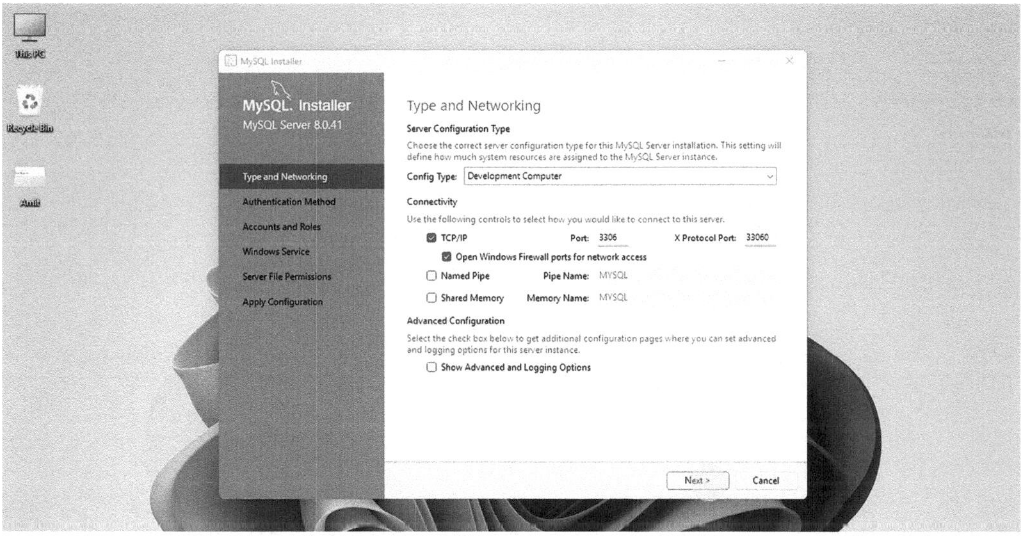

Figure 1.12: *Type and Networking section*

Step 5: Authentication

We will reach the **`Authentication Method`** section. Keep the default, that is, **`Use String Password`** as it is recommended. Click **`Next:`**

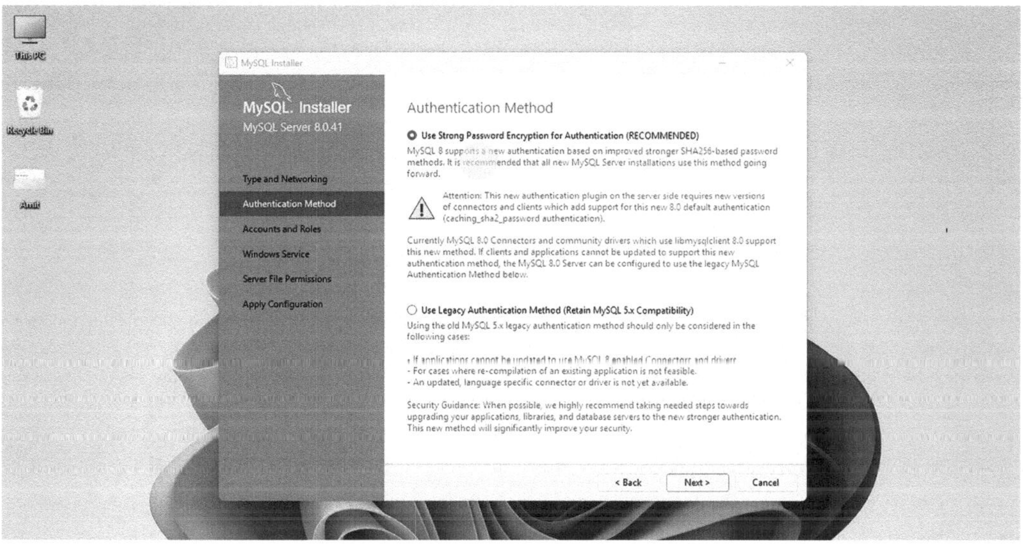

Figure 1.13: *Use Strong Password Encryption*

The **`Accounts and Roles`** section can now be seen. Set the password for the root. The username for the admin is **`root.`** Add any password and click **`Next:`**

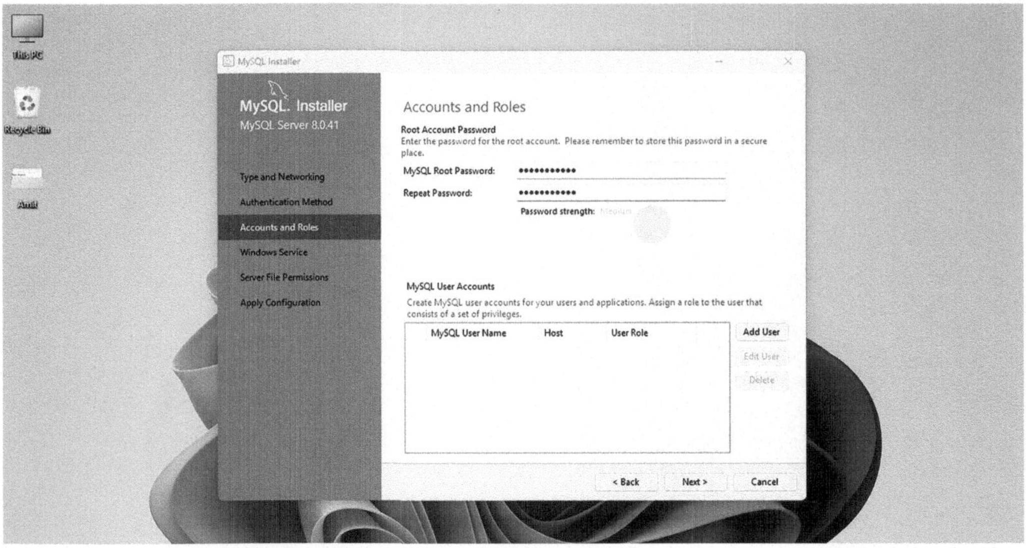

Figure 1.14: *Set a password for the MySQL Server*

Step 6: Windows Service

The Windows service section is visible. Keep it as it is and click **Next**:

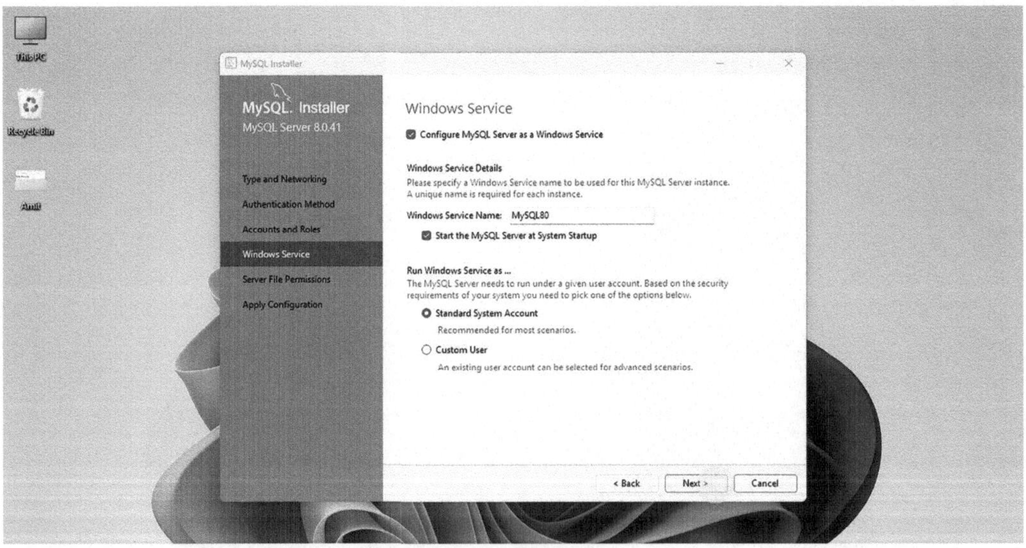

Figure 1.15: *Windows Service*

Step 7: Server File Permissions

The Server File Permissions section is visible. This is the location where your databases will get saved. Keep it as it is, that is, **`Yes, grant full access...`**" and click **Next**:

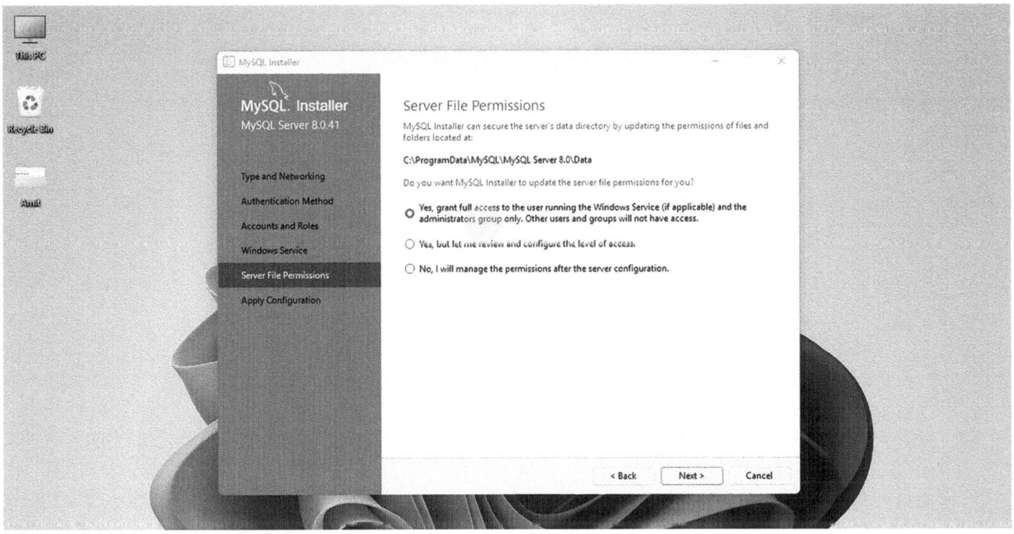

Figure 1.16: *Server File Permissions*

Step 8: Apply Configuration

We have reached the **Apply Configuration** section. Click **Execute**:

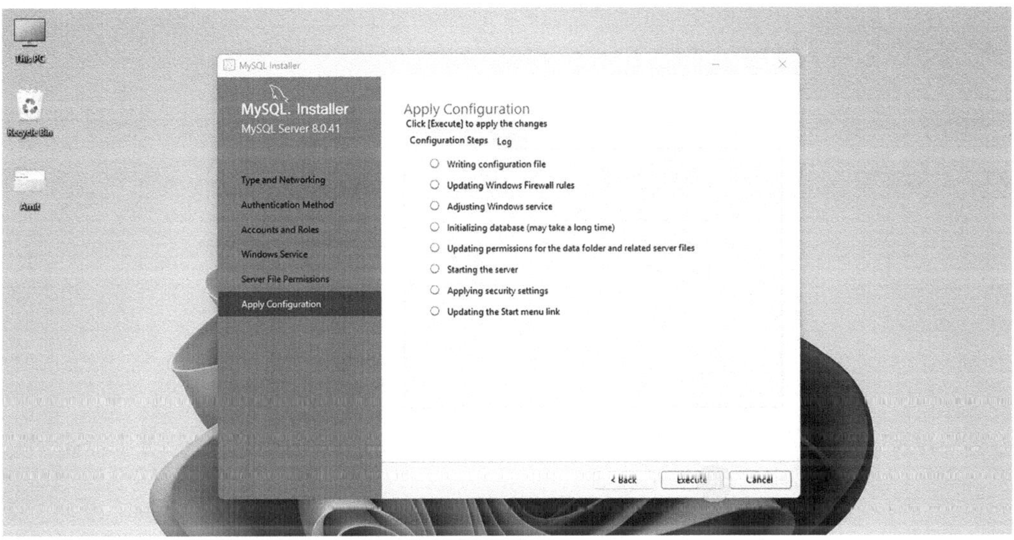

Figure 1.17: *Apply configuration*

After the above is completed, the following will be visible, that is, the configuration will be successful. Click **Finish**:

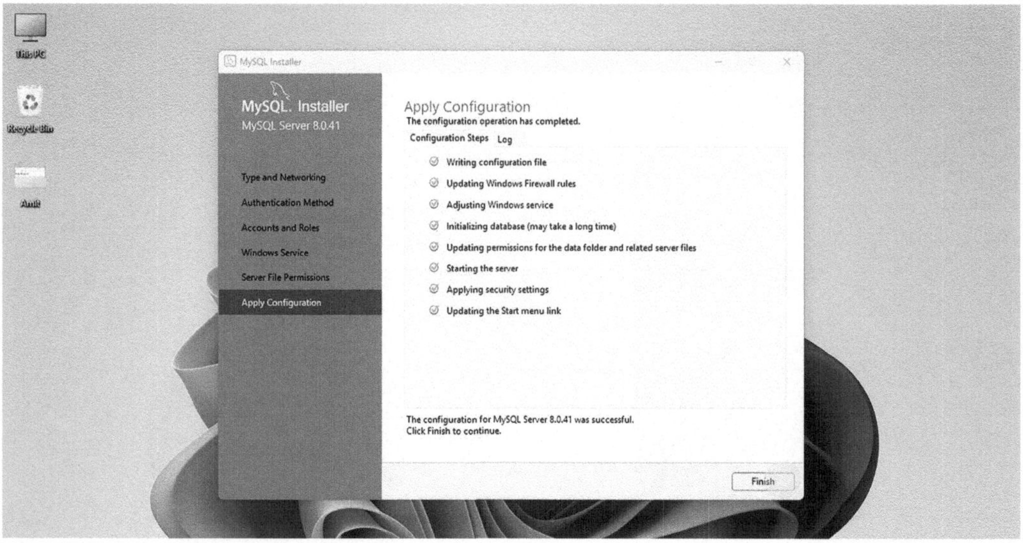

***Figure 1.18:** MySQL configuration is successful*

Installation completed successfully. On clicking **`Finish`**, the shell and workbench will open:

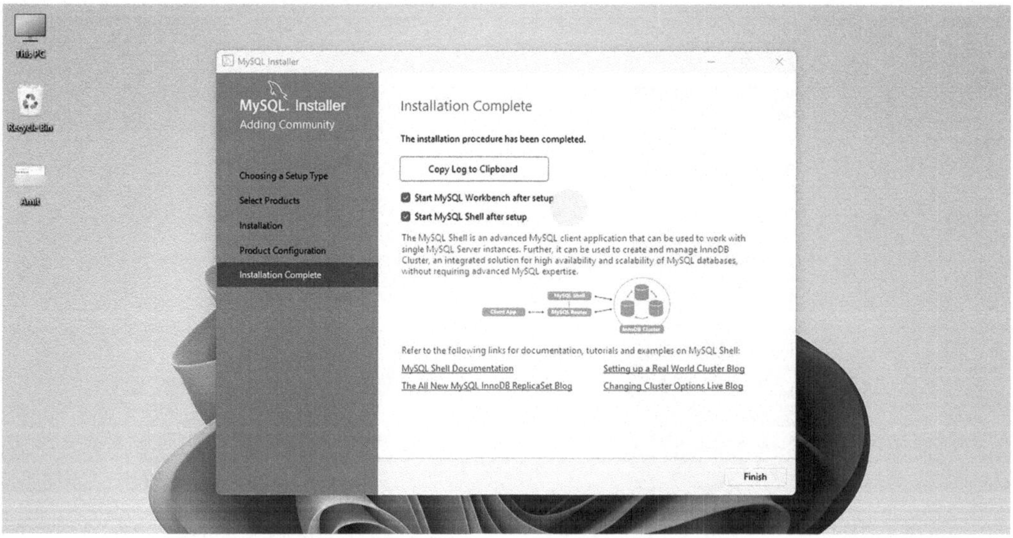

***Figure 1.19:** MySQL installation completed*

The shell and workbench open:

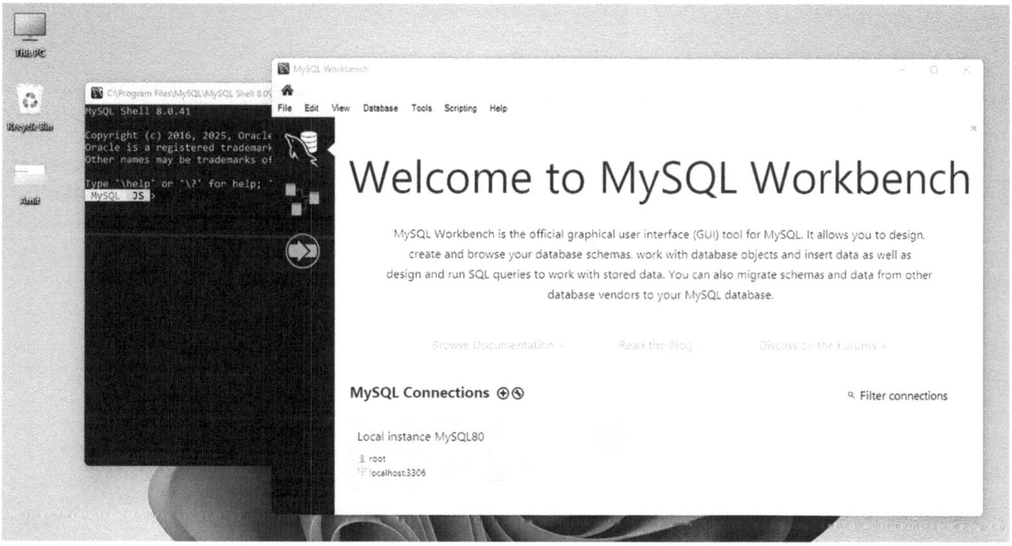

Figure 1.20: *MySQL Workbench opens up*

Step 8: Set the Environment Variables

Before moving further, set the MySQL path. This will allow us to start the MySQL Server from anywhere without reaching the MySQL bin path.

Go to the location where we installed MySQL, that is, the C: drive. Get the following **`bin`** path:

C:\Program Files\MySQL\MySQL Server 8.0\bin

Copy the **`bin`** path, as shown in the following screenshot:

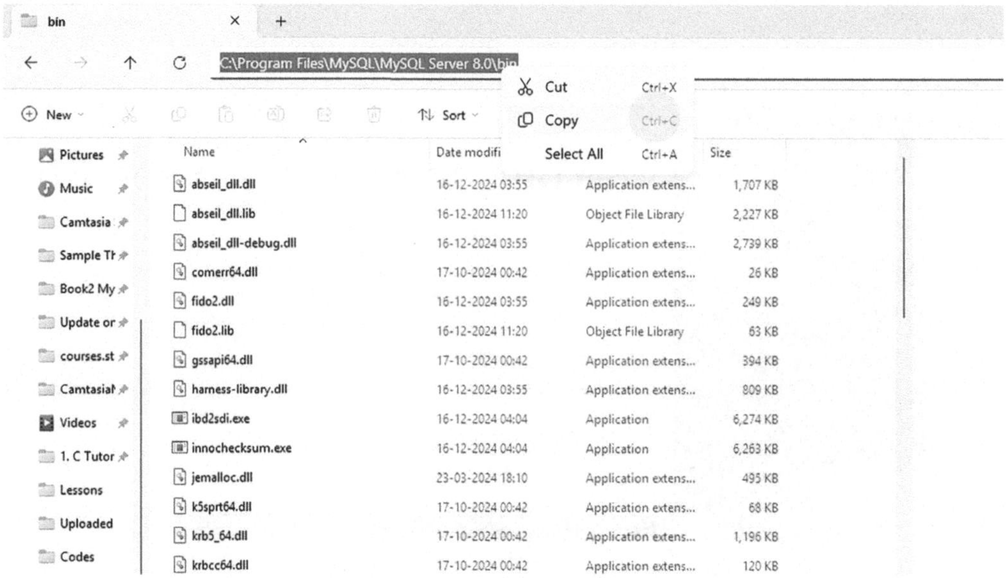

Figure 1.21: *Copy the bin path*

Go to **`START`**, type **`Environment Variables`**, and click **`Open`** to **`Edit the system environment variables`**, as shown in *Figure 1.22*:

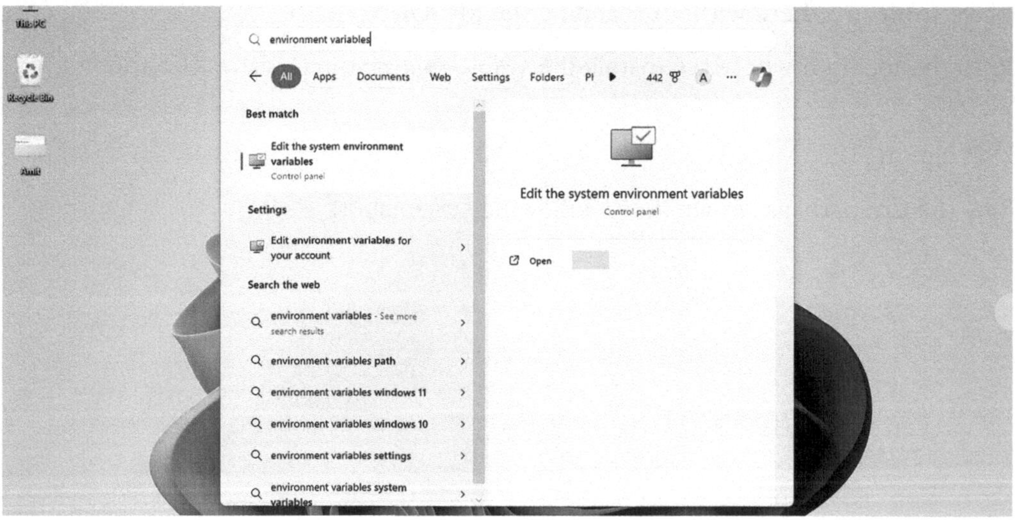

Figure 1.22: *Open the system environment variables*

Under **`System Properties`**, click **`Environment Variables`**. Now, double-click the **`Path`** under the **`System Variables`**, as shown in *Figure 1.23*:

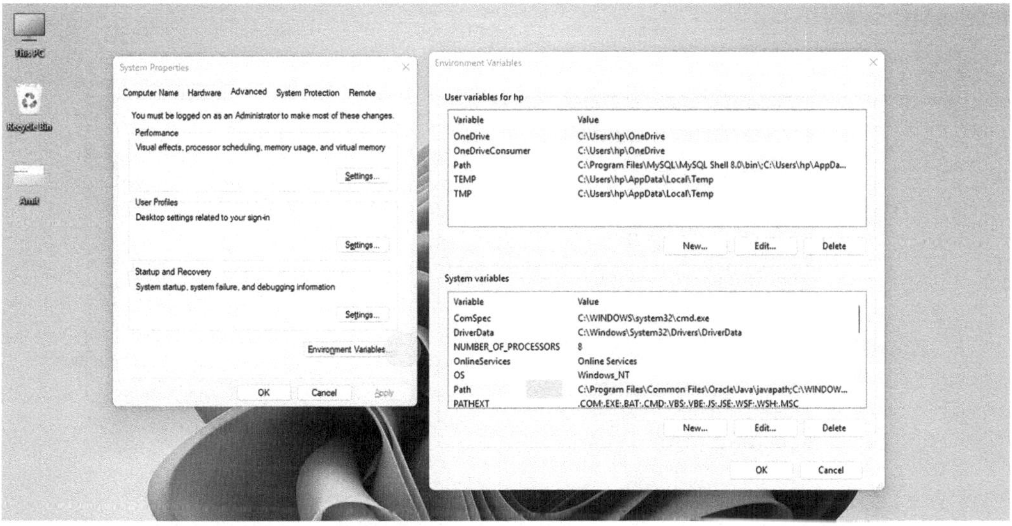

Figure 1.23: *Double-click the path*

We copied the **`bin`** path above. Paste the same path after clicking **`New`**. After that, click **`OK`**:

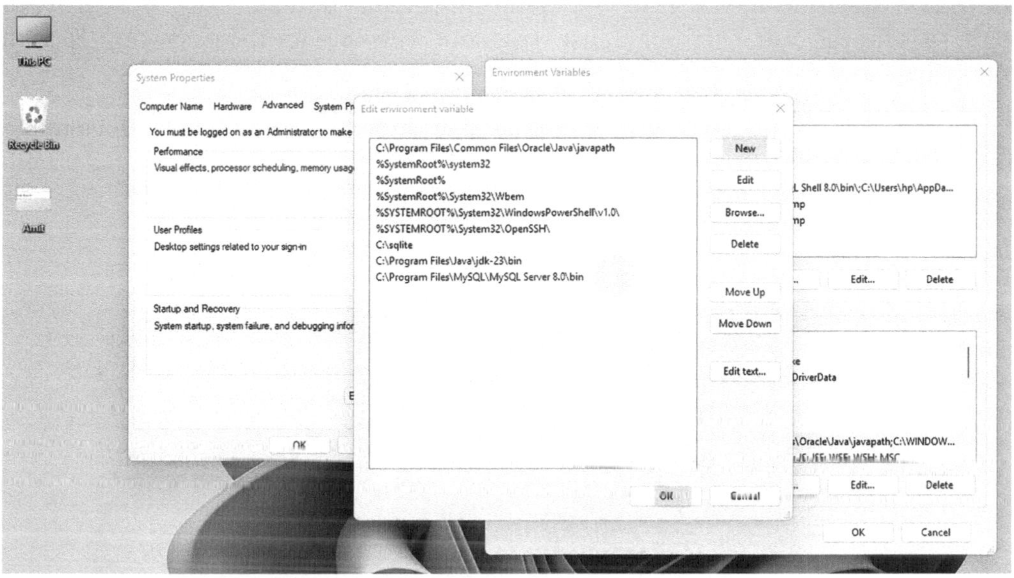

Figure 1.24: *Create a new path*

Step 9: Verify the MySQL installation

Go to **`START`**, and type **`CMD`**. Open the CMD (command prompt). Type the following command to verify the MySQL installation:

```
mysql --version
```

Here is the screenshot:

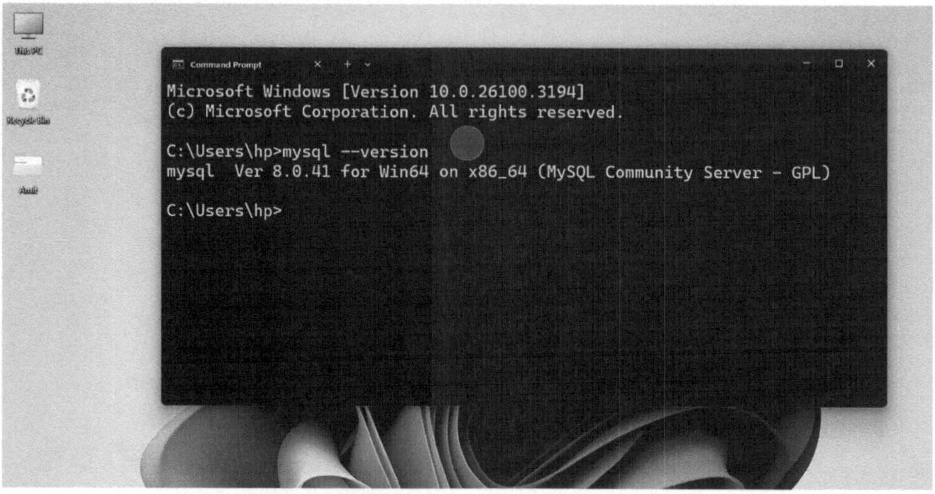

Figure 1.25: *MySQL installation verified*

Step 10: Start the MySQL Server

Let us now start the server. Type the following command to start the MySQL Server. Here, `-u` is for the user. Our default user was root. The `-p` is for the password. Type the command and press *Enter*:

Note: *Since we set the* ***`bin`*** *path before, we will directly use the following command to start the server, that is, no need to reach the bin path on the command prompt:*

```
mysql -u root -p
```

Here is the screenshot:

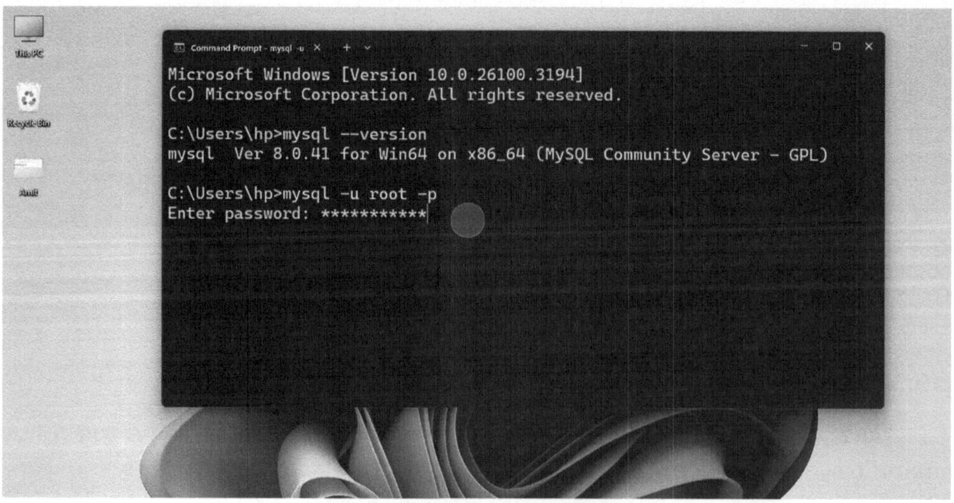

Figure 1.26: *Start the Server*

Now, enter the admin password which we have set before, and press *Enter*:

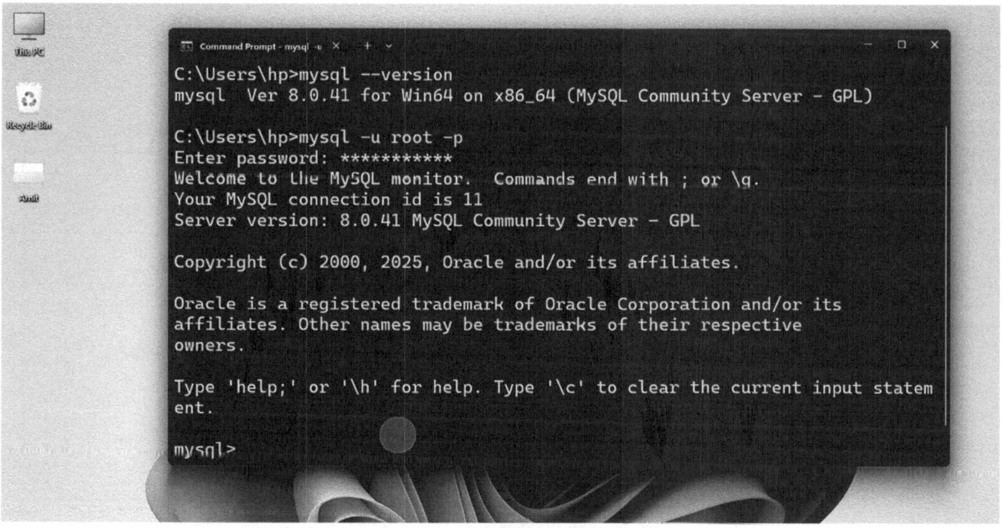

Figure 1.27: MySQL Server started

The MySQL Server was installed and started successfully.

Note: *We will create a new database and table in the next lesson. The commands will be typed here only.*

MySQL Workbench opened after the installation was completed. Click **`Local Instance`**:

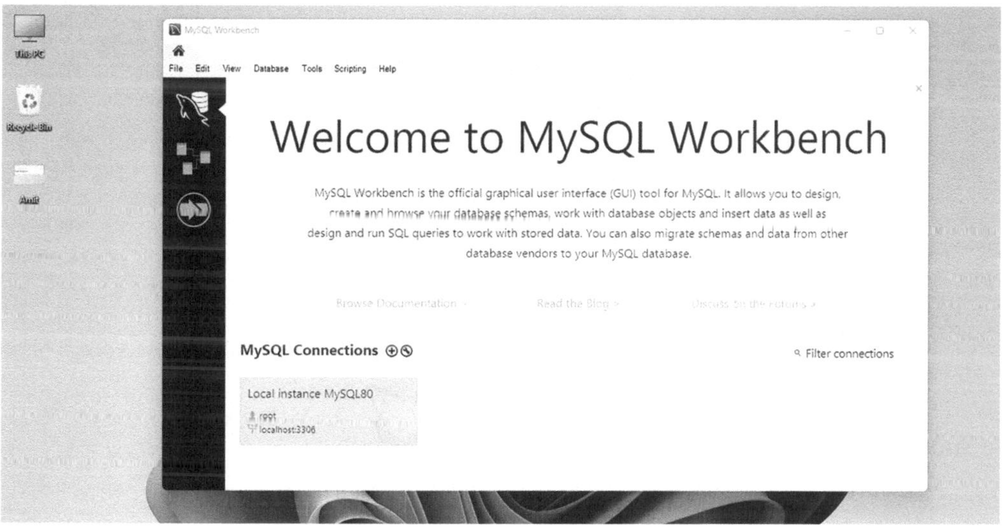

Figure 1.28: Open MySQL Workbench

Enter the same password that we set before and click **OK**:

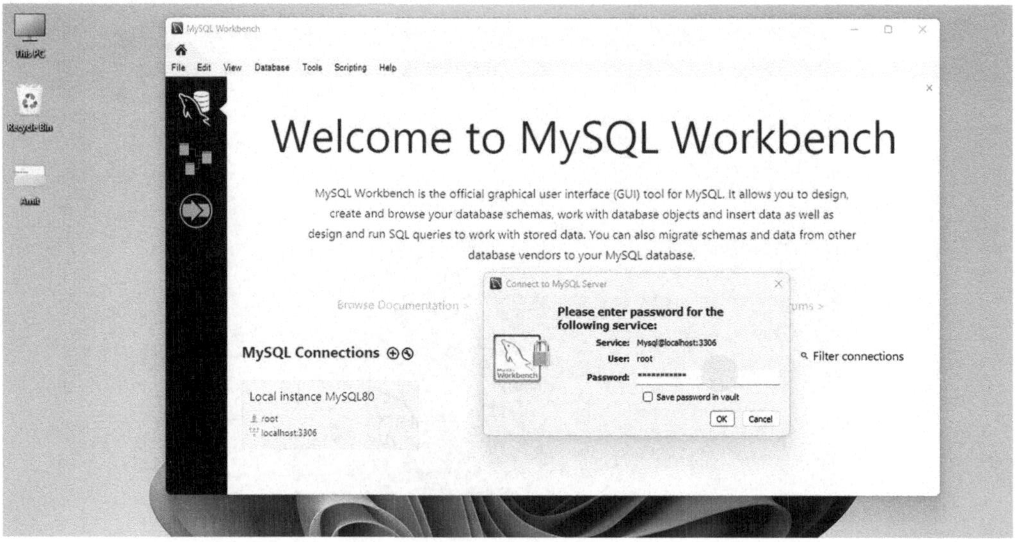

Figure 1.29: Add the password for MySQL Workbench

MySQL Workbench opened successfully:

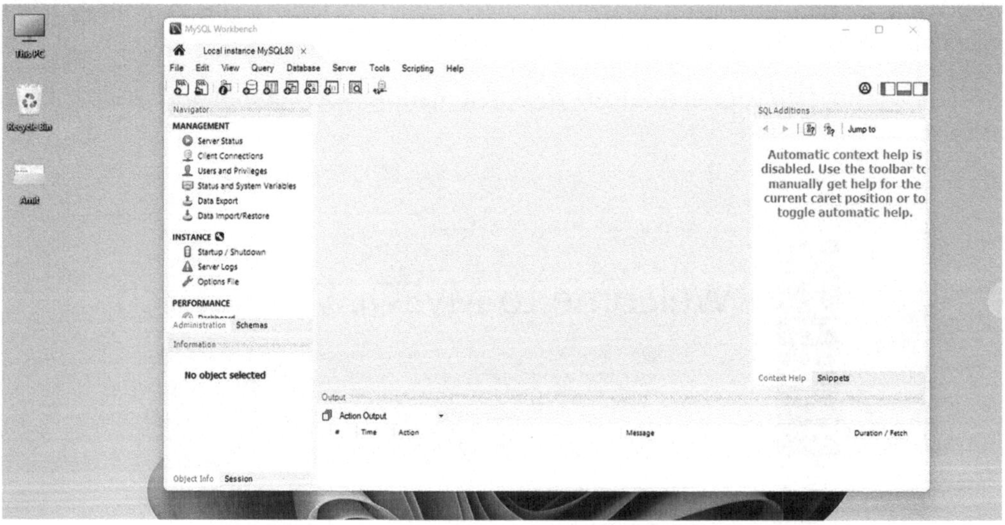

Figure 1.30: MySQL Workbench opened

We successfully installed MySQL Server and Workbench.

Notes: *Video Tutorials:*

Install MySQL on Windows 10: https://youtu.be/35hSyyBhPT0

Install MySQL on Windows 11: https://youtu.be/If_racf2ocM

While installing MySQL, if you face any errors or issues, refer to our free YouTube playlist. It fixes over 10 issues related to MySQL installation:

https://www.youtube.com/playlist?list=PLSwH4ViBDl2RrLZg3yZ5EXG1LUXAr9l2s

MySQL Workbench is a powerful graphical user interface tool designed for Database Administrators (DBAs) and developers. Let us understand more about MySQL Workbench.

MySQL Workbench

MySQL Workbench is a unified visual tool for database architects, developers, and DBAs. It provides data modeling, SQL development, and comprehensive administration tools for server configuration, user administration, and much more. MySQL Workbench is available on Windows, Linux, and macOS.

Note: *In the last lesson, we installed Workbench as well, However, we will focus on the command-line MySQL and type the commands explained in the upcoming lesson.*

Features of MySQL Workbench

The following are the features of MySQL Workbench:

- **SQL Development:**
    - **SQL Editor**: Write, edit, and execute SQL queries.
    - **Syntax Highlighting**: Helps in writing error-free SQL code.
    - **Query Results**: View and export query results in various formats.
    - **Execution Plan**: Visualize and optimize query performance.
- **Data Modeling (Design):**
    - **ER Diagrams**: Create and manage Entity-Relationship diagrams.
    - **Forward and Reverse Engineering**: Generate database schemas from models and vice versa.
    - **Synchronization**: Keep the model and database in sync.
- **Database Administration:**
    - **Server Configuration**: Manage server settings and configurations.
    - **User Administration**: Create and manage user accounts and privileges.
    - **Backup and Restore**: Perform database backups and restore.
    - **Server Logs**: View and analyze server logs.

- **Data Migration:**
  - **Migration Wizard**: Migrate data from other database systems to MySQL.
  - **Compatibility Checks**: Ensure compatibility between different database systems.
- **Performance Tuning:**
  - **Performance Dashboard**: Monitor and analyze server performance.
  - **Index Advisor**: Get recommendations for improving query performance.

For a quick overview of MySQL Workbench, refer to our free video tutorial:

https://youtu.be/UzodkZUt5JY

Conclusion

RDBMS and MySQL provide a structured, reliable approach to data management, ideal for structured data and complex queries. Meanwhile, NoSQL offers flexibility and scalability for unstructured data and real-time applications, making the choice dependent on specific project needs.

In the next lesson, we will learn how to create a database and tables. We will also insert records and understand the data types of MySQL with some other topics, such as the LIMIT Clause, Auto Increment, and so on.

Points to Remember

- RDBMS is a structured way to store data using tables and relationships.
- MySQL is a popular open-source RDBMS known for its performance, scalability, and ease of use.
- SQL databases are ideal for structured data and complex queries, while NoSQL databases are better suited for unstructured data and high scalability.

Multiple Choice Questions

1. What does RDBMS stand for?
   a. Relational Data Business Management System
   b. Relational Database Management System
   c. Random Database Management System
   d. Real-time Database Management System

2. Which of the following is a key feature of MySQL?
    a. Schema-less design
    b. Horizontal scaling only
    c. ACID compliance
    d. No support for stored procedures
3. What is the primary purpose of a foreign key in an RDBMS?
    a. To uniquely identify a record in a table
    b. To establish relationships between tables
    c. To encrypt data in a table
    d. To optimize query performance
4. Which of the following is a NoSQL database?
    a. MongoDB
    b. PostgreSQL
    c. MySQL
    d. Oracle
5. What is the main advantage of NoSQL databases over SQL databases?
    a. Better support for complex joins
    b. Fixed schema for structured data
    c. Horizontal scalability and flexibility
    d. Strict ACID compliance
6. Which of the following is NOT a characteristic of MySQL?
    a. Open-source
    b. Cross-platform compatibility
    c. Schema-less design
    d. Support for stored procedures

Answers

1. b
2. c
3. b
4. a
5. c
6. c

Questions

1. What is the full form of RDBMS, and what is its primary function?
2. Explain the difference between a primary key and a foreign key in an RDBMS.
3. What are the ACID properties in a database, and why are they important?
4. List three key features of MySQL that make it a popular choice for web applications.
5. What is normalization in the context of RDBMS, and what are its benefits?
6. Compare SQL and NoSQL databases in terms of data structure, scalability, and use cases.
7. Why would you choose a NoSQL database over a traditional SQL database for a specific project? Provide an example.
8. What is the role of SQL in an RDBMS, and name three common SQL commands used for data manipulation?

Key Terms

- **RDBMS (Relational Database Management System):** A system that stores data in a structured format using tables, rows, and columns, and establishes relationships between tables using keys.
- **ACID Properties:** A set of properties (Atomicity, Consistency, Isolation, Durability) that ensure reliable processing of database transactions, maintaining data integrity.
- **Normalization:** The process of organizing data in a database to reduce redundancy and improve data integrity by dividing tables and establishing relationships.

- **NoSQL:** A type of database that provides a flexible, schema-less approach to storing unstructured or semi-structured data, often used for big data and real-time applications.
- **Structured Data:** It refers to data that is organized in a predefined format, typically within a database or a spreadsheet, where it is arranged in rows and columns.
- **Unstructured Data:** It refers to data that does not have a predefined format or organization. Unstructured data is often text-heavy but can also include other types of data such as images, videos, audio, and more.

CHAPTER 2
Getting Started with MySQL

Introduction

This chapter covers how to create a new database and table after installing MySQL. We will also insert records and understand the data types of MySQL with some other topics, such as the LIMIT Clause, Auto Increment, and so on.

After completing this chapter, the readers will be able to create a database or table, insert records, and understand some other MySQL concepts, such as database, alias, where clause, limit clause, and more.

Structure

In this chapter, we will discuss the following topics:

- Creating a Database
- Creating a Table
- Inserting Records
- Adding a comment in MySQL
- SELECT Statement in MySQL
- SELECT DISTINCT Statement in MySQL
- WHERE Clause in MySQL
- MySQL Datatypes
- LIMIT Clause
- Alias
- Auto Increment
- Practical Exercise

Create a Database

A database is a structured collection of data. In MySQL, you create a database using the **CREATE DATABASE** statement.

Creating a database is the very first step in working with MySQL. A database is like a container that holds all your tables, views, and other database objects. Without a database, you cannot create tables or store data.

Note: *Database and table names are* ***case-insensitive***. ***MyTable*** and ***mytable*** refer to the same table. Similarly, column names, statements, commands, and so on are also case-insensitive.

Tip: *Use consistent naming conventions (for example, lowercase for table and column names) to avoid issues.*

Defining a Database

A **database** is an organized collection of data stored in a structured format. In MySQL, a database contains:

- **Tables**: To store data in rows and columns.
- **Views**: Virtual tables based on the result of a query.
- **Stored Procedures**: Reusable SQL code blocks.
- **Functions**: Reusable code that returns a value.

And more!

Creating a Database

To create a database, you use the **CREATE DATABASE** statement.

yntax:

```
CREATE DATABASE database name;
```

Here, **database_name** is the name of the database you want to create. It should be unique within the MySQL server.

Example: Creating a Database

Let us create a database called **school_db**:

```
CREATE DATABASE school_db;
```

Type the above command on the command prompt. We already started the server in the previous lesson. Here is the screenshot to display how a command is typed on cmd after starting the server. Type the command and press *Enter* as shown in the following screenshot:

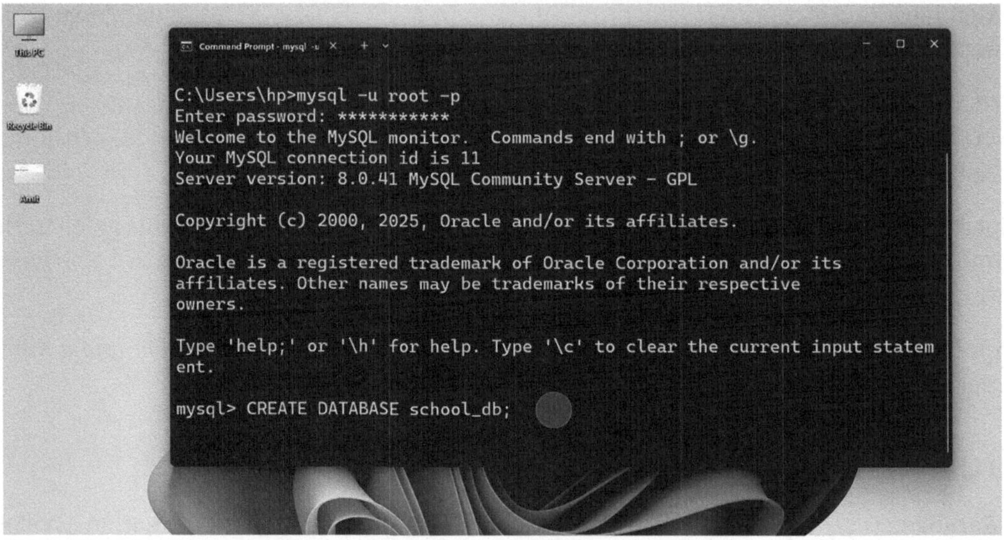

Figure 2.1: *Creating a new database in MySQL*

Under the next steps, we will display the command with its output. Type them on the same command prompt as shown in the *Figure 2.1*

Verifying the Database

After creating the database, you can verify it by listing all databases:

```
SHOW DATABASES;
```

This will display a list of all databases, including the one you just created (**`school_db`**).

Selecting a Database

Before you can create tables or perform any operations, you need to **select** the database using the **`USE`** statement.

Syntax:

```
USE database_name;
```

Example:

```
USE school_db;
```

Now, all subsequent queries will be executed in the **`school_db`** database.

Best Practices for Naming Databases

The following are some best practices to name databases in MySQL:

- Use meaningful and descriptive names (for example, **`school_db`**, **`ecommerce_db`**, **`students`**).
- Use lowercase letters and underscores (_) to separate words.
- Avoid using special characters or spaces in database names.

Creating a Table

A table in MySQL is like a spreadsheet with rows and columns. Each row represents a single record, and each column represents a specific piece of information about that record. A table is a structured way of organizing rows and columns as shown:

```
+------------+--------------+------+-------+
| student_id | name         | age  | grade |
+------------+--------------+------+-------+
| 1001       | Alice Chen   | 16   | A     |   ← Row (Record)
| 1002       | David Smith  | 17   | B+    |   ← Another Row
| 1003       | Maria Garcia | 16   | A-    |   ← Another Row
+------------+--------------+------+-------+
       ↑             ↑          ↑      ↑
    Column        Column     Column  Column
```

Figure 2.2: *Displaying rows and columns in a table*

In *Figure 2.2*, rows are horizontal, and columns are vertical.

For example, if you are creating a table to store information about students, the columns might include:

- **`student_id`**
- **`name`**
- **`age`**
- **`grade`**

Syntax

The syntax to create a table is:

```
CREATE TABLE table_name (
    column1_name data_type,
```

```
        column2_name data_type,
        column3_name data_type,
        ...
    );
```

Here,

- **CREATE TABLE**: This is the command to create a new table.
- **table_name**: Replace this with the name you want to give your table (for example, students).
- **column_name**: Replace this with the name of the column (for example, name, age).
- **data_type**: This defines the type of data the column will store (for example, numbers, text, dates).

Common Data Types

Here are some basic data types you will use often:

- **INT**: For whole numbers (for example, age, ID).
- **VARCHAR(size)**: For text (for example, names, emails). The size is the maximum number of characters it can store.
- **DATE**: For dates (for example, birthdate).
- **DECIMAL(total_digits, decimal_places)**: For numbers with decimals (for example, salary, price).

Note: *MySQL Datatypes are covered in the* **Datatypes** *lesson. For this, we have considered only the above four data types.*

Example: Creating a Simple Table

Let us create a table called **students** with the following columns:

- **student_id** (a number to uniquely identify each student)
- **name** (the student's name)
- **age** (the student's age)
- **grade** (the student's grade, for example, A, B, C)

Here is how you can create a new table in MySQL:

```
CREATE TABLE students (
    student_id INT,
    name VARCHAR(50),
```

```
        age INT,
        grade VARCHAR(2)
    );
```

Here,

- **CREATE TABLE students**: This creates a new table called students.
- **student_id INT**: This creates a column called **student_id** that will store whole numbers (for example, 1, 2, 3).
- **name VARCHAR(50)**: This creates a column called name that will store text up to 50 characters long.
- **age INT**: This creates a column called age that will store whole numbers (for example, 15, 16, 17).
- **grade VARCHAR(2)**: This creates a column called grade that will store text up to 2 characters long (for example, A, B, C).

Verifying the Table

After creating the table, you can verify it by running:

```
DESCRIBE students;
```

This will show you the structure of the **students** table, including the column names.

Inserting Records

Now that we have created the **students** table, let us learn how to insert records into it. Inserting records means adding rows of data to the table. This is done using the **INSERT INTO** statement.

Understanding Inserting Records

When you insert a record into a table, you are adding a new row of data. For example, if your table has columns such as **student_id**, **name**, **age**, and **grade**, inserting a record means providing values for each of these columns.

Basic Syntax for Inserting Records

The basic syntax for inserting a single record is:

```
INSERT INTO table_name (column1, column2, column3, ...)
VALUES (value1, value2, value3, ...);
```

Here,

- **INSERT INTO table_name**: This specifies the table where you want to insert the data.
- **(column1, column2, column3, ...)**: Lists the columns you want to insert data into.
- **VALUES (value1, value2, value3, ...)**: Provides the actual data for each column.

Example: Inserting a Single Record

Let us insert a record into the **students** table we created earlier. The table has the following columns:

- **student_id**
- **name**
- **age**
- **grade**

Here is how you can insert a record for a student named "**John Doe**" with **student_id = 1**, **age = 16**, and **grade = 'A'**:

```
INSERT INTO students (student_id, name, age, grade)
VALUES (1, 'John Doe', 16, 'A');
```

Here,

- **INSERT INTO students**: This tells MySQL that we want to insert data into the **students** table.
- **(student_id, name, age, grade)**: These are the columns we are inserting data into.
- **VALUES (1, 'John Doe', 16, 'A')**: These are the actual values for the columns:
  - student_id = 1
  - name = 'John Doe'
  - age = 16
  - grade = 'A'

Inserting Multiple Records

You can also insert multiple records at once by separating each set of values with a comma. For example:

```
INSERT INTO students (student_id, name, age, grade)
VALUES
    (2, 'Jane Smith', 15, 'B'),
    (3, 'Alice Johnson', 17, 'A'),
    (4, 'Bob Brown', 16, 'C'),
    (5, 'Emily Davis', 14, 'B')
    (6, 'Michael Wilson', 18, 'A');
```

This will insert five new records into the **students** table.

Verifying the Inserted Data

After inserting records, you can check if the data was added successfully by running a **SELECT** statement:

```
SELECT * FROM students;
```

This will display all the records in the **students** table. For example:

STUDENT_ID	NAME	AGE	GRADE
1	JOHN DOE	16	A
2	JANE SMITH	15	B
3	ALICE JOHNSON	17	A
4	BOB BROWN	16	C
5	Emily Davis	14	B
6	Michael Wilson	18	A

Table 2.1: *Students table output*

Important Notes

- **Order of Columns**: The order of the columns in the **INSERT INTO** statement must match the order of the values in the **VALUES** clause.
- **Data Types**: Make sure the data you are inserting matches the data type of the column. For example:
    - **student_id** and **age** should be numbers.
    - **name** and **grade** should be text.
- **Quotes for Text**: Always use single quotes (' ') for text values such as names or grades. Numbers do not need quotes.

SELECT Statement in MySQL

Now that we have created a table (students) and inserted some records into it, let us learn about the **SELECT** statement. The **SELECT** statement is one of the most important and frequently used commands in MySQL. It allows you to retrieve data from one or more tables.

Define SELECT Statement

The **SELECT** statement is used to **query** (fetch) data from a database. You can use it to:

- Retrieve all rows and columns from a table.
- Retrieve specific columns.
- Filter rows based on conditions.
- Sort the results.

Basic Syntax of SELECT

The simplest form of the **SELECT** statement is:

```
SELECT column1, column2, ...
FROM table_name;
```

Here,

- **SELECT**: Specifies the columns you want to retrieve.
- **FROM**: Specifies the table from which to retrieve the data.

If you want to retrieve all columns, you can use the * wildcard:

```
SELECT * FROM table_name;
```

Example: Retrieving Data from the students Table

Let us retrieve all the records from the **students** table we created earlier:

```
SELECT * FROM students;
```

This will display all the rows and columns in the **students** table. For example:

STUDENT_ID	NAME	AGE	GRADE
1	John Doe	16	A
2	Jane Smith	15	B

3	Alice Johnson	17	A
4	Bob Brown	16	C
5	Emily Davis	14	B
6	Michael Wilson	18	A

Table 2.2: *Students table records*

Retrieving Specific Columns

If you only want to retrieve specific columns, list them after the **SELECT** keyword. For example, to retrieve only the name and grade columns:

```
SELECT name, grade
FROM students;
```

This will return:

name	**grade**
John Doe	A
Jane Smith	B
Alice Johnson	A
Bob Brown	C
Emily Davis	B
Michael Wilson	A

Table 2.3: *Output showing specific columns from a table*

WHERE Clause in MySQL

The WHERE clause is one of the most powerful tools in MySQL. It allows you to **filter** rows based on specific conditions. This means you can retrieve only the data that meets certain criteria, making your queries more precise and efficient.

The **WHERE** clause is used in a **SELECT** statement (and other statements such as **UPDATE** and **DELETE**) to specify a condition. Only rows that satisfy the condition will be included in the result.

Basic Syntax of the WHERE Clause

The basic syntax of a **SELECT** statement with a **WHERE** clause is:

```
SELECT column1, column2, ...
FROM table_name
WHERE condition;
```

Here, **condition** is a logical expression that evaluates to TRUE or FALSE for each row. Only rows where the condition is TRUE are included in the result.

Common Operators in the `WHERE` Clause

Here are some common operators you can use in the **WHERE** clause:

Operator	Description	Example
=	Equal to	age = 16
<> or !=	Not equal to	grade <> 'A'
>	Greater than	age > 15
<	Less than	age < 18
>=	Greater than or equal to	age >= 16
<=	Less than or equal to	age <= 17
IS NULL	Check for NULL values	grade IS NULL

Table 2.4: *Operators in the `WHERE` clause*

Examples of the `WHERE` Clause

Let us use the students table we created earlier:

student_id	name	age	grade
1	John Doe	16	A
2	Jane Smith	15	B
3	Alice Johnson	17	A
4	Bob Brown	16	C
5	Emily Davis	14	B
6	Michael Wilson	18	A

Table 2.5: *Students table*

Example 1: Retrieve Students with a Specific Age

To retrieve students who are **16 years old**:

```
SELECT * FROM students
WHERE age = 16;
```

Result:

student_id	name	age	grade
1	John Doe	16	A
4	Bob Brown	16	C

Table 2.6: *Output showing students with a specific age*

Example 2: Retrieve Students Older Than 15

To retrieve students who are **older than 15**:

```
SELECT * FROM students
WHERE age > 15;
```

Result:

student_id	name	age	grade
1	John Doe	16	A
3	Alice Johnson	17	A
4	Bob Brown	16	C
6	Michael Wilson	18	A

Table 2.7: *Output showing students older than age 15*

Example 3: Retrieve Students with a Specific Grade

To retrieve students who have a grade of '**A**':

```
SELECT * FROM students
WHERE grade = 'A';
```

Result:

student_id	name	age	grade
1	John Doe	16	A
3	Alice Johnson	17	A
6	Michael Wilson	18	A

Table 2.8: *Output showing students with a specific grade*

Example 4: Retrieve Students with Missing Grades

If some students do not have a grade (for example, the **grade** column is **NULL**), you can find them using:

```
SELECT * FROM students
WHERE grade IS NULL;
```

SELECT DISTINCT Statement in MySQL

The **SELECT DISTINCT** statement is a handy tool in MySQL that allows you to **retrieve unique values** from a column or a set of columns. This is particularly useful when you want to eliminate duplicate values from your query results.

Define SELECT DISTINCT

The **SELECT DISTINCT** statement is used to return only **unique (distinct)** values from a column or a combination of columns. It removes duplicate values from the result set.

Syntax of SELECT DISTINCT

The syntax of **SELECT DISTINCT** is:

```
SELECT DISTINCT column1, column2, ...
FROM table_name;
```

Here,

- **DISTINCT**: This keyword ensures that unique values are returned.
- **column1, column2, ...**: The columns from which you want to retrieve unique values.
- **table_name:** The table from which you are retrieving the data.

Example Table

Let us use the **students** table we created earlier:

student_id	name	age	grade
1	John Doe	16	A
2	Jane Smith	15	B
3	Alice Johnson	17	A
4	Bob Brown	16	C

5	Emily Davis	14	B
6	Michael Wilson	18	A

Table 2.9: *Records of the students table*

Example 1: Retrieve Unique Grades

To retrieve all the unique grades from the **students** table:

```
SELECT DISTINCT grade
FROM students;
```

Result:

grade
A
B
C

Table 2.10: *Output displaying unique grades*

Explanation:

The **DISTINCT** keyword removes duplicate grades, so even though there are multiple students with grades A and B, each grade appears only once in the result.

Example 2: Retrieve Unique Ages

To retrieve all the unique ages from the **students** table:

```
SELECT DISTINCT age
FROM students;
```

Result:

age
16
15
17
14
18

Table 2.11: *Output displaying unique ages*

Explanation:

The **`DISTINCT`** keyword ensures that each age appears only once, even though multiple students may share the same age.

Example 3: Retrieve Unique Combinations of Columns

You can also use **`DISTINCT`** with multiple columns to retrieve unique combinations of values. For example, to retrieve unique combinations of **`age`** and **`grade`**:

```
SELECT DISTINCT age, grade
FROM students;
```

Result:

age	grade
16	A
15	B
17	A
16	C
14	B
18	A

Table 2.12: *Output displaying unique combinations of columns*

Explanation:

Each combination of **`age`** and **`grade`** is unique in the result set.

Example 4: `DISTINCT` with `WHERE` Clause

You can combine **`DISTINCT`** with the **`WHERE`** clause to filter the results. For example, to retrieve unique grades for students older than 15:

```
SELECT DISTINCT grade
FROM students
WHERE age > 15;
```

Result:

grade
A
C

Table 2.13: *Output displaying filtered records*

Explanation:

Only students older than 15 are considered, and the **`DISTINCT`** keyword ensures that each grade appears only once.

MySQL Data Types

MySQL data types define the type of data that can be stored in a column. They ensure data integrity and optimize storage. Here are the main categories of MySQL data types:

Let us understand them with examples:

- Numeric Datatypes
- String Datatypes
- Date and Time Data Types
- Boolean Datatypes
- Binary Datatypes
- Enum and Set Data Types

Numeric Data types

The numeric data types in MySQL store numbers (integers, decimals, and so on). Let us see some types of numeric data types with examples:

`INT`

Stores whole numbers:

```
age INT
```

`FLOAT`

Stores approximate floating-point numbers.

```
price FLOAT(5, 2) -- Stores up to 5 digits, 2 after the decimal
```

`DECIMAL`

Stores exact fixed-point numbers.

```
salary DECIMAL(10, 2) -- Stores up to 10 digits, 2 after the decimal
```

String Data types

The string data types in MySQL store text or binary data. Let us see some types of string data types with examples:

VARCHAR

Stores variable-length strings (up to 65,535 characters).:

```
name VARCHAR(100) -- Stores a string of up to 100 characters
```

CHAR

Stores fixed-length strings (padded with spaces).

```
code CHAR(5) -- Always stores 5 characters
```

TEXT

Stores large text data (up to 65,535 characters).

```
description TEXT
```

Date and Time Data Types

The data and time data types in MySQL store dates, times, or both. Let us see some types of date and time data types with examples:

DATE

Stores a date in YYYY-MM-DD format.

```
birthdate DATE
```

DATETIME

Stores both date and time in YYYY-MM-DD HH:MM:SS format.

```
created_at DATETIME
```

TIMESTAMP

Stores a timestamp (auto-updates on row modification).

```
updated_at TIMESTAMP
```

Boolean Data Type

The boolean data type stores TRUE (1) or FALSE (0). It simplifies logical conditions in queries. Here, 1 = TRUE and 0 = FALSE.

Example:

```
is_active BOOLEAN
```

Binary Data Types

The binary data types store binary data such as images or files. Let us see some types of binary data types with examples:

Examples:

BLOB: Stores binary large objects (up to 65,535 bytes):

```
image BLOB
```

LONGBLOB: Stores larger binary objects (up to 4GB):

```
file LONGBLOB
```

Enum and Set Data Types

MySQL provides specialized string data types called **ENUM** and **SET** that allow you to define columns with specific allowed values.

ENUM: Stores a single value from a predefined list.

The **ENUM** type is a string object with a value chosen from a predefined list of permitted values.

Here are the features::

- Can store one value from a predefined list
- Values are stored as integers (indexes) internally, making them compact
- Maximum of 65,535 distinct elements
- Sorting is based on index numbers (insertion order), not string values

Here is an example:

```
size ENUM('Small', 'Medium', 'Large')
```

SET: Stores multiple values from a predefined list.

The SET type is a string object that can have zero or more values, each of which must be chosen from a predefined list of permitted values.

Here are the features:

- Can store multiple values from a predefined list
- Maximum of 64 members
- Values are stored as a bitmap (very space-efficient)
- Values are stored as strings but represented as numbers internally

Here is an example:

```
colors SET('Red', 'Green', 'Blue')
```

Let us see an example that includes all the data types:

```
CREATE TABLE users (
    id INT PRIMARY KEY AUTO_INCREMENT,
    username VARCHAR(50) NOT NULL,
    password CHAR(60) NOT NULL,
    email VARCHAR(100),
    birthdate DATE,
    salary DECIMAL(10, 2),
```

```
        is_active BOOLEAN DEFAULT TRUE,
        created_at DATETIME DEFAULT CURRENT_TIMESTAMP
    );
```

Note: *The above example is unrelated to our initial examples from* Lesson 2 *that continue in the next lesson as well.*

Key Points to Remember

The following are some key points regarding data types in MySQL:

- Choose the appropriate datatype to optimize storage and performance.
- Use **VARCHAR** for variable-length; **STRINGS** and **CHAR** for fixed-length strings.
- Use **INT** for whole numbers and **DECIMAL** for precise decimal values.
- Use **DATETIME** or **TIMESTAMP** for date and time storage.
- Avoid using overly large data types unless necessary to save space.

Adding a comment in MySQL

Adding **comments** in MySQL is a useful way to document your SQL code, making it easier to understand and maintain. Comments can be added to explain the purpose of a query, describe a column, or provide any other relevant information.

In MySQL, there are **three ways** to add comments:

- **Single-line comments** (using -- or #).
- **Multi-line comments** (using /* ... */).

Single-Line Comments

Single-line comments are used to add short explanations or notes that fit on a single line.

Method 1: Using –

Let us see how to add a single-line comment in MySQL:

- Syntax: -- Your comment here
- The comment starts with -- and ends at the end of the line.
- There must be at least one space after --.

Example:

```
-- This is a single-line comment
SELECT * FROM students; -- Retrieves all rows from the students table
```

Method 2: Using

Let us see the alternative way to add a single-line comment in MySQL:

- Syntax: # Your comment here
- The comment starts with # and ends at the end of the line.

Example:

```
# This is another single-line comment
SELECT * FROM students; # Retrieves all rows from the students table
```

Multi-Line Comments

Multi-line comments are used for longer explanations or to comment out multiple lines of code.

Method: Using /* ... */

Let us see how to create multi-line comments in MySQL:

- Syntax: /* Your comment here */
- The comment starts with /* and ends with */.
- It can span multiple lines.

Example:

```
/*
This is a multi-line comment.
It can span multiple lines.
Useful for detailed explanations.
*/
SELECT * FROM students;
```

Using Comments in Code

Comments can be added anywhere in your SQL code, such as:

- At the top of a script to describe its purpose.
- Next to a query to explain its logic.
- To temporarily disable a part of the code (commenting out).

Example: Commenting in a Script

The following is an example to add comments. Add what the script is about, its author, date of creation, and so on.

```
-- This script retrieves student data from the database
-- Created by: Amit Diwan
-- Date: 2025-03-15

/*
Table: students
Columns:
- student_id: Unique ID for each student
- name: Student's full name
- age: Student's age
- grade: Student's grade (A, B, C, etc.)
*/

-- Retrieve all students
SELECT * FROM students;

-- Retrieve students older than 15
SELECT * FROM students
WHERE age > 15; # Filters students by age
```

Example: Commenting Out Code

You can use comments to temporarily disable part of your SQL code without deleting it.

```
-- Retrieve all students
SELECT * FROM students;

/*
-- Retrieve students older than 15 (commented out for now)
SELECT * FROM students
WHERE age > 15;
*/

-- Retrieve students with grade 'A'
SELECT * FROM students
WHERE grade = 'A';
```

Adding Comments to Table and Column Definitions

You can also add comments when creating or altering tables and columns. This is useful for documenting the purpose of a table or column directly in the database schema.

Syntax for Table Comments:

The following is the syntax to add table comments in MySQL:

```
CREATE TABLE table_name (
    column1 data_type COMMENT 'Your comment here',
    column2 data_type COMMENT 'Your comment here'
) COMMENT = 'Your table comment here';
```

Syntax for Column Comments:

The following is the syntax to add column comments in MySQL:

```
ALTER TABLE table_name
MODIFY column_name data_type COMMENT 'Your comment here';
```

Example: Adding Comments to a Table

The following is an example of how to add comments to a table in MySQL:

```
CREATE TABLE employees (
    id INT AUTO_INCREMENT PRIMARY KEY COMMENT 'Unique employee ID',
    name VARCHAR(50) NOT NULL COMMENT 'Employee full name',
    department VARCHAR(50) COMMENT 'Employee department'
) COMMENT = 'Stores employee information';
```

Example: Adding Comments to an Existing Column

The following is an example of how to add comments to an existing column in MySQL:

```
ALTER TABLE employees
MODIFY department VARCHAR(50) COMMENT 'Employee department (e.g.,
HR, IT)';
```

Viewing Comments in MySQL

To view the comments for a table or column, you can use the **`SHOW CREATE TABLE`** statement or query the **`information_schema`** database.

Example: View Table and Column Comments

Let us see how to display the definition of the table, and also the comments:

```
SHOW CREATE TABLE employees;
```

This will display the table definition, including comments.

`LIMIT` Clause

The **`LIMIT`** clause is a very useful feature in MySQL that allows you to **restrict the number of rows** returned by a query. This is particularly helpful when you are working with large datasets and only need a subset of the data, such as the top 10 results or the first 5 rows.

Define the `LIMIT` Clause

The LIMIT clause is used to specify the **maximum number of rows** to return from a query. It is often used in combination with **`SELECT`** statements to control the size of the result set.

Basic Syntax of the `LIMIT` Clause

The basic syntax of the `LIMIT` clause is:

```
SELECT column1, column2, ...
FROM table_name
LIMIT number_of_rows;
```

Here, **`number_of_rows`**: The maximum number of rows to return.

You can also specify an **`offset`** to skip a certain number of rows before starting to return the results:

```
SELECT column1, column2, ...
FROM table_name
LIMIT offset, number_of_rows;
```

Here,

- **`offset`**: The number of rows to skip before starting to return rows.
- **`number_of_rows`**: The maximum number of rows to return after the offset.

Example of the `Limit` Clause

Let us see some examples:

Example Table

Let us use the **`students`** table we created earlier:

student_id	name	age	grade
1	John Doe	16	A
2	Jane Smith	15	B

3	Alice Johnson	17	A
4	Bob Brown	16	C
5	Emily Davis	14	B
6	Michael Wilson	18	A

Table 2.14: *Students table*

Example 1: Retrieve the First 3 Rows

To retrieve the first 3 rows from the **students** table:

```
SELECT * FROM students
LIMIT 3;
```

Result:

student_id	name	age	grade
1	John Doe	16	A
2	Jane Smith	15	B
3	Alice Johnson	17	A

Table 2.15: *Output displaying the first 3 rows*

Example 2: Retrieve Rows with an Offset

To skip the first 2 rows and retrieve the next 3 rows:

```
SELECT * FROM students
LIMIT 2, 3;
```

Explanation:

- **2**: Skip the first 2 rows.
- **3**: Return the next 3 rows.

Result:

student_id	name	age	grade
3	Alice Johnson	17	A
4	Bob Brown	16	C
5	Emily Davis	14	B

Table 2.16: *Output displaying rows with an offset*

Example 3: Combine `LIMIT` with `WHERE`

You can also use **`LIMIT`** with the **`WHERE`** clause to filter rows before limiting the results. For example, to retrieve the first 2 students with a grade of '**A**':

```
SELECT * FROM students
WHERE grade = 'A'
LIMIT 2;
```

Result:

student_id	name	age	grade
1	John Doe	16	A
3	Alice Johnson	17	A

Table 2.17: *Output combining clauses*

Example 4: Pagination with `LIMIT`

The **`LIMIT`** clause is often used for **pagination** (displaying a subset of results per page). For example, to retrieve rows 4 to 6 (page 2 with 3 rows per page):

```
SELECT * FROM students
LIMIT 3, 3;
```

Explanation:

- **3**: Skip the first 3 rows.
- **3**: Return the next 3 rows.

Result:

student_id	name	age	grade
4	Bob Brown	16	C
5	Emily Davis	14	B
6	Michael Wilson	18	A

Table 2.18: *Output displaying pagination with limit*

Alias

Aliases in MySQL are used to give a temporary name (or nickname) to a table or a column in a query. They make your queries more readable and concise, especially when working with long table or column names or when performing calculations or joins.

An **alias** is a temporary name assigned to a table or column in a query. It exists only for the duration of the query and does not change the actual name of the table or column in the database.

Reasons to Use Aliases

The following are some reasons to use aliases in MySQL:

- **Improve Readability**: Shorten long table or column names.
- **Simplify Queries**: Make complex queries easier to write and understand.
- **Handle Duplicate Column Names**: This is useful when joining tables with columns of the same name.
- **Customize Output**: Rename columns in the result set for better presentation.

Types of Aliases

The following are the two types of aliases in MySQL:

- **Column Aliases**: Used to rename a column in the result set.
- **Table Aliases**: Used to rename a table in the query.

Column Aliases

A column alias is used to rename a column in the result set:

Syntax of the Column Aliases

The following is the syntax of the column aliases in MySQL:

```
SELECT column_name AS alias_name
FROM table_name;
```

Here,

- **`AS`**: Optional keyword used to assign an alias. You can skip it, but it is good practice to include it for clarity.
- **`alias_name`**: The temporary name you want to assign to the column.

Example 1: Rename a Column in the Result Set

Let us retrieve the **`name`** and **`grade`** columns from the **`students`** table, but rename **`name`** to **`student_name`** and **`grade`** to **`student_grade`**:

```
SELECT name AS student_name, grade AS student_grade
FROM students;
```

Result:

student_name	student_grade
John Doe	A
Jane Smith	B
Alice Johnson	A
Bob Brown	C
Emily Davis	B
Michael Wilson	A

Table 2.19: *Output displaying renaming a column*

Example 2: Alias Without AS

You can also assign an alias without using the **AS** keyword:

```
SELECT name student_name, grade student_grade
FROM students;
```

This will produce the same result as above.

Example 3: Alias for Calculated Columns

If you perform calculations in your query, you can use an alias to give the result a meaningful name. For example, let us calculate the birth year of each student (assuming the current year is 2025):

```
SELECT name, 2025 - age AS birth_year
FROM students;
```

Result:

name	birth_year
John Doe	2007
Jane Smith	2008
Alice Johnson	2006
Bob Brown	2007
Emily Davis	2009
Michael Wilson	2005

Table 2.20: *Output displaying the usage of Alias*

Table Aliases

A table alias is used to rename a table in the query

Syntax of the Table Alias

The following is the syntax of creating a table alias in MySQL:

```
SELECT column_name
FROM table_name AS alias_name;
```

Here,

`alias_name`: The temporary name you want to assign to the table.

Example 4: Rename a Table in a Query

Let us retrieve the **`name`** and **`grade`** columns from the **`students`** table, but give the table an alias **`s`**:

```
SELECT s.name, s.grade
FROM students AS s;
```

Result:

name	grade
John Doe	A
Jane Smith	B
Alice Johnson	A
Bob Brown	C
Emily Davis	B
Michael Wilson	A

Table 2.21: *Output renaming the table*

Example 5: Table Alias Without AS

You can also assign a table alias without using the **`AS`** keyword:

```
SELECT s.name, s.grade
FROM students s;
```

This will produce the same result as above.

Auto Increment in MySQL

Auto Increment is a very useful feature in MySQL that allows you to automatically generate a unique number for a column whenever a new record is inserted into a table. This is especially helpful for creating primary keys, which uniquely identify each row in a table.

Defining Auto Increment

Let us define auto increment and understand what it is in MySQL:

- **Auto Increment** is a property that can be assigned to a column (usually an integer column) in a table.
- When a new record is inserted, MySQL automatically assigns the next available number to the column, starting from 1 (by default).
- This ensures that each row has a unique value in the auto-increment column.

Reasons to Use Auto Increment

Let us see what is the purpose of using Auto Increment in MySQL:

- **Unique Identifiers**: Automatically generate unique values for primary keys.
- **Simplify Insertions**: You do not need to manually specify a value for the auto-increment column when inserting data.
- **Avoid Duplicates**: This ensures that no two rows have the same value in the auto-increment column.

Auto Increment Column

To define an auto-increment column, you use the **`AUTO_INCREMENT`** keyword when creating or altering a table. The column must be of an integer type (for example, **`INT`**, **`BIGINT`**).

Example: Creating a Table with Auto Increment

Let us create a table called **`employees`** with an auto-increment column **`id`**:

```
CREATE TABLE employees (
    id INT AUTO_INCREMENT PRIMARY KEY,
    name VARCHAR(50) NOT NULL,
    department VARCHAR(50)
);
```

Explanation:

- **`id INT AUTO_INCREMENT PRIMARY KEY`**:
  - **`id`** is the column name.
  - **`INT`** is the data type (an integer).
  - **`AUTO_INCREMENT`** ensures the column automatically generates a unique value for each new row.

- **`PRIMARY KEY`** ensures the column is unique and not null.

Inserting Data into an Auto-Increment Table

When inserting data into a table with an auto-increment column, you **do not need to specify a value** for the auto-increment column. MySQL will automatically assign the next available number.

Example: Inserting Records

Let's insert some records into the **employees** table:

```
INSERT INTO employees (name, department)
VALUES ('John Doe', 'HR'),
       ('Jane Smith', 'Finance'),
       ('Alice Johnson', 'IT');
```

Resulting Table:

id	name	department
1	John Doe	HR
2	Jane Smith	Finance
3	Alice Johnson	IT

Table 2.22: *Output displaying a table with 3 columns*

Explanation:

The **`id`** column is automatically populated with unique **`values`** (1, 2, 3).

Manually Inserting a Value into an Auto Increment Column

If you want to manually specify a value for the auto-increment column, you can do so. However, you must ensure the value is unique and not already used in the column.

Example: Manual Insert

Let us see how to manually insert a value for the auto-increment column:

```
INSERT INTO employees (id, name, department)
VALUES (10, 'Bob Brown', 'Marketing');
```

Resulting Table:

id	name	department
1	John Doe	HR
2	Jane Smith	Finance
3	Alice Johnson	IT
10	Bob Brown	Marketing

Table 2.23: *Output displaying the auto-increment column inserted manually*

Explanation:

- The `id` value 10 was manually specified.
- The next auto-increment value will start from 11.

Important Notes

Let us see some important notes related to Auto-Increment in MySQL:

- **Primary Key Requirement**: An auto-increment column is typically used as the primary key to ensure uniqueness.
- **Gaps in Values**: If you delete rows or manually insert values, there may be gaps in the auto-increment sequence. This is normal and does not affect functionality.
- **Maximum Value**: The maximum value for an auto-increment column depends on the data type (for example, INT can go up to 2,147,483,647). If the limit is reached, you will need to alter the column to a larger data type (for example, BIGINT).

Practical Exercise

Here is a practical exercise that covers all the MySQL topics we covered in this chapter. This exercise will guide you through creating a database, defining tables, inserting records, querying data, and using various MySQL features.

Exercise: Employee Management System

Let us now see an **Employee Management System** covering whatever we discussed in the preceding lesson.

Step 1: Create a Database

Create a database named **employee_management**.

```
CREATE DATABASE employee_management;
USE employee_management;
```

Step 2: Create a Table

Create a table named **employees** with the following columns:

- **id** (INT, Primary Key, Auto Increment)
- **name** (VARCHAR(50))
- **department** (VARCHAR(50))
- **salary** (DECIMAL(10, 2))
- **join_date** (DATE)
- Add a comment to the table: "**Stores employee details**".

Here is the query:

```
CREATE TABLE employees (
    id INT PRIMARY KEY AUTO_INCREMENT COMMENT 'Unique employee ID',
    name VARCHAR(50) NOT NULL,
    department VARCHAR(50) NOT NULL,
    salary DECIMAL(10, 2) NOT NULL,
    join_date DATE NOT NULL
) COMMENT='Stores employee details';
```

Step 3: Insert Records

Insert the following records into the **employees** table:

id	name	department	salary	join_date
1	John Doe	HR	50000.00	2024-01-15
2	Jane Smith	IT	60000.00	2024-03-22
3	Alice Johnson	Finance	55000.00	2024-07-30
4	Bob Brown	IT	62000.00	2025-02-10
5	Charlie Davis	HR	48000.00	2025-05-05

Table 2.24: *The employees table after inserting some records*

Here is the query:

```
INSERT INTO employees (name, department, salary, join_date)
VALUES
('John Doe', 'HR', 50000.00, '2024-01-15'),
('Jane Smith', 'IT', 60000.00, '2024-03-22'),
```

```
('Alice Johnson', 'Finance', 55000.00, '2024-07-30'),
('Bob Brown', 'IT', 62000.00, '2025-02-10'),
('Charlie Davis', 'HR', 48000.00, '2025-05-05');
```

Step 4: Add a Comment

Add a comment to the **salary** column: "**Employee's monthly salary**":

```
ALTER TABLE employees MODIFY salary DECIMAL(10, 2) COMMENT
"Employee's monthly salary";
```

Step 5: SELECT Statement

Retrieve all records from the **employees** table:

```
SELECT * FROM employees;
```

Step 6: SELECT DISTINCT Statement

Retrieve a list of unique departments from the **employees** table:

```
SELECT DISTINCT department FROM employees;
```

Step 7: WHERE Clause

Retrieve all employees who work in the IT department:

```
SELECT * FROM employees WHERE department = 'IT';
```

Step 8: MySQL Datatypes

Add a new column **email (VARCHAR(100))** to the **employees** table:

```
ALTER TABLE employees ADD COLUMN email VARCHAR(100);
```

Step 9: LIMIT Clause

Retrieve the first 3 records from the **employees** table.

```
SESELECT * FROM employees LIMIT 3;
```

Step 10: Alias

Retrieve the **name** and **salary** columns, but display name as **Employee Name** and **salary** as **Monthly Salary**.

```
SELECT name AS 'Employee Name', salary AS 'Monthly Salary' FROM
employees;
```

Step 11: Auto Increment

Insert a new employee without specifying the **id** (let it auto-increment):

```
INSERT INTO employees (name, department, salary, join_date)
VALUES
('Eva Green', 'Finance', 58000.00, '2025-01-10');
```

Step 12: Verify Data

Retrieve all records from the employees table to verify the new employee and changes:

```
SELECT * FROM employees;
```

Final Queries

We have shown the step-by-step queries. Now, let us see all the queries:

```
CREATE DATABASE employee_management;
USE employee_management;

CREATE TABLE employees (
    id INT PRIMARY KEY AUTO_INCREMENT COMMENT 'Unique employee
ID',
    name VARCHAR(50) NOT NULL,
    department VARCHAR(50) NOT NULL,
    salary DECIMAL(10, 2) NOT NULL,
    join_date DATE NOT NULL
) COMMENT='Stores employee details';

INSERT INTO employees (name, department, salary, join_date)
VALUES
('John Doe', 'HR', 50000.00, '2024-01-15'),
('Jane Smith', 'IT', 60000.00, '2024-03-22'),
('Alice Johnson', 'Finance', 55000.00, '2024-07-30'),
('Bob Brown', 'IT', 62000.00, '2025-02-10'),
('Charlie Davis', 'HR', 48000.00, '2025-05-05');

ALTER TABLE employees MODIFY salary DECIMAL(10, 2) COMMENT
"Employee's monthly salary";

SELECT * FROM employees;

SELECT DISTINCT department FROM employees;

SELECT * FROM employees WHERE department = 'IT';

ALTER TABLE employees ADD COLUMN email VARCHAR(100);

SELECT * FROM employees LIMIT 3;

SELECT name AS 'Employee Name', salary AS 'Monthly Salary' FROM
employees;
```

```
INSERT INTO employees (name, department, salary, join_date)
VALUES
('Eva Green', 'Finance', 58000.00, '2025-01-10');

SELECT * FROM employees;
```

Expected Output

After completing the exercise, you should have:

- A database named **`employee_management`**.
- A table named **`employees`** with 6 records.
- Applied comments to the table and **`salary`** column.
- Used **`SELECT`**, **`SELECT DISTINCT`**, **`WHERE`**, **`LIMIT`**, and **`Alias`** to query data.
- Added a new column (**email**) and inserted a new record with auto-increment.

This exercise covers all the topics of this lesson and provides hands-on practice with MySQL database and table creation.

Conclusion

We are now familiar with creating and managing a MySQL database, including defining tables, inserting records, and using queries such as SELECT, WHERE, and LIMIT for data retrieval. Understanding data types, aliases, and auto-increment ensures efficient data organization. Comments enhance code readability, while DISTINCT filters unique values, optimizing database functionality and performance.

In the next chapter, we will learn about constraints in MySQL. Different types of constraints and their usages will also be covered with examples.

Points to Remember

- Define a database and tables with appropriate structure and data types to ensure data integrity and efficiency.
- Use INSERT to add records and SELECT with WHERE and LIMIT to retrieve specific data.
- Utilize SELECT DISTINCT to filter duplicate values and fetch unique records.
- Apply aliases for readability and use AUTO_INCREMENT for unique primary keys.
- Add comments in MySQL to improve code understanding and maintainability.

Multiple Choice Questions

1. What is the purpose of the AUTO_INCREMENT attribute in MySQL?
   a. To delete records automatically
   b. To generate a unique number for each new record
   c. To limit the number of records in a table
   d. To add comments to a table
2. Which SQL statement is used to retrieve unique values from a column?
   a. SELECT
   b. SELECT UNIQUE
   c. SELECT DISTINCT
   d. SELECT DIFFERENT
3. What does the LIMIT clause do in MySQL?
   a. Restricts the number of rows returned in a query
   b. Limits the number of columns in a table
   c. Adds a comment to a query
   d. Filters data based on a condition
4. How do you add a comment in MySQL?
   a. Using -- or /* */
   b. Using # or //
   c. Using the COMMENT keyword
   d. Using the REMARK keyword

Answer

1. b
2. c
3. a
4. a

Questions

1. Explain the steps to create a database and a table in MySQL. What are the key considerations when defining table columns?
2. How does the INSERT statement work in MySQL? Provide an example of inserting multiple records into a table.
3. What is the purpose of the WHERE clause in MySQL? Write a query to retrieve records from a table where the age is greater than 25.
4. Describe the difference between the SELECT and SELECT DISTINCT statements in MySQL. Provide an example for each.
5. What are MySQL data types? List and explain at least three commonly used datatypes and their applications.

Key Terms

- **Database**: A structured collection of data stored and organized for easy access, management, and updating.
- **Table**: A set of related data stored in rows and columns within a database.
- **`SELECT` Statement**: A SQL command used to retrieve data from one or more tables.
- **`AUTO_INCREMENT`**: A MySQL attribute that automatically generates a unique number for a column when a new record is inserted.
- **WHERE Clause**: A SQL clause used to filter records based on specified conditions.
- **Datatype**: Defines the type of data a column can hold, such as **`INT`**, **`VARCHAR`**, or **`DATE`**, ensuring data integrity.
- **Alias**: A temporary name assigned to a table or column in a query to improve readability or simplify references.

CHAPTER 3
Constraints in MySQL

Introduction

This chapter covers the constraints in MySQL with example queries. The rules for the data in a table are called constraints. We will discuss the types of constraints with examples, including Primary Key, Foreign Key, Not Null, Check, and so on. In the later part of the chapter, we will add constraints to existing tables and also how to drop a constraint easily.

Structure

In this chapter, we will discuss the following topics:

- Defining Constraints in MySQL
- Primary Key Constraint
- Foreign Key Constraint
- Unique Constraint
- Not Null Constraint
- CHECK Constraint
- Default Constraint
- Adding Constraints to Existing Tables
- Dropping Constraints
- Practical Exercise

Defining Constraints in MySQL

In MySQL, constraints are predefined rules applied to columns or tables to uphold data integrity and guarantee the reliability and accuracy of stored information. These constraints ensure database consistency by limiting the kinds of data that can be added, modified, or removed.

Constraints in MySQL are rules applied to table columns to enforce data integrity, accuracy, and consistency. They help maintain reliable and meaningful data in a database. Here are the key advantages:

Ensures Data Integrity:

- **Prevents Invalid Data:** Constraints such as `NOT NULL`, `CHECK`, and `FOREIGN KEY` ensure only valid data is stored.
- **Avoids Duplicate Records:** `PRIMARY KEY` and `UNIQUE` constraints prevent duplicate entries.

Maintains Referential Integrity (Foreign Keys)

- **Ensures Valid Relationships:** A `FOREIGN KEY` constraint links tables and prevents orphaned records.
- **Prevents Accidental Deletion:** Prevents deleting a parent record if child records exist (unless `ON DELETE CASCADE` is used).

Improves Query Performance

- **Indexing:** Constraints such as `PRIMARY KEY` and `UNIQUE` automatically create indexes, speeding up searches.
- **Optimized Joins:** Foreign keys improve join operations between related tables.

Enforces Business Rules

- **Custom Validation:** `CHECK` constraints enforce specific conditions (for example, salary > 0, email format).
- **Domain Integrity:** Restricts column values to valid options (for example, `ENUM('Male','Female')`).

Simplifies Error Handling

- **Clear Error Messages:** MySQL rejects invalid data with explicit errors (for example, "Duplicate entry for `PRIMARY KEY`").
- **Early Detection:** Issues are caught at the database level rather than in the application code.

Supports Data Consistency in Transactions

ACID Compliance: Constraints work with transactions to ensure all operations follow rules (for example, rolling back invalid inserts).

Here are the main types of constraints in MySQL:

Define the Primary Key Constraint

The primary key constraint ensures that a column or a combination of columns uniquely identifies each row within a table. Key aspects include:

- A table can have only a single primary key.

- Columns designated as the primary key must not contain NULL values.
- Example:

```
CREATE TABLE Employees (
    EmployeeID INT PRIMARY KEY,
    FirstName VARCHAR(50),
    LastName VARCHAR(50)
);
```

Define Foreign Key Constraint

The foreign key constraint enforces referential integrity between two tables. Here are some key points:

- A foreign key in one table references the primary key of another table.
- Prevents actions that would destroy the link between the tables.
- Example:

```
CREATE TABLE Orders (
    OrderID INT PRIMARY KEY,
    OrderDate DATE,
    EmployeeID INT,
    FOREIGN KEY (EmployeeID) REFERENCES Employees(EmployeeID)
);
```

Define Unique Constraint

The unique constraint guarantees that all entries in a column, or a combination of columns, are distinct and not duplicated.

Here are some key points:

- Unlike a primary key, a table can have multiple unique constraints.
- Allows **NULL** values (unless explicitly restricted).
- Example:

```
CREATE TABLE Users (
    UserID INT PRIMARY KEY,
    Email VARCHAR(100) UNIQUE,
    Username VARCHAR(50) UNIQUE
);
```

Define `Not Null` Constraint

The Not Null constraint ensures that a column cannot have **NULL** values.

Example:

```
CREATE TABLE Customers (
    CustomerID INT PRIMARY KEY,
    FirstName VARCHAR(50) NOT NULL,
    LastName VARCHAR(50) NOT NULL
);
```

Define `CHECK` Constraint

The **`CHECK`** constraint ensures that all values in a column satisfy a specific condition.

Example:

```
CREATE TABLE Products (
    ProductID INT PRIMARY KEY,
    ProductName VARCHAR(100),
    Price DECIMAL(10, 2) CHECK (Price > 0)
);
```

Define `Default` Constraint

The default constraint assigns a predefined value to a column when no specific value is provided during data insertion.

Example:

```
CREATE TABLE Orders (
    OrderID INT PRIMARY KEY,
    OrderDate DATE DEFAULT CURRENT_DATE
);
```

Constraints play a vital role in preserving data integrity and ensuring the proper functioning of the database.

They help prevent invalid data entry and enforce relationships between tables.

Now, we will understand the types of constraints in detail.

Primary Key Constraint

The **Primary Key Constraint** in MySQL is a fundamental concept used to uniquely identify each row in a table. It ensures that the column (or set of columns) designated as the primary key contains unique and non-NULL values.

In MySQL, the primary key is a fundamental feature that guarantees data integrity by requiring uniqueness and non-NULL values in a column or a combination of columns. It is commonly employed to uniquely distinguish rows in a table and to create relationships between tables.

Features of Primary Key Constraints

The following are the features of primary key constraint:

- **Uniqueness**: Each value in the primary key column(s) must be unique. No two rows can have the same primary key value.
- **Non-NULL**: The primary key column(s) cannot contain NULL values. Every row must have a valid, non-NULL value in the primary key column(s).
- **Single Primary Key per Table**: A table can have only one primary key, but this primary key can consist of one or multiple columns (composite key).
- **Indexing**: MySQL automatically creates an index for the primary key column(s), which speeds up queries that search or filter based on the primary key.

Defining a Primary Key

You can define a primary key when creating a table or alter an existing table to add a primary key.

Defining Primary Key During Table Creation

- Single-column primary key:

```
CREATE TABLE Employees (
    EmployeeID INT PRIMARY KEY,
    FirstName VARCHAR(50),
    LastName VARCHAR(50)
      );
```

- Composite primary key (multiple columns):

```
CREATE TABLE Orders (
    OrderID INT,
    ProductID INT,
    Quantity INT,
    PRIMARY KEY (OrderID, ProductID)
      );
```

Adding Primary Key to an Existing Table

To add a primary key to an existing table, you can use the **`ALTER TABLE`** statement.

```
ALTER TABLE Employees
ADD PRIMARY KEY (EmployeeID);
```

Example of Primary Key Usage

Let us see some examples of using the primary key, including single-column and composite primary key:

Table with Single-Column Primary Key

Here, the **StudentID** is set as the primary key:

```
CREATE TABLE Students (
    StudentID INT PRIMARY KEY,
    Name VARCHAR(100),
    Age INT
);
```

In this example, **StudentID** is the primary key. Each student must have a unique **StudentID**, and it cannot be **NULL**.

Table with Composite Primary Key

Here, the combination of **OrderID** and **ProductID** forms the primary key. This ensures that each product in an order is unique.

```
CREATE TABLE OrderDetails (
    OrderID INT,
    ProductID INT,
    Quantity INT,
    PRIMARY KEY (OrderID, ProductID)
);
```

Important Notes

- **Auto Increment**: Often, the primary key column is paired with the **AUTO_INCREMENT** attribute to automatically generate unique values for each row:

  ```
  CREATE TABLE Customers (
      CustomerID INT PRIMARY KEY AUTO_INCREMENT,
      Name VARCHAR(100)
        );
  ```

- **Foreign Key Relationship**: The primary key of one table is often referenced as a foreign key in another table to establish relationships between tables.
- **Performance**: Since the primary key is indexed, it improves the performance of queries that search, filter, or join tables based on the primary key.

Foreign Key Constraint

In MySQL, the **Foreign Key Constraint** ensures referential integrity by linking two tables. It mandates that the value in a column (or group of columns) in one table corresponds to the primary key or unique key in another table. This relationship helps maintain consistency and avoids the creation of orphaned records.

It is a powerful feature in MySQL that establishes a relationship between the child table (containing the foreign key) and the parent table (containing the referenced primary key or unique key). By using foreign keys, you can maintain data consistency and prevent invalid data entries.

Features of Foreign Key Constraints

The following are the features of the foreign key constraint:

- **Referential Integrity**: Ensures that the value in the foreign key column(s) must exist in the referenced primary key or unique key column(s) of the parent table.
- **Parent-Child Relationship**: The table with the foreign key is called **the child table**, and the table being referenced is called the **parent table**.
- **Actions on Update/Delete**: You can define what happens to the child table when the referenced row in the parent table is updated or deleted. Common actions include:
    - **`CASCADE`:** Automatically propagates updates or deletions in the parent table to the corresponding rows in the child table.
    - **`SET NULL`**: Assigns NULL to the foreign key column(s) in the child table when the related row in the parent table is updated or removed.
    - **`RESTRICT`:** Prevent the update or deletion of the referenced row in the parent table if dependent rows exist in the child table.
    - **`NO ACTION`:** Similar to **`RESTRICT`**, but the behavior depends on the database engine.
- **Indexing**: MySQL automatically creates an index on the foreign key column(s) to improve query performance.

Defining a Foreign Key

You can define a foreign key when creating a table or alter an existing table to add a foreign key.

Defining Foreign Key During Table Creation

```
CREATE TABLE Orders (
    OrderID INT PRIMARY KEY,
    OrderDate DATE,
    CustomerID INT,
    FOREIGN KEY (CustomerID) REFERENCES Customers(CustomerID)
);
```

Adding a Foreign Key to an Existing Table

If the table already exists, use the **ALTER TABLE** statement to add a foreign key:

```
ALTER TABLE Orders
ADD CONSTRAINT FK_Customer
FOREIGN KEY (CustomerID) REFERENCES Customers(CustomerID);
```

Example of Foreign Key Usage

Let us see an example of the usage of foreign keys in MySQL. We have created both the parent and the child table:

- **Parent Table (Customers)**

```
CREATE TABLE Customers (
    CustomerID INT PRIMARY KEY,
    Name VARCHAR(100),
    Email VARCHAR(100)
       );
```

- **Child Table (Orders)**

```
CREATE TABLE Orders (
    OrderID INT PRIMARY KEY,
    OrderDate DATE,
    CustomerID INT,
    FOREIGN KEY (CustomerID) REFERENCES Customers(CustomerID)
       );
```

In this example, the **CustomerID** column in the **Orders** table serves as a foreign key, linking to the **CustomerID** column in the **Customers** table. This ensures that every order is associated with a valid customer.

Here is a graphic representation of the relationship discussed:

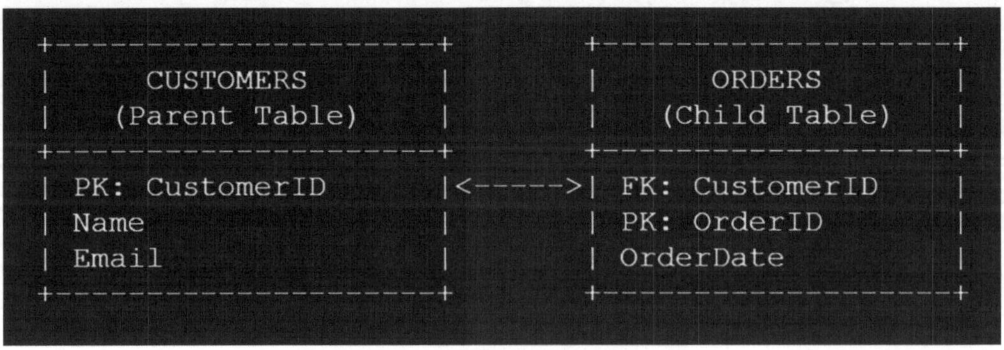

Figure 3.1: *Foreign Key relationship*

Actions on `Update/Delete`

You can define the actions to be taken when the referenced row in the parent table is modified or removed. For example:

```
CREATE TABLE Orders (
    OrderID INT PRIMARY KEY,
    OrderDate DATE,
    CustomerID INT,
    FOREIGN KEY (CustomerID) REFERENCES Customers(CustomerID)
    ON DELETE CASCADE
    ON UPDATE CASCADE
);
```

Here,

- **`ON DELETE CASCADE`**: If a customer is deleted from the **`Customers`** table, all their orders in the **Orders** table will also be deleted.
- **`ON UPDATE CASCADE`**: If a **`CustomerID`** is updated in the **`Customers`** table, the corresponding **`CustomerID`** in the Orders table will also be updated.

Important Notes

- **Data Types**: The foreign key column(s) and the referenced column(s) must have the same data type.
- **Indexing**: The referenced column(s) in the parent table must be indexed (for example, a primary key or unique key).
- **Referential Actions**: Choose the appropriate action (**`CASCADE, SET NULL, RESTRICT, NO ACTION`**) based on your application's requirements.
- **Storage Engine**: Foreign keys are supported only by the **InnoDB** storage engine in MySQL. If you are using a different storage engine (for example, MyISAM), foreign keys will not work.

Unique Constraint

The **Unique Constraint** in MySQL ensures that all values in a column are distinct. This works for a set of columns as well. Unlike the **Primary Key Constraint**, a table can have multiple unique constraints, and the unique column(s) can contain NULL values (though only one NULL is allowed per column if the column is unique). It is useful for enforcing data integrity when you need to prevent duplicate values in specific columns.

Features of Unique Constraints

The following are the features of Unique Constraints:

- **Uniqueness**: Ensures that all values in the column(s) are unique. No two rows can have the same value(s) in the unique column(s).
- **Multiple Unique Constraints**: A table can have more than one unique constraint.
- **NULL Values**: Unique columns can contain **NULL** values, but only one **NULL** is allowed per column (since **NULL** is considered a distinct value in MySQL).
- **Indexing**: MySQL automatically creates an index on the unique column(s) to enforce uniqueness and improve query performance.

Differences Between UNIQUE and PRIMARY KEY Constraints in MySQL

Both **UNIQUE** and **PRIMARY KEY** enforce uniqueness in a column (or set of columns), but they have key differences. Students often get confused between unique and primary key constraints. Let us see the differences:

Feature	PRIMARY KEY	UNIQUE KEY
Uniqueness	Must be unique (no duplicates).	Must be unique (no duplicates).
NULL Values	**Cannot** contain NULL values.	**Can** contain one NULL (unless NOT NULL is also set).
Number per Table	Only **one** per table.	**Multiple** allowed per table.
Auto-Increment	Often used with AUTO_INCREMENT.	Rarely used with auto-increment.
Indexing	Automatically creates a **clustered index** (faster retrieval).	Creates a **non-clustered index**.
Purpose	Used to **uniquely identify each row** (for example, id).	Used to enforce uniqueness in non-primary columns (for example, email, username).
Foreign Key	Can be referenced by FOREIGN KEY.	Can also be referenced, but less common.

Table 1.1: *Differences between PRIMARY KEY and UNIQUE constraints*

Defining a Unique Constraint

A unique constraint can be specified during table creation or added to an existing table using the **`ALTER TABLE`** statement.

Defining Unique Constraints During Table Creation

Let us define the unique constraint while creating a table. Here, we will cover the single-column and composite unique constraints:

- Single-column unique constraint:

```
CREATE TABLE Users (
    UserID INT PRIMARY KEY,
    Username VARCHAR(50) UNIQUE,
    Email VARCHAR(100) UNIQUE
      );
```

- Composite unique constraint (multiple columns):

```
CREATE TABLE Orders (
    OrderID INT,
    ProductID INT,
    Quantity INT,
    UNIQUE (OrderID, ProductID)
      );
```

Adding Unique Constraints to an Existing Table

If a table is already created, the **ALTER TABLE** statement can be used to introduce a unique constraint.

```
ALTER TABLE Users
ADD CONSTRAINT UQ_Email UNIQUE (Email);
```

Example of Unique Constraint Usage

Here are some examples of using the unique constraint, including single-column and composite unique constraint:

- Table with Single-Column Unique Constraint

```
CREATE TABLE Employees (
    EmployeeID INT PRIMARY KEY,
    Email VARCHAR(100) UNIQUE,
    Phone VARCHAR(15) UNIQUE
);
```

In this example, the **Email** and **Phone** columns must contain unique values. No two employees can have the same email or phone number.

- Table with Composite Unique Constraint

```
CREATE TABLE OrderItems (
    OrderID INT,
    ProductID INT,
```

```
    Quantity INT,
    UNIQUE (OrderID, ProductID)
);
```

Here, the combination of **OrderID** and **ProductID** must be unique. This ensures that the same product cannot be added more than once to the same order.

Important Notes

- **NULL Values**: Unique constraints allow NULL values, but only one NULL is allowed per column. For example:

  ```
  INSERT INTO Users (UserID, Email) VALUES (1, NULL); -- Allowed
  INSERT INTO Users (UserID, Email) VALUES (2, NULL); -- Allowed in
  some databases, but not in MySQL
  ```

- **Difference from Primary Key**:
  - A table can have only one primary key, but multiple unique constraints.
  - The primary key column(s) cannot contain NULL values, but unique columns can.
- **Performance**: Unique constraints automatically create an index, which improves the performance of queries that search or filter based on the unique column(s).
- **Composite Unique Constraint**: When using a composite unique constraint, the combination of values in the specified columns must be unique, but individual columns can have duplicate values.

Not Null Constraint

The **NOT NULL** constraint in MySQL guarantees that a column must always have a value and cannot be left empty (**NULL**). It enforces that a column must always have a value, preventing the insertion or update of rows with missing data in that column. It makes it mandatory for every row to have a value in that column. It is a simple yet powerful tool for enforcing data integrity and preventing incomplete or missing data.

Features of NOT NULL Constraint

The following are the features of the NOT NULL Constraint:

- **Mandatory Value**: Ensures that a column must always have a value. **NULL** values are not allowed.
- **Data Integrity**: It ensures data integrity by preventing incomplete or missing data in critical columns.

- **No Default Value**: Unlike the **`DEFAULT`** constraint, the **`NOT NULL`** constraint does not provide a default value. It simply enforces that a value must be explicitly provided.
- **Applicable to Any Data Type**: Can be applied to columns of any data type (for example, **`INT, VARCHAR, DATE`**, and so on).

Defining a NOT NULL Constraint

You can define a **`NOT NULL`** constraint when creating a table or alter an existing table to add the constraint.

Defining NOT NULL During Table Creation

Let us create a table and set **`NOT NULL`** for some columns while creating a table:

```
CREATE TABLE Employees (
    EmployeeID INT PRIMARY KEY,
    FirstName VARCHAR(50) NOT NULL,
    LastName VARCHAR(50) NOT NULL,
    Email VARCHAR(100)
);
```

In this example, the **`FirstName`** and **`LastName`** columns cannot contain NULL values.

Adding NOT NULL to an Existing Table

If the table already exists, use the **`ALTER TABLE`** statement and add the **`NOT NULL`** constraint:

```
ALTER TABLE Employees
MODIFY Email VARCHAR(100) NOT NULL;
```

Example of NOT NULL Usage

Let us see some examples to understand how the **`NOT NULL`** constraint works while creating tables:

Table with NOT NULL Columns

In this example, the **`Name`** and **`Age`** columns must have values, while the Grade column can contain **`NULL`**.

```
CREATE TABLE Students (
    StudentID INT PRIMARY KEY,
    Name VARCHAR(100) NOT NULL,
    Age INT NOT NULL,
```

```
    Grade CHAR(1)
);
```

Inserting Data

Let us now insert records in a table where we have set the Not Null constraint:

- Valid insertion:

  ```
  INSERT INTO Students (StudentID, Name, Age) VALUES (1, 'John
  Doe', 20);
  ```

- Invalid insertion (will fail because **Name** is **NULL**):

  ```
  INSERT INTO Students (StudentID, Name, Age) VALUES (2, NULL, 22);
  ```

Important Notes

- **Combining with DEFAULT**: You can combine the **NOT NULL** constraint with the **DEFAULT** constraint to ensure that a column always has a value, even if one is not explicitly provided:

  ```
  CREATE TABLE Orders (
      OrderID INT PRIMARY KEY,
      OrderDate DATE NOT NULL DEFAULT CURRENT_DATE
        );
  ```

- **Primary Key Columns**: Primary key columns implicitly have the **NOT NULL** constraint, so you do not need to specify it explicitly.
- **Error Handling**: If you try to insert or update a row with a **NULL** value in a **NOT NULL** column, MySQL will raise an error.
- **Use Cases**: Use the **NOT NULL** constraint for columns that are critical to the table's functionality, such as:
  - User names, email addresses, or IDs.
  - Dates, amounts, or other mandatory fields.

Check Constraint

The **Check Constraint** in MySQL is used to enforce a condition on the values that can be inserted or updated in a column. It ensures that the data in a column meets a specific requirement, such as a range, pattern, or logical condition. If the condition is not satisfied, MySQL will reject the insert or update operation.

It is a powerful tool for enforcing specific conditions on the data in a table. Utilizing check constraints helps preserve data integrity and ensures that invalid data cannot be inserted or modified within your database.

Features of Check Constraints

The following are the features of check constraints:

- **Condition Enforcement**: Ensures that the values in a column satisfy a specified condition.
- **Flexible Conditions**: The condition can be based on logical expressions, mathematical comparisons, or even references to other columns in the same row.
- **Applicable to Insert and Update Operations**: The check constraint is enforced during both **INSERT** and **UPDATE** operations.
- **Column-Level or Table-Level**: Apply it to a single column easily, However, it can be applied to multiple columns (table-level) as well.

Defining a Check Constraint

You can define a check constraint when creating a table or alter an existing table to add the constraint.

Defining Check Constraints During Table Creation

Let us see an example to define check constraints at the column and table level while creating tables:

- Column-level check constraint:

```
CREATE TABLE Employees (
    EmployeeID INT PRIMARY KEY,
    FirstName VARCHAR(50),
    LastName VARCHAR(50),
    Age INT CHECK (Age >= 18)
      );
```

- Table-level check constraint (involving multiple columns):

```
CREATE TABLE Orders (
    OrderID INT PRIMARY KEY,
    OrderDate DATE,
    TotalAmount DECIMAL(10, 2),
    Discount DECIMAL(10, 2),
    CHECK (TotalAmount >= Discount)
);
```

Adding Check Constraint to an Existing Table

If the table is already created, you can utilize the **ALTER TABLE** statement to include a check constraint.

```
ALTER TABLE Employees
ADD CONSTRAINT CHK_Age CHECK (Age >= 18);
```

Example of Check Constraint Usage

Let us see some examples related to check constraints at the column and table levels:

- **Table with Column-Level Check Constraint**

```
CREATE TABLE Students (
    StudentID INT PRIMARY KEY,
    Name VARCHAR(100),
    Age INT CHECK (Age BETWEEN 10 AND 20),
    Grade CHAR(1) CHECK (Grade IN ('A', 'B', 'C', 'D', 'F'))
);
```

In this example:

- The **Age** column must be between 10 and 20.
- The **Grade** column must be one of the specified values (**A**, **B**, **C**, **D**, or **F**).
- **Table with Table-Level Check Constraint**

```
CREATE TABLE Products (
    ProductID INT PRIMARY KEY,
    ProductName VARCHAR(100),
    Price DECIMAL(10, 2),
    Quantity INT,
    CHECK (Price > 0 AND Quantity >= 0)
);
```

Here, the **Price** must be greater than 0, and the **Quantity** must be non-negative.

Inserting Data with Check Constraints

Consider the **Students** table, where we have set check constraints for the **Age** and **Grade** columns. Let us insert data to the same table with check constraints:

- Valid insertion:

```
INSERT INTO Students (StudentID, Name, Age, Grade) VALUES (1,
'John Doe', 15, 'A');
```

- Invalid insertion (will fail because **Age** is out of range):

```
INSERT INTO Students (StudentID, Name, Age, Grade) VALUES (2,
'Jane Smith', 25, 'B');
```

Notes:

- **MySQL Version Support**: *Check constraints are fully supported starting from* **MySQL 8.0.16**. *If you are using an older version, the check constraint syntax will be accepted, but it will not be enforced.*
- **Error Handling**: *If a check constraint is violated during an* ***INSERT*** *or* ***UPDATE*** *operation, MySQL will raise an error and reject the operation.*
- **Combining with Other Constraints**: *Check constraints can be used alongside other constraints such as* ***NOT NULL***, ***UNIQUE***, *and* ***FOREIGN KEY***.
- **Complex Conditions**: *You can use complex logical expressions in check constraints, such as:*

```
CREATE TABLE Employees (
    EmployeeID INT PRIMARY KEY,
    Salary DECIMAL(10, 2),
    Bonus DECIMAL(10, 2),
    CHECK (Salary > 0 AND Bonus <= Salary * 0.2)
      );
```

Default Constraint

The **Default Constraint** in MySQL is used to define a predetermined (default) value for a column. If no value is provided for the column during an INSERT operation, the default value is automatically assigned. This ensures that the column always has a value, even if one is not explicitly provided.

Default constraints are commonly used for columns such as dates, statuses, or numeric fields, and they help maintain data consistency and integrity.

Features of Default Constraint

The following are the features of default constraint:

- **Default Value:** Assigns a fallback value to a column when no explicit value is provided during an INSERT operation.
- **Applicable to All Data Types:** Can be used with columns of any data type (for example, **INT, VARCHAR, DATE**, and so on).
- **Optional**: If a value is explicitly provided for the column, the default value is ignored.

- **NULL Handling**: If the column allows **NULL** values and no default value is specified, **NULL** is used as the default.

Syntax for Defining a `Default` Constraint

You can define a default constraint when creating a table or alter an existing table to add a default value.

Defining `Default` Constraints During Table Creation

Let us see how we can define a default constraint for a column while creating a table:

```
CREATE TABLE Employees (
    EmployeeID INT PRIMARY KEY,
    FirstName VARCHAR(50),
    LastName VARCHAR(50),
    HireDate DATE DEFAULT CURRENT_DATE,
    Salary DECIMAL(10, 2) DEFAULT 0.00
);
```

In this example:

- The **`HireDate`** column will default to the current date if no value is provided.
- The **`Salary`** column will default to 0.00 if no value is provided.

Adding Default Constraints to an Existing Table

If the table already exists, use the **`ALTER TABLE`** statement in MySQL to add a default value:

```
ALTER TABLE Employees
ALTER HireDate SET DEFAULT CURRENT_DATE;
```

Example of Default Constraint Usage

Let us see some examples of default constraints in MySQL:

Table with Default Values

```
CREATE TABLE Orders (
    OrderID INT PRIMARY KEY,
    OrderDate DATE DEFAULT CURRENT_DATE,
    TotalAmount DECIMAL(10, 2) DEFAULT 0.00,
    Status VARCHAR(20) DEFAULT 'Pending'
);
```

In this example:

- The **OrderDate** column defaults to the current date.
- The **TotalAmount** column defaults to **0.00**.
- The **Status** column defaults to '**Pending**'.

Inserting Data

We will now insert some data in the table:

- Inserting a row without specifying values for columns with default constraints:
  ```
  INSERT INTO Orders (OrderID) VALUES (1);
  ```
  Result:
  - **OrderDate** will be set to the current date.
  - **TotalAmount** will be set to **0.00**.
  - Status will be set to '**Pending**'.
- Inserting a row with explicit values:
  ```
  INSERT INTO Orders (OrderID, OrderDate, TotalAmount, Status)
  VALUES (2, '2025-10-01', 100.50, 'Completed');
  ```
  The default values are ignored because explicit values are provided.

Notes:

- **NULL Values**: *If a column permits NULL values and lacks a specified default,* **NULL** *will be used as the default.*
- **Expressions as Default Values**: *MySQL allows certain expressions as default values, such as* ***CURRENT_DATE*** *or* ***CURRENT_TIMESTAMP****. However, not all expressions are supported.*
- **Combining with *NOT NULL***: *If a column has both a* ***NOT NULL*** *constraint and a default value, the default value will be used when no value is provided, ensuring the column is never* ***NULL****.*
- **Use Cases**: *Default constraints are useful for columns such as:*
  - *Dates (for example, default to the current date).*
  - *Status fields (for example, default to '****Pending****').*
  - *Numeric fields (for example, default to 0).*

Adding Constraints to Existing Tables

In MySQL, you can add constraints to existing tables. To achieve this, use the ALTER TABLE statement. Constraints help enforce data integrity and ensure that the data in your tables meets specific rules.

Examples of Adding Various Types of Constraints to Existing Tables

The following are examples of how to add various types of constraints to an existing table:

Adding a `Primary Key` Constraint

Let us see how to add a primary key constraint to an existing table in MySQL:

```
ALTER TABLE Employees
ADD PRIMARY KEY (EmployeeID);
```

This makes the **`EmployeeID`** column the primary key of the **`Employees`** table.

Adding a `Foreign Key` Constraint

Let us see how to add a foreign key constraint to an existing table in MySQL:

```
ALTER TABLE Orders
ADD CONSTRAINT FK_Customer
FOREIGN KEY (CustomerID) REFERENCES Customers(CustomerID);
```

This creates a foreign key relationship between the **`CustomerID`** column in the **`Orders`** table and the **`CustomerID`** column in the **`Customers`** table.

Adding a `Unique` Constraint

Let us see how to add a unique constraint to an existing table in MySQL:

```
ALTER TABLE Users
ADD CONSTRAINT UQ_Email UNIQUE (Email);
```

This ensures that the **`Email`** column in the **`Users`** table contains unique values.

Adding a `NOT NULL` Constraint

Let us see how to add a NOT NULL constraint to an existing table in MySQL:

```
ALTER TABLE Employees
MODIFY FirstName VARCHAR(50) NOT NULL;
```

This ensures that the **`FirstName`** column in the **`Employees`** table cannot contain **`NULL`** values.

Adding a `CHECK` Constraint

Let us see how to add a **`CHECK`** constraint to an existing table in MySQL using **`CHECK`**:

```
ALTER TABLE Products
ADD CONSTRAINT CHK_Price CHECK (Price > 0);
```

This ensures that the **`Price`** column in the **`Products`** table must be greater than 0.

Adding a Default Constraint

Let us see how to add a default constraint to an existing table in MySQL using **`DEFAULT`**:

```
ALTER TABLE Orders
ALTER OrderDate SET DEFAULT CURRENT_DATE;
```

This sets the default value of the **`OrderDate`** column in the **`Orders`** table to the current date.

Examples of Adding Constraints

Let us see some examples to learn how to add constraints in MySQL:

Example 1: Adding Multiple Constraints

Suppose you have a table **`Students`** and want to add a primary key, a unique constraint, and a check constraint:

```
ALTER TABLE Students
ADD PRIMARY KEY (StudentID),
ADD CONSTRAINT UQ_Email UNIQUE (Email),
ADD CONSTRAINT CHK_Age CHECK (Age >= 10);
```

Example 2: Adding a Foreign Key with `ON DELETE CASCADE`

To add a foreign key that cascades delete from the parent table to the child table:

```
ALTER TABLE Orders
ADD CONSTRAINT FK_Customer
FOREIGN KEY (CustomerID) REFERENCES Customers(CustomerID)
ON DELETE CASCADE;
ALTER TABLE Orders
ALTER OrderDate DROP DEFAULT;
```

Notes:

1. **Data Validation**: *When adding constraints to an existing table, MySQL will validate the existing data to ensure it complies with the new constraint. If any data violates the constraint, the operation will fail.*
2. **Indexing**: *Adding a primary key or unique constraint automatically creates an index on the column(s).*
3. **Foreign Key Requirements**: *The referenced column(s) in the parent table must have a primary key or unique constraint.*
4. **MySQL Version**: *Ensure you are using a MySQL version that supports the constraint you want to add. For example, check constraints are fully supported starting from MySQL 8.0.16.*

You can add constraints to existing tables in MySQL using the **`ALTER TABLE`** statement. This allows you to enforce data integrity rules, such as primary keys, foreign keys, unique constraints, **`NOT NULL`** constraints, check constraints, and default values. Always ensure that existing data complies with the new constraints before adding them.

Dropping Constraints

In MySQL, you can **easily drop** (remove) constraints from a table. To achieve this, use the **`ALTER TABLE`** statement. Dropping constraints is useful when you no longer need to enforce certain rules on your data or when you want to modify the table's structure.

Each type of constraint (primary key, foreign key, unique, check, **`NOT NULL`**, and default) has its syntax for removal. Always verify the impact of dropping a constraint on your data integrity and application logic before proceeding.

Examples of Dropping Various Types of Constraints

The following are examples of how to drop various types of constraints:

Dropping a `Primary Key` Constraint

Let us see how to drop a primary key constraint:

```
ALTER TABLE Employees
DROP PRIMARY KEY;
```

This removes the primary key constraint from the **Employees** table.

Note: *A table can have only one primary key, so you do not need to specify the column name.*

Dropping a Foreign Key Constraint

Let us see how to drop a foreign key constraint:

```
ALTER TABLE Orders
DROP FOREIGN KEY FK_Customer;
```

This removes the foreign key constraint named **FK_Customer** from the **Orders** table.

Note: *You need to know the name of the foreign key constraint. You can find it using the* ***SHOW CREATE TABLE*** *statement*:

```
SHOW CREATE TABLE Orders;
```

Dropping a Unique Constraint

Let us see how to drop a unique constraint:

```
ALTER TABLE Users
DROP INDEX UQ_Email;
```

This removes the unique constraint named **UQ_Email** from the **Users** table.

Note: *In MySQL, a unique constraint is implemented as an index, so you use* ***DROP INDEX*** *to remove it.*

Dropping a Check Constraint

Let us see how to drop a check constraint:

```
ALTER TABLE Products
DROP CONSTRAINT CHK_Price;
```

This removes the check constraint named **CHK_Price** from the **Products** table.

Note: *Check constraints are supported starting from* MySQL 8.0.16.

Removing a NOT NULL Constraint

To remove a **NOT NULL** constraint:

```
ALTER TABLE Employees
MODIFY FirstName VARCHAR(50);
```

This modifies the **FirstName** column to allow **NULL** values, effectively removing the **NOT NULL** constraint.

Removing a `Default` Constraint

Let us see how to remove a value from a column:

```
ALTER TABLE Orders
ALTER OrderDate DROP DEFAULT;
```

This removes the default value from the **`OrderDate`** column in the **`Orders`** table.

Examples of Dropping Constraints

Let us see some examples to learn how to drop constraints in MySQL:

Example 1: Dropping Multiple Constraints

Let us say, you want to drop a primary key and a foreign key from a table:

```
ALTER TABLE Employees
DROP PRIMARY KEY,
DROP FOREIGN KEY FK_Department;
```

Example 2: Dropping a Unique Constraint and Removing `NOT NULL`

To drop a unique constraint and remove the **`NOT NULL`** constraint from a column:

]

```
ALTER TABLE Users
DROP INDEX UQ_Email,
MODIFY Email VARCHAR(100);
```

Notes:

1. **Foreign Key Names**: *When dropping a foreign key, you need to specify the constraint name, not the column name. Use* ***`SHOW CREATE TABLE`*** *to find the constraint name.*
2. **Indexes**: *Dropping a unique constraint removes the associated index. If you need the index for performance reasons, you may want to recreate it separately.*
3. **Data Integrity**: *Dropping constraints can affect data integrity. Ensure that removing a constraint will not lead to invalid or inconsistent data.*
4. **MySQL Version**: *Some constraints (for example, check constraints) are only supported in newer versions of MySQL (8.0.16 and above).*

Practical Exercise

Here is a practical exercise that builds on the previous **Employee Management System** and incorporates the MySQL topics of this lesson. This exercise will guide you through creating tables with constraints, modifying existing tables, and working with primary keys, foreign keys, unique constraints, and more.

Exercise: Enhanced Employee Management System

Here is a practical exercise that covers all the MySQL topics we covered. This exercise will guide you through creating a database, defining tables, inserting records, and using various MySQL constraints.

Step 1: Create a Database

Create a databasc namcd **`employee_management_advanced`**.

```
CREATE DATABASE employee_management_advanced;
USE employee_management_advanced;
```

Step 2: Create Tables with Constraints

Create two tables:

- **departments**: Stores department details.
  - `department_id (INT, Primary Key, Auto Increment)`
  - `department_name (VARCHAR(50), Unique, Not Null`
  - Add a comment: "`Stores department details`".
- **employees**: Stores employee details.
  - `id (INT, Primary Key, Auto Increment)`
  - `name (VARCHAR(50), Not Null`
  - `department_id (INT, Foreign Key referencing departments.department_id)`
  - `salary (DECIMAL(10, 2), Not Null, Check Constraint (salary > 0)`
  - `join_date (DATE, Not Null, Default Constraint (CURRENT_DATE)`
  - Add a comment: "`Stores employee details`".

Here are the queries:

```
CREATE TABLE departments (
    department_id INT PRIMARY KEY AUTO_INCREMENT COMMENT 'Unique
department ID',
    department_name VARCHAR(50) NOT NULL UNIQUE COMMENT 'Name of the
department'
) COMMENT='Stores department details';

CREATE TABLE employees (
    id INT PRIMARY KEY AUTO_INCREMENT COMMENT 'Unique employee ID',
    name VARCHAR(50) NOT NULL COMMENT 'Employee name',
    department_id INT NOT NULL COMMENT 'Department ID',
    salary DECIMAL(10, 2) NOT NULL CHECK (salary > 0) COMMENT
'Employee salary',
    join_date DATE NOT NULL DEFAULT (CURRENT_DATE) COMMENT 'Employee
join date',
    FOREIGN KEY (department_id) REFERENCES departments(department_
id)
) COMMENT='Stores employee details';
```

Step 3: Insert Records

Insert records into the **departments** and **employees** tables.

```
-- Insert departments
INSERT INTO departments (department_name) VALUES
('HR'),
('IT'),
('Finance');

-- Insert employees
INSERT INTO employees (name, department_id, salary, join_date)
VALUES
('John Doe', 1, 50000.00, '2024-01-15'),
('Jane Smith', 2, 60000.00, '2024-03-22'),
('Alice Johnson', 3, 55000.00, '2024-07-30'),
('Bob Brown', 2, 62000.00, '2025-02-10'),
('Charlie Davis', 1, 48000.00, '2025-05-05');
```

Step 4: Test Constraints

Test the constraints by attempting to insert invalid data:

- Try inserting a duplicate department name.
- Try inserting an employee with a negative salary.
- Try inserting an employee without a name.

Let us see how to test:

```
-- Duplicate department name
INSERT INTO departments (department_name) VALUES ('HR'); -- Should
fail (Unique Constraint)

-- Negative salary
INSERT INTO employees (name, department_id, salary, join_date)
VALUES
('Eva Green', 3, -1000.00, '2025-01-10'); -- Should fail (Check
Constraint)

-- Missing name
INSERT INTO employees (department_id, salary, join_date) VALUES
(3, 58000.00, '2025-01-10'); -- Should fail (Not Null Constraint)
```

Step 5: Add Constraints to Existing Tables

Add a **UNIQUE** constraint to the **email** column in the **employees** table and a **DEFAULT** constraint for the **department_id** column.

```
-- Add email column
ALTER TABLE employees ADD COLUMN email VARCHAR(100);

-- Add Unique Constraint to email
ALTER TABLE employees ADD CONSTRAINT unique_email UNIQUE (email);

-- Add Default Constraint to department_id
ALTER TABLE employees MODIFY department_id INT DEFAULT 1;
```

Step 6: Insert Records with New Constraints

Insert records to test the new constraints.

```
-- Insert employee with email
INSERT INTO employees (name, department_id, salary, join_date,
email) VALUES
('Eva Green', 3, 58000.00, '2025-01-10', 'eva.green@example.com');

-- Insert employee without department_id (should use default value
1)
INSERT INTO employees (name, salary, join_date, email) VALUES
('Frank White', 52000.00, '2025-02-15', 'frank.white@example.com');
```

Step 7: Drop Constraints

Drop the **UNIQUE** constraint on the **email** column and the **CHECK** constraint on the **salary** column.

```
-- Drop Unique Constraint on email
ALTER TABLE employees DROP CONSTRAINT unique_email;

-- Drop Check Constraint on salary (MySQL does not support dropping
CHECK constraints directly, so recreate the column)
ALTER TABLE employees MODIFY salary DECIMAL(10, 2) NOT NULL;
```

Step 8: Verify Data

Retrieve all records from the **departments** and **employees** tables to verify the changes.

```
SELECT * FROM departments;
SELECT * FROM employees;
```

Final Queries

We added the following queries above:

```
CREATE DATABASE employee_management_advanced;
USE employee_management_advanced;

CREATE TABLE departments (
    department_id INT PRIMARY KEY AUTO_INCREMENT COMMENT 'Unique
department ID',
    department_name VARCHAR(50) NOT NULL UNIQUE COMMENT 'Name of the
department'
) COMMENT='Stores department details';

CREATE TABLE employees (
    id INT PRIMARY KEY AUTO_INCREMENT COMMENT 'Unique employee ID',
    name VARCHAR(50) NOT NULL COMMENT 'Employee name',
    department_id INT NOT NULL COMMENT 'Department ID',
    salary DECIMAL(10, 2) NOT NULL CHECK (salary > 0) COMMENT
'Employee salary',
    join_date DATE NOT NULL DEFAULT (CURRENT_DATE) COMMENT 'Employee
join date',
    FOREIGN KEY (department_id) REFERENCES departments(department_
id)
) COMMENT='Stores employee details';

-- Insert departments
INSERT INTO departments (department_name) VALUES
('HR'),
('IT'),
('Finance');
```

```
-- Insert employees
INSERT INTO employees (name, department_id, salary, join_date)
VALUES
('John Doe', 1, 50000.00, '2024-01-15'),
('Jane Smith', 2, 60000.00, '2024-03-22'),
('Alice Johnson', 3, 55000.00, '2024-07-30'),
('Bob Brown', 2, 62000.00, '2025-02-10'),
('Charlie Davis', 1, 48000.00, '2025-05-05');

-- Duplicate department name
INSERT INTO departments (department_name) VALUES ('HR'); -- Should
fail (Unique Constraint)

-- Negative salary
INSERT INTO employees (name, department_id, salary, join_date)
VALUES
('Eva Green', 3, -1000.00, '2025-01-10'); -- Should fail (Check
Constraint)

-- Missing name
INSERT INTO employees (department_id, salary, join_date) VALUES
(3, 58000.00, '2025-01-10'); -- Should fail (Not Null Constraint)

-- Add email column
ALTER TABLE employees ADD COLUMN email VARCHAR(100);

-- Add Unique Constraint to email
ALTER TABLE employees ADD CONSTRAINT unique_email UNIQUE (email);

-- Add Default Constraint to department_id
ALTER TABLE employees MODIFY department_id INT DEFAULT 1;

-- Insert employee with email
INSERT INTO employees (name, department_id, salary, join_date,
email) VALUES
('Eva Green', 3, 58000.00, '2025-01-10', 'eva.green@example.com');

-- Insert employee without department_id (should use default value
1)
INSERT INTO employees (name, salary, join_date, email) VALUES
('Frank White', 52000.00, '2025-02-15', 'frank.white@example.com');

-- Drop Unique Constraint on email
ALTER TABLE employees DROP CONSTRAINT unique_email;

-- Drop Check Constraint on salary (MySQL does not support dropping
```

```
CHECK constraints directly, so recreate the column)
ALTER TABLE employees MODIFY salary DECIMAL(10, 2) NOT NULL;

SELECT * FROM departments;
SELECT * FROM employees;
```

Expected Output

After completing the exercise, you should have:

- A database named **`employee_management_advanced`**.
- Two tables: departments and employees.
- Applied constraints: Primary Key, Foreign Key, Unique, Not Null, Check, and Default.
- Tested constraints by attempting to insert invalid data.
- Added and dropped constraints on existing tables.
- Verified the data in both tables.

Conclusion

We are now familiar with constraints in MySQL. MySQL constraints, such as **`NOT NULL`**, **`PRIMARY KEY`**, **`UNIQUE`**, **`DEFAULT`**, **`CHECK`**, and **`FOREIGN KEY`**, are essential tools for maintaining data integrity and consistency in a database. They enforce rules that ensure accurate and valid data, prevent duplicates, and establish relationships between tables.

By using constraints effectively, you can build robust and reliable database systems that meet your application's requirements. Always test constraints thoroughly to ensure they behave as expected.

In the next chapter, we will learn about operators in MySQL.

Points to Remember

- A primary key column cannot have **`NULL`** values.
- A table can have a single primary key, which may comprise multiple columns (composite key).
- A table can have multiple **`UNIQUE`** constraints.
- Constraints can be added during table creation or later. Use **`CREATE TABLE`** or **`ALTER TABLE`** to add constraints.
- Constraints can be dropped or modified. Use ALTER TABLE to remove or change constraints.

Multiple Choice Questions

1. Which of the following is true about the PRIMARY KEY constraint?
   a. A table can consist of multiple primary keys.
   b. A primary key column can contain NULL values.
   c. A primary key serves to distinctly identify each row within a table.
   d. A primary key is the same as a UNIQUE constraint.
2. Which version of MySQL introduced support for the CHECK constraint?
   a. MySQL 5.0
   b. MySQL 8.0.11
   c. MySQL 8.0.16
   d. MySQL 4.0
3. What is the purpose of a FOREIGN KEY constraint?
   a. To ensure that a column contains unique values.
   b. To establish a connection between a column in one table and the primary key in another table.
   c. To provide a default value for a column.
   d. To ensure that a column is required to contain a value and cannot be left as NULL.

Answer

1. c
2. c
3. b

Questions

1. Explain the purpose of the **`NOT NULL`** constraint in MySQL. Provide an example of a scenario where this constraint would be useful.
2. What is the significance of the **`PRIMARY KEY`** constraint in a database table? How does it differ from the **`UNIQUE`** constraint? Provide an example of a table where a primary key is essential.

3. Describe the **UNIQUE** constraint in MySQL. How does it ensure data integrity? Can a column with a **UNIQUE** constraint contain NULL values? Explain with an example.

4. What is the role of the **DEFAULT** constraint in MySQL? Provide an example of a situation where using a **DEFAULT** constraint would be beneficial.

5. Explain the purpose of the **CHECK** constraint in MySQL. Provide an example of a table where a **CHECK** constraint would be used to enforce a specific condition on a column. What happens if the condition is not met?

Key Terms

- **NOT NULL:** Guarantees that a column cannot have NULL values.
- **PRIMARY KEY:** Distinguishes each row uniquely and prohibits NULL values.
- **UNIQUE**: Ensures that all entries in a column are distinct, permitting a single NULL value.
- **DEFAULT:** Provides a default value if none is specified.
- **CHECK:** Ensures values meet a specific condition.
- **FOREIGN KEY:** Links two tables and enforces referential integrity.

CHAPTER 4
Operators in MySQL

Introduction

This chapter covers the operators in MySQL. Operators are symbols or keywords to perform operations on data in queries. We will understand the types of operators, such as **`AND`**, **`OR`**, **`NOT`**, **`IN`**, **`LIKE`**, and so on. Bitwise, logical, arithmetic, and comparison operators will also be covered with examples.

Structure

In this chapter, we will discuss the following topics:

- Operator in MySQL
- **`AND`** in MySQL
- **`OR`** Operator in MySQL
- **`NOT`** Operator in MySQL
- **`IN`** Operator in MySQL
- **`LIKE`** Operator in MySQL
- **`BETWEEN`** Operator in MySQL
- Practical Exercise

Operator in MySQL

In MySQL, an **operator** is a symbol or keyword used to perform operations on data. Operators are used in SQL statements to manipulate data, compare values, and perform calculations. They are essential for constructing queries, filtering results, and performing logical or arithmetic operations.

Here are the main types of operators in MySQL:

Arithmetic Operators

Arithmetic Operators are used to perform mathematical calculations on numeric data. The following are the types of Arithmetic Operators in MySQL:

- **+** (Addition)
- **-** (Subtraction)
- ***** (Multiplication)
- **/** (Division)
- **%** or MOD (Modulus, returns the remainder)

Example:

```
SELECT 10 + 5; -- Returns 15
SELECT 10 * 2; -- Returns 20
SELECT 10 % 3; -- Returns 1
```

Comparison Operators

Comparison Operators are used to compare two values and return a Boolean result (**TRUE**, **FALSE**, or **NULL**). The following are the types of Comparison Operators in MySQL:

- **=** (Equal to)
- **!=** or <> (Not equal to)
- **>** (Greater than)
- **<** (Less than)
- **>=** (Greater than or equal to)
- **<=** (Less than or equal to)
- **<=>** (NULL-safe equal to, returns TRUE even if both operands are NULL)

Example:

```
SELECT * FROM employees WHERE salary > 50000;
SELECT * FROM products WHERE price <= 100;
```

Logical Operators

Logical Operators are used to combine multiple conditions in a query. The following are the types of Logical Operators in MySQL:

- **AND** (Returns TRUE if all conditions are TRUE)
- **OR** (Returns TRUE if at least one condition is TRUE)

- **NOT** (Negates a condition)
- **XOR** (Returns TRUE if only one of the conditions is TRUE)

Example:

```
SELECT * FROM employees WHERE salary > 50000 AND department =
'Sales';
SELECT * FROM products WHERE price < 50 OR stock > 100;
```

Bitwise Operators

Bitwise Operators are used to perform bit-level operations on integer values. The following are the types of Bitwise Operators in MySQL:

- **&** (Bitwise AND)
- **|** (Bitwise OR)
- ^ (Bitwise XOR)
- ~ (Bitwise NOT)
- << (Left shift)
- >> (Right shift)

Example:

```
SELECT 5 & 3; -- Returns 1 (binary AND operation)
SELECT 5 | 3; -- Returns 7 (binary OR operation)
```

Assignment Operators

Assignment Operators are used to assign a value to a variable or column. The assignment operator is = (Assignment).

Example:

```
SET @x = 10;    Assigns the value 10 to the variable @x
```

String Operators

String Operators are used for manipulating and comparing string values. The following are the types of String Operators in MySQL:

- **||** or **CONCAT()** (Concatenates strings)
- **LIKE** (Pattern matching)
- **NOT LIKE** (Negation of pattern matching)
- **REGEXP** or **RLIKE** (Regular expression matching)

Example:

```
SELECT CONCAT(first_name, ' ', last_name) AS full_name FROM
employees;
SELECT * FROM products WHERE name LIKE 'App%';
```

NULL Operators

Null Operators are used to check for **NULL** values. The following are the types of **NULL** Operators in MySQL:

- **IS NULL** (Checks if a value is **NULL**)
- **IS NOT NULL** (Checks if a value is not **NULL**)

Example:

```
SELECT * FROM employees WHERE manager_id IS NULL;
```

IN Operator

The **IN** Operator is used to check if a value matches any value in a list. The following are the types of IN Operators in MySQL:

- **IN** (Matches any value in a list)
- **NOT IN** (Does not match any value in a list)

Example:

```
SELECT * FROM employees WHERE department_id IN (1, 2, 3);
BETWEEN Operator
```

The **BETWEEN** Operator is used to check if a value lies within a range. The following are the types of BETWEEN Operators in MySQL:

- **BETWEEN** (Checks if a value is within a range, inclusive)
- **NOT BETWEEN** (Checks if a value is outside a range)

Example:

```
SELECT * FROM products WHERE price BETWEEN 50 AND 100;
```

CASE Operator

The **CASE** Operator is used for conditional logic in queries. The **CASE** evaluates conditions and returns a value.

Example:

```
SELECT
    name,
```

```
        CASE
            WHEN salary > 50000 THEN 'High'
            WHEN salary > 30000 THEN 'Medium'
            ELSE 'Low'
        END AS salary_level
    FROM employees;
```

UNION Operator

The **UNION** Operator is used to combine the results of two or more **SELECT** queries. The following are the types of UNION Operators in MySQL:

- **UNION** (Combines results and removes duplicates)
- **UNION ALL** (Combines results without removing duplicates)

Example:

```
SELECT name FROM employees
UNION
SELECT name FROM contractors;
```

Operators are fundamental to writing effective SQL queries in MySQL. They allow you to filter, manipulate, and analyze data efficiently.

Let us now understand the key operators, **AND**, **OR**, **NOT**, **IN**, **LIKE**, and **BETWEEN** in detail.

AND Operator

The **AND** operator in MySQL is a **logical operator** used to combine multiple conditions in a query. It ensures that all the specified conditions must be true for a row to be included in the result set. If any of the conditions are false, the row is excluded.

Syntax of AND Operator

```
SELECT column1, column2, ...
FROM table_name
WHERE condition1 AND condition2 AND condition3 ...;
```

Here,

- **condition1, condition2, and so on**: These are the conditions that must all evaluate to **TRUE** for a row to be selected.
- The **AND** operator can be used to combine **two or more conditions**.

Examples of the AND Operator

Example 1: Simple AND Condition

```
SELECT * FROM employees
WHERE department = 'Sales' AND salary > 50000;
```

This query retrieves all employees who:

- Work in the **Sales** department **and**
- Have a salary greater than **50,000**.

Example 2: Multiple AND Conditions

```
SELECT * FROM employees
WHERE department = 'Sales' AND salary > 50000 AND hire_date >
'2024-01-01';
```

This query retrieves all employees who:

- Work in the **Sales** department **and**
- Have a salary greater than **50,000** and
- Were hired after **January 1, 2024**.

Example 3: Combining AND with Other Operators

```
SELECT * FROM products
WHERE price > 100 AND stock > 0 AND category = 'Electronics';
```

This query retrieves all products that:

- Have a price greater than **100 and**
- Are in stock (stock > 0) **and**
- Belong to the **Electronics** category.

Key Points About the AND Operator:

- **All Conditions Must Be True**:
  - The **AND** operator requires **every condition** to be true for a row to be included in the result set.
  - If even one condition is false, the row is excluded.
- **Combining with Other Operators**:
  - The **AND** operator is often used with other operators such as **OR, NOT, BETWEEN, IN**, and so on, to create more complex queries.

- **Order of Evaluation**:
    - In a query with multiple logical operators (**AND, OR**), the **AND** operator has **higher precedence** than **OR**. Use parentheses () to explicitly define the order of evaluation if needed.

Example with AND and OR

```
SELECT * FROM employees
WHERE (department = 'Sales' AND salary > 50000)
   OR (department = 'Marketing' AND salary > 60000);
```

This query retrieves employees who:

- Work in the **Sales** department **and** have a salary greater than **50,000**, **or**
- Work in the **Marketing** department **and** have a salary greater than **60,000**.

When to Use AND

- Use the **AND** operator when you want to filter rows that meet **all** the specified conditions.
- It is commonly used in **SELECT, UPDATE, DELETE**, and **INSERT...SELECT** statements.

OR Operator

The **OR operator** in MySQL is a logical operator used to combine multiple conditions in a query. It ensures that at least one of the specified conditions must be true for a row to be included in the result set. If any of the conditions are true, the row is included.

Syntax of OR Operator

```
SELECT column1, column2, ...
FROM table_name
WHERE condition1 OR condition2 OR condition3 ...;
```

Here,

- **condition1, condition2, and so on**: These are the conditions where **at least one** must evaluate to **TRUE** for a row to be selected.
- The **OR** operator can be used to combine **two or more conditions**.

Examples of OR Operator

Example 1: Simple OR Condition

```
SELECT * FROM employees
WHERE department = 'Sales' OR department = 'Marketing';
```

This query retrieves all employees who:

- Work in the **Sales** department **or**
- Work in the **Marketing** department.

Example 2: Multiple OR Conditions

```
SELECT * FROM employees
WHERE department = 'Sales' OR department = 'Marketing' OR
department = 'HR';
```

This query retrieves all employees who:

- Work in the **Sales** department **or**
- Work in the **Marketing** department **or**
- Work in the **HR** department.

Example 3: Combining OR with Other Operators

```
SELECT * FROM products
WHERE price < 50 OR stock = 0;
```

This query retrieves all products that:

- Have a price less than **50** **or**
- Are out of stock (**stock = 0**).

Key Points About the OR Operator

- **At Least One Condition Must Be True**:
    - The **OR** operator requires **at least one condition** to be true for a row to be included in the result set.
    - If all conditions are false, the row is excluded.
- **Combining with Other Operators**:
    - The **OR** operator is often used with other operators such as **AND, NOT, BETWEEN, IN,** and so on, to create more complex queries.

- **Order of Evaluation**:
  - In a query with multiple logical operators (**AND, OR**), the **AND** operator has **higher precedence** than **OR**. Use parentheses () to explicitly define the order of evaluation if needed.

When to Use OR

- Use the **OR** operator when you want to filter rows that meet **at least one** of the specified conditions.
- It is commonly used in **SELECT, UPDATE, DELETE,** and **INSERT...SELECT** statements.

Difference Between AND and OR

Operator	Description
AND	Returns rows where **all** conditions are true.
OR	Returns rows where **at least one** condition is true.

Table 4.1: *Differences between AND and OR*

NOT Operator

The **NOT** operator in MySQL is a **logical operator** used to **negate** a condition. It returns **TRUE** if the condition is **FALSE** and **FALSE** if the condition is **TRUE**. It is commonly used in the **WHERE** clause to exclude rows that meet a specific condition.

Syntax of NOT Operator

```
SELECT column1, column2, ...
FROM table_name
WHERE NOT condition;
```

Here,

- **condition**: The condition that you want to negate.
- The **NOT** operator can be used with other operators such as **AND, OR, IN, BETWEEN, LIKE**, and so on.

Examples of NOT Operator

Example 1: Simple NOT Condition

```
SELECT * FROM employees
WHERE NOT department = 'Sales';
```

This query retrieves all employees who **do not** work in the **`Sales`** department.

Example 2: `NOT` with AND

```
SELECT * FROM employees
WHERE NOT department = 'Sales' AND salary > 50000;
```

This query retrieves all employees who:

- **Do not** work in the **`Sales`** department **and**
- Have a salary greater than **`50,000`**.

Example 3: `NOT` with `IN`

```
SELECT * FROM employees
WHERE department NOT IN ('Sales', 'Marketing');
```

This query retrieves all employees who **do not** work in the **`Sales`** or **`Marketing`** departments.

Example 4: `NOT` with `BETWEEN`

```
SELECT * FROM products
WHERE price NOT BETWEEN 50 AND 100;
```

This query retrieves all products whose price is **not between 50 and 100**.

Example 5: `NOT` with `LIKE`

```
SELECT * FROM employees
WHERE first_name NOT LIKE 'A%';
```

This query retrieves all employees whose first name **does not start with the letter 'A'**.

Example 6: `NOT` with `IS NULL`

```
SELECT * FROM employees
WHERE manager_id IS NOT NULL;
```

This query retrieves all employees who **have a manager** (i.e., **`manager_id`** is **`NOT NULL`**).

Key Points About the `NOT` Operator:

- **Negates a Condition**: The **`NOT`** operator reverses the result of a condition. If the condition is **`TRUE`**, **`NOT`** makes it **`FALSE`**, and vice versa.
- **Combining with Other Operators**: The **`NOT`** operator is often used with other

operators such as **AND, OR, IN, BETWEEN, LIKE**, and so on, to create more complex queries.

- **Use with NULL**: When working with **NULL** values, use **IS NOT NULL** or **IS NULL** instead of **= NULL** or != **NULL.**
- **Readability**: Using **NOT** can sometimes make queries harder to read. Consider rewriting the condition for better clarity if needed.

Example with NOT, AND, and OR

```
SELECT * FROM employees
WHERE (NOT department = 'Sales')
   AND (salary > 50000 OR hire_date > '2024-01-01');
```

This query retrieves employees who:

- **Do not** work in the **Sales** department **and**
- Either have a salary greater than **50,000 or** were hired after **January 1, 2024**.

When to Use NOT

- Use the **NOT** operator when you want to **exclude rows** that meet a specific condition.
- It is commonly used **in SELECT, UPDATE, DELETE**, and **INSERT...SELECT** statements.

IN Operator

The **IN** operator in MySQL is used to check if a value matches any value in a **list of specified values.** It is a shorthand for multiple OR conditions and is commonly used in the WHERE clause to filter rows based on a set of possible values.

Syntax of IN Operator

```
SELECT column1, column2, ...
FROM table_name
WHERE column_name IN (value1, value2, value3, ...);
```

Here,

- **column_name**: The column to be evaluated.
- **value1, value2, ...**: A list of values to compare against the column. If the column value matches **any** of these values, the row is included in the result set.

Examples of `IN` Operator

Example 1: Simple `IN` Condition

```
SELECT * FROM employees
WHERE department IN ('Sales', 'Marketing', 'HR');
```

This query retrieves all employees who work in the **`Sales`**, **`Marketing`**, or **`HR`** departments.

Example 2: `IN` with Numbers

```
SELECT * FROM products
WHERE category_id IN (1, 3, 5);
```

This query retrieves all products that belong to categories with IDs **1**, **3**, or **5**.

Example 3: IN with Subquery

```
SELECT * FROM employees
WHERE department_id IN (SELECT department_id FROM departments
WHERE location = 'New York');
```

This query retrieves all employees who work in departments located in **`New York`**.

Example 4: `NOT IN`

```
SELECT * FROM employees
WHERE department NOT IN ('Sales', 'Marketing');
```

This query retrieves all employees who **do not** work in the **`Sales`** or **`Marketing`** departments.

Key Points About the `IN` Operator

- **Shorthand for Multiple OR Conditions**: The **`IN`** operator simplifies queries by replacing multiple **`OR`** conditions. For example:

  ```
  WHERE column_name = value1 OR column_name = value2 OR column_name
  = value3;
  ```

  can be written as:

  ```
  WHERE column_name IN (value1, value2, value3);
  ```

- **Works with Lists and Subqueries**: The **`IN`** operator can be used with a list of values or a subquery that returns a list of values.
- **Performance**: Using **`IN`** with a large list of values or a subquery can impact performance. Ensure proper indexing on the column being evaluated.

- **NULL Handling**: If the list contains **`NULL`**, the **`IN`** operator will **not** match **`NULL`** values. Use **`IS NULL`** to check for **`NULL`** explicitly.

Comparison with `OR`

Operator	Description
IN	Checks if a value matches any value in a list.
OR	Checks if at least one of multiple conditions is true.

Table 4.2: *Differences between IN and OR*

Example:

```
-- Using OR
SELECT * FROM employees
WHERE department = 'Sales' OR department = 'Marketing' OR
department = 'HR';

-- Using IN
SELECT * FROM employees
WHERE department IN ('Sales', 'Marketing', 'HR');
```

Both queries return the same result, but the **`IN`** operator is more concise.

When to Use `IN`

- Use the **IN** operator when you want to filter rows based on a **list of possible values**.
- It is commonly used in **`SELECT`**, **`UPDATE`**, **`DELETE`**, and **`INSERT...SELECT`** statements.

Example with `IN` and `AND`

```
SELECT * FROM employees
WHERE department IN ('Sales', 'Marketing')
  AND salary > 50000;
```

This query retrieves employees who:

- Work in the **`Sales`** or **`Marketing`** departments **and**
- Have a salary greater than **`50,000`**.

`LIKE` Operator

The **`LIKE`** operator in MySQL is used to search for a **specified pattern** in a column. It is commonly used in the **`WHERE`** clause of **a `SELECT`**, **`UPDATE`**, or **`DELETE`** statement to filter rows based on partial matches. The **`LIKE`** operator is case-insensitive by default in MySQL, but this behavior can vary depending on the collation of the column.

Syntax of `LIKE` Operator

```
SELECT column1, column2, ...
FROM table_name
WHERE column_name LIKE 'pattern';
```

Here,

- **`column_name`**: The column to be evaluated.
- **`pattern`**: The pattern to search for. It can include two wildcard characters:
    - **%** (percent sign): Matches **zero or more characters**.
    - **_** (underscore): Matches **exactly one character**.

Wildcard Characters in `LIKE`

1. **% (Percent Sign)**:
    - Represents **zero, one, or multiple characters**.
    - Example: '**a%**' matches any string that starts with ‹a›.
2. **_ (Underscore)**:
    - Represents **exactly one character**.
    - Example: '**a_**' matches any two-character string that starts with '**a**'.

Examples of `LIKE` Operator

Example 1: Match Strings Starting with a Specific Pattern

```
SELECT * FROM employees
WHERE first_name LIKE 'Jo%';
```

This query retrieves all employees whose first name starts with **`Jo`** (for example, **John, Joan, Joseph**).

Example 2: Match Strings Ending with a Specific Pattern

```
SELECT * FROM employees
WHERE last_name LIKE '%son';
```

This query retrieves all employees whose last name ends with **son** (for example, **Johnson**, **Wilson**).

Example 3: Match Strings Containing a Specific Pattern

```
SELECT * FROM employees
WHERE email LIKE '%@gmail.com';
```

This query retrieves all employees whose email contains **@gmail.com**.

Example 4: Match Strings with a Specific Length

```
SELECT * FROM employees
WHERE first_name LIKE '___';
```

This query retrieves all employees whose first name is **exactly 3 characters long** (for example, **Bob**, **Eve**).

Example 5: Match Strings with a Specific Character at a Specific Position

```
SELECT * FROM employees
WHERE first_name LIKE '_a%';
```

This query retrieves all employees whose first name has **a as the second character** (for example, **Sam**, **Pat**).

Using `NOT LIKE`

The **`NOT LIKE`** operator is used to exclude rows that match a specified pattern.

Example:

```
SELECT * FROM employees
WHERE first_name NOT LIKE 'A%';
```

This query retrieves all employees whose first name **does not start with A**.

Key Points about the `LIKE` Operator

- **Case Sensitivity:**
    - By default, **`LIKE`** is **case-insensitive** in MySQL. However, this depends on the collation of the column. For case-sensitive searches, use a case-sensitive collation (for example, **utf8mb4_bin**).

- **Wildcard Characters**:
    - Use **%** to match **any sequence of characters**.
    - Use _ to match **a single character**.
- **Performance:**
    - Using **LIKE** with a leading wildcard (for example, '**%pattern**') can be slow because it prevents the use of indexes. Avoid leading wildcards if possible.
- **Escaping Wildcards:**
    - If you need to search for literal **%** or _, use the **ESCAPE** keyword. For example:

    ```
    SELECT * FROM employees
    WHERE notes LIKE '%\%%' ESCAPE '\';
    ```

    - This query retrieves rows where the **notes** column contains a **%** character.

Difference between LIKE and = Operator

Operator	Description
LIKE	Matches a pattern using wildcards (**%** and _).
=	Matches an exact value (no wildcards).

Table 4.3: *Differences between LIKE and =*

Example:

```
-- Using =
SELECT * FROM employees
WHERE first_name = 'John';

-- Using LIKE
SELECT * FROM employees
WHERE first_name LIKE 'Jo%';
```

When to Use LIKE

- Use the **LIKE** operator when you need to search for **partial matches** or patterns in a column.
- It is commonly used in **SELECT**, **UPDATE**, and **DELETE** statements.

Example with LIKE and AND

```
SELECT * FROM employees
WHERE first_name LIKE 'J%' AND department = 'Sales';
```

This query retrieves employees whose:

- The first name starts with **J and**
- The **department** is **Sales**.

BETWEEN Operator

The **BETWEEN** operator in MySQL is used to filter results within a **specified range**. It is commonly used in the **WHERE** clause of a **SELECT, UPDATE,** or **DELETE** statement to retrieve rows where a column's value lies between two values (inclusive).

Syntax of BETWEEN Operator

```
SELECT column1, column2, ...
FROM table_name
WHERE column_name BETWEEN value1 AND value2;
```

Here,

- **column_name**: The column to be evaluated.
- **value1 and value2**: The range of values to compare against. The **BETWEEN** operator is **inclusive**, meaning it includes the boundary values (**value1** and **value2**).

Examples of the BETWEEN Operator

Example 1: Numeric Range

```
SELECT * FROM employees
WHERE salary BETWEEN 30000 AND 50000;
```

This query retrieves all employees whose salary is **between 30,000 and 50,000** (inclusive).

Example 2: Date Range

```
SELECT * FROM orders
WHERE order_date BETWEEN '2024-01-01' AND '2024-12-31';
```

This query retrieves all orders placed **between January 1, 2024, and December 31, 2024.**

Example 3: String Range

```
SELECT * FROM products
WHERE product_name BETWEEN 'A' AND 'D';
```

This query retrieves all products whose names start with **A, B, C, or D**.

Using `NOT BETWEEN`

The **`NOT BETWEEN`** operator is used to exclude rows that fall within a specified range.

Example:

```
SELECT * FROM employees
WHERE salary NOT BETWEEN 30000 AND 50000;
```

This query retrieves all employees whose salary is **not between 30,000 and 50,000**.

Key Points About the `BETWEEN` Operator:

- **Inclusive Range**: The **`BETWEEN`** operator includes the boundary values (**`value1`** and **`value2`**).
- **Works with Numeric, Date, and String Values**: The **`BETWEEN`** operator can be used with **numbers**, **dates**, and **strings**.
- **Performance**: The **`BETWEEN`** operator can use indexes efficiently when applied to indexed columns.
- **Equivalent to >= and <=**: The **`BETWEEN`** operator is equivalent to combining **>=** and **<=**:|

  ```
  WHERE column_name >= value1 AND column_name <= value2;
  ```

Difference between `IN` Operator and `BETWEEN`

Operator	**Description**
BETWEEN	Filters rows within a **range** of values (inclusive).
IN	Filters rows that match **any value in a list.**

Table 4.4: *Differences between BETWEEN and IN*

Example:

```
-- Using BETWEEN
SELECT * FROM employees
WHERE salary BETWEEN 30000 AND 50000;

-- Using IN
SELECT * FROM employees
WHERE salary IN (30000, 40000, 50000);
```

When to Use `BETWEEN`

- Use the **`BETWEEN`** operator when you want to filter rows based on a **range of values**.

- It is commonly used in **SELECT**, **UPDATE**, and **DELETE** statements.

Example with BETWEEN and AND

```
SELECT * FROM employees
WHERE salary BETWEEN 30000 AND 50000
  AND department = 'Sales';
```

This query retrieves employees whose:

- The **salary** is **between 30,000 and 50,000 and**
- The **department** is **Sales**.

Example with BETWEEN and Dates

```
SELECT * FROM orders
WHERE order_date BETWEEN '2024-01-01' AND '2024-12-31'
  AND status = 'Shipped';
```

This query retrieves all orders that:

- Were placed **between January 1, 2024, and December 31, 2024, and**
- Have a status of **Shipped**.

Practical Exercise

Here is a practical exercise that builds on the previous **Employee Management System** and incorporates the MySQL topics of this lesson. This exercise will guide you through querying data using logical operators (AND, OR, NOT), as well as filtering data using IN, LIKE, and BETWEEN.

Exercise: Querying Employee Data

Step 1: Use the Existing Database

Use the **employee_management_advanced** database created in the previous exercise.

```
USE employee_management_advanced;
```

Step 2: Insert Additional Records

Insert additional records into the **employees** table to make the queries more meaningful.

```
INSERT INTO employees (name, department_id, salary, join_date,
email) VALUES
```

```
('Grace Lee', 2, 65000.00, '2024-03-01', 'grace.lee@example.
com'),
('Henry Brown', 1, 52000.00, '2024-04-15', 'henry.brown@example.
com'),
('Ivy Davis', 3, 58000.00, '2024-05-10', 'ivy.davis@example.
com'),
('Jack Wilson', 2, 70000.00, '2024-06-20', 'jack.wilson@example.
com'),
('Karen White', 1, 53000.00, '2024-07-05', 'karen.white@example.
com');
```

Step 3: AND Operator

Retrieve employees who work in the IT department (**department_id = 2**) and have a salary greater than 60000.

```
SELECT * FROM employees
WHERE department_id = 2 AND salary > 60000;
```

Step 4: OR Operator

Retrieve employees who work in either the HR department (**department_id = 1**) or the Finance department (**department_id = 3**).

```
SELECT * FROM employees
WHERE department_id = 1 OR department_id = 3;
```

Step 5: NOT Operator

Retrieve employees who do **not** work in the IT department (**department_id = 2**).

```
SELECT * FROM employees
WHERE NOT department_id = 2;
```

Step 6: IN Operator

Retrieve employees who work in the HR or Finance departments using the **IN** operator.

```
SELECT * FROM employees
WHERE department_id IN (1, 3);
```

Step 7: LIKE Operator

Retrieve employees whose names start with the letter **J**.

```
SELECT * FROM employees
WHERE name LIKE 'J%';
```

Step 8: BETWEEN Operator

Retrieve employees who joined between **2024-01-01** and **2025-01-30**.

```
SELECT * FROM employees
WHERE join_date BETWEEN '2024-01-01' AND '2025-01-30';
```

Step 9: Combining Operators

Retrieve employees who:

- Work in the IT department (department_id = 2), **AND**
- Have a salary between 60000 and 70000, **AND**
- Joined after 2024-01-01.

Here is the query:

```
SELECT * FROM employees
WHERE department_id = 2
  AND salary BETWEEN 60000 AND 70000
  AND join_date > '2024-01-01';
```

Step 10: Verify Data

Retrieve all records from the employees table to verify the results of your queries.

```
SELECT * FROM employees;
```

Final Queries

```
USE employee_management_advanced;
INSERT INTO employees (name, department_id, salary, join_date,
email) VALUES
('Grace Lee', 2, 65000.00, '2024-03-01', 'grace.lee@example.
com'),
('Henry Brown', 1, 52000.00, '2024-04-15', 'henry.brown@example.
com'),
('Ivy Davis', 3, 58000.00, '2024-05-10', 'ivy.davis@example.
com'),
('Jack Wilson', 2, 70000.00, '2024-06-20', 'jack.wilson@example.
com'),
('Karen White', 1, 53000.00, '2024-07-05', 'karen.white@example.
com');

SELECT * FROM employees
WHERE department_id = 2 AND salary > 60000;
```

```
SELECT * FROM employees
WHERE department_id = 1 OR department_id = 3;

SELECT * FROM employees
WHERE NOT department_id = 2;

SELECT * FROM employees
WHERE department_id IN (1, 3);

SELECT * FROM employees
WHERE name LIKE 'J%';

SELECT * FROM employees
WHERE join_date BETWEEN '2024-01-01' AND '2025-01-30';

SELECT * FROM employees
WHERE department_id = 2
  AND salary BETWEEN 60000 AND 70000
  AND join_date > '2024-01-01';

SELECT * FROM employees;
```

Expected Output

After completing the exercise, you should have:

- Used the AND, OR, and NOT operators to filter data.
- Used the IN operator to filter data based on multiple values.
- Used the LIKE operator to filter data based on patterns.
- Used the BETWEEN operator to filter data within a range.
- Combined multiple operators to create complex queries.
- Verified the results by querying the **employees** table.

This exercise provides hands-on practice with MySQL operators.

Conclusion

MySQL operators such as AND, OR, NOT, IN, LIKE, and BETWEEN are essential tools for filtering and manipulating data in SQL queries. They allow you to specify conditions, combine multiple criteria, and search for patterns or ranges efficiently. Mastering these operators enables you to write precise and powerful queries to retrieve the exact data you need.

In the next lesson, we will cover the built-in functions provided by MySQL.

Points to Remember

- Combine multiple conditions (all conditions must be true) in a WHERE clause with the AND operator.
- Combine multiple conditions (at least one condition must be true) in a WHERE clause with the OR operator.
- Negate a condition with the NOT operator.
- Search for a specified pattern in a column using the LIKE operator.
- Filter results within a specified range (inclusive) using the BETWEEN operator.

Multiple Choice Questions

1. What does the AND operator do in MySQL?
    a. Combines multiple conditions, and at least one must be true.
    b. Combines multiple conditions, and all must be true.
    c. Negates a condition.
    d. Filters results within a specified range.
2. Which operator is used to negate a condition in MySQL?
    a. `AND`
    b. `OR`
    c. `IN`
    d. `NOT`
3. What does the IN operator do in MySQL?
    a. Searches for a specified pattern in a column.
    b. Filters results within a specified range.
    c. Matches any value in a list of specified values.
    d. Combines multiple conditions.
4. Which wildcard character is used with the LIKE operator to represent zero or more characters?
    a. _
    b. %

   c. *

   d. ?

5. What does the BETWEEN operator do in MySQL?

   a. Combines multiple conditions.

   b. Filters results within a specified range (inclusive).

   c. Negates a condition.

   d. Matches any value in a list.

6. Which operator would you use to retrieve records where the salary is either 50,000 or 60,000?

   a. IN

   b. OR

   c. AND

   d. LIKE

Answers

1. b
2. d
3. c
4. b
5. b
6. a

Questions

1. What is the purpose of the **`AND`** operator in MySQL, and how does it differ from the **`OR`** operator?
2. How does the **`NOT`** operator work in a MySQL query? Provide an example of its usage.
3. Explain the **`IN`** operator in MySQL. How is it useful for simplifying queries with multiple OR conditions?

4. What are the wildcard characters used with the **LIKE** operator, and how do they function in pattern matching?
5. Describe the **BETWEEN** operator in MySQL. Can it be used with non-numeric data types such as dates or text?
6. Write a MySQL query to retrieve all employees whose names start with "A" and work in either the "Sales" or "Marketing" department.

Key Terms

- **AND**: Combines multiple conditions (all must be true).
- **OR**: Combines multiple conditions (at least one must be true).
- **NOT**: Negates a condition.
- **IN**: Matches any value in a list.
- **LIKE**: Matches a pattern using wildcards.
- **BETWEEN**: Filters results within a range.

CHAPTER 5
MySQL Built-in Functions

Introduction

This chapter covers the pre-defined, that is, the built-in functions provided by MySQL. We will understand the functions for string, including concatenation, padding, search, and so on, and numeric operations, including trigonometric, logarithmic, and so on. Furthermore, date-time and aggregate functions are covered with examples.

Structure

In this chapter, we will discuss the following topics:

- String Built-in Functions in MySQL
- Numeric Built-in Functions in MySQL
- Date Built-in Functions in MySQL
- Aggregate Built-in Functions in MySQL
- Practical Exercise

String Built-in Functions

MySQL provides a variety of built-in string functions that allow you to manipulate and process text data. The following is a list of commonly used string functions in MySQL:

String Concatenation

String Concatenation means combining multiple strings into one.

- **CONCAT(str1, str2, ...)**: Combines two or more strings into one.

  ```
  SELECT CONCAT('Hello', ' ', 'World'); -- Output: 'Hello World'
  ```

- **CONCAT_WS(separator, str1, str2, ...)**: Concatenates strings with a specified separator.
  `SELECT CONCAT_WS('-', '2023', '10', '05'); -- Output: '2023-10-05'`

String Length

String Length means measuring the number of bytes or characters in a string.

- **LENGTH(str)**: Returns the length of the string in bytes.
  `SELECT LENGTH('MySQL'); -- Output: 5`
- **CHAR_LENGTH(str)**: Returns the length of the string in characters.
  `SELECT CHAR_LENGTH('MySQL'); -- Output: 5`

Substring Extraction

Substring Extraction means extracting a part of a string.

- **SUBSTRING(str, start, length)**: Extracts a substring from a string.
  `SELECT SUBSTRING('Hello World', 7, 5); -- Output: 'World'`
- **LEFT(str, length)**: Returns the leftmost **length** characters of the string.
  `SELECT LEFT('Hello World', 5); -- Output: 'Hello'`
- **RIGHT(str, length)**: Returns the rightmost **length** characters of the string.
  `SELECT RIGHT('Hello World', 5); -- Output: 'World'`

String Search

String Search means finding the position of a substring within a string.

- **LOCATE(substr, str, start)**: Returns the position of the first occurrence of **substr** in **str**.
  `SELECT LOCATE('World', 'Hello World'); -- Output: 7`
- **INSTR(str, substr)**: Similar to **LOCATE**, but the arguments are reversed.
  `SELECT INSTR('Hello World', 'World'); -- Output: 7`
- **POSITION(substr IN str)**: Returns the position of **substr** in **str**.
  `SELECT POSITION('World' IN 'Hello World'); -- Output: 7`

String Modification

String Modification means replacing, inserting, or trimming parts of a string.

- **REPLACE(str, from_str, to_str)**: Replaces all occurrences of **from_str** with **to_str**.
  `SELECT REPLACE('Hello World', 'World', 'MySQL'); -- Output: 'Hello MySQL'`

- **INSERT(str, pos, len, new_str)**: Inserts **new_str** into str at position **pos**, replacing **len** characters.
  ```
  SELECT INSERT('Hello World', 7, 5, 'MySQL'); -- Output: 'Hello MySQL'
  ```
- **TRIM([{BOTH | LEADING | TRAILING} [remstr] FROM] str)**: Removes leading, trailing, or both spaces (or specified characters) from a string.
  ```
  SELECT TRIM('  Hello World  '); -- Output: 'Hello World'
  SELECT TRIM(LEADING 'x' FROM 'xxxHello'); -- Output: 'Hello'
  ```
- **LTRIM(str)**: Removes leading spaces from a string.
  ```
  SELECT LTRIM('  Hello'); -- Output: 'Hello'
  ```
- **RTRIM(str)**: Removes trailing spaces from a string.
  ```
  SELECT RTRIM('Hello  '); -- Output: 'Hello'
  ```

Case Conversion

Case Conversion means changing text to uppercase or lowercase.

- **UPPER(str)**: Converts the string to uppercase.
  ```
  SELECT UPPER('Hello'); -- Output: 'HELLO'
  ```
- **LOWER(str)**: Converts the string to lowercase.
  ```
  SELECT LOWER('Hello'); -- Output: 'hello'
  ```

String Padding

String Padding means adding characters to the left or right of a string.

- **LPAD(str, len, padstr)**: Pads the string to the left with **padstr** until it reaches length **len**.
  ```
  SELECT LPAD('Hello', 10, '*'); -- Output: '*****Hello'
  ```
- **RPAD(str, len, padstr)**: Pads the string to the right with **padstr** until it reaches length **len**.
  ```
  SELECT RPAD('Hello', 10, '*'); -- Output: 'Hello*****'
  ```

String Comparison

String Comparison means checking if two strings are equal or determining their order.

- **STRCMP(str1, str2)**: Compares two strings. Returns **0** if equal, **-1** if **str1 < str2**, and **1** if **str1 > str2**.
  ```
  SELECT STRCMP('Hello', 'Hello'); -- Output: 0
  SELECT STRCMP('Hello', 'World'); -- Output: -1
  ```

String Reversal

String Reversal means flipping the order of characters in a string.

- **REVERSE(str)**: Reverses the characters in a string.
  ```
  SELECT REVERSE('Hello'); -- Output: 'olleH'
  ```

String Formatting

String Formatting means formatting numbers with commas and decimal places.

- **FORMAT(X, D)**: Formats a number **X** with **D** decimal places and adds commas as thousand separators.
  ```
  SELECT FORMAT(1234567.89, 2); -- Output: '1,234,567.89'
  ```

String Repetition

String Repetition means repeating a string a specified number of times.

- **REPEAT(str, count)**: Repeats a string **count** times.
  ```
  SELECT REPEAT('MySQL ', 3); -- Output: 'MySQL MySQL MySQL '
  ```

String Splitting

String Splitting means extracting text based on a delimiter.

- **SUBSTRING_INDEX(str, delim, count)**: Returns a substring from **str** before **count** occurrences of **delim**.
  ```
  SELECT SUBSTRING_INDEX('www.example.com', '.', 2); -- Output:
  'www.example'
  ```

These functions are powerful tools for manipulating and processing strings in MySQL. You can combine them to achieve more complex operations.

Numeric Built-in Functions

MySQL provides a wide range of built-in numeric functions for performing mathematical operations, rounding, formatting, and more. Here is a list of commonly used numeric functions in MySQL:

Basic Arithmetic Functions

Basic Arithmetic Functions include performing fundamental mathematical operations such as absolute value, rounding, and truncation.

- **ABS(x)**: Returns the absolute value of **x**.
  ```
  SELECT ABS(-10); -- Output: 10
  ```
- **CEIL(x)**: Returns the smallest integer greater than or equal to **x**.
  ```
  SELECT CEIL(10.1); -- Output: 11
  ```
- **FLOOR(x)**: Returns the largest integer less than or equal to **x**.
  ```
  SELECT FLOOR(10.9); -- Output: 10
  ```
- **ROUND(x, d)**: Rounds **x** to **d** decimal places. If **d** is omitted, it rounds to the nearest integer.
  ```
  SELECT ROUND(10.567, 2); -- Output: 10.57
  SELECT ROUND(10.567); -- Output: 11
  ```
- **TRUNCATE(x, d)**: Truncates **x** to **d** decimal places.
  ```
  SELECT TRUNCATE(10.567, 2); -- Output: 10.56
  ```

Power and Logarithmic Functions

Power and Logarithmic Functions include calculating exponents, roots, and logarithms.

- **POW(x, y) or POWER(x, y)**: Returns **x** raised to the power of **y**.
  ```
  SELECT POW(2, 3); -- Output: 8
  ```
- **SQRT(x)**: Returns the square root of **x**.
  ```
  SELECT SQRT(16); -- Output: 4
  ```
- **EXP(x)**: Returns the value of **e** raised to the power of **x**.
  ```
  SELECT EXP(1); -- Output: 2.718281828459045
  ```
- **LOG(x)**: Returns the natural logarithm of **x**.
  ```
  SELECT LOG(2.718281828459045); -- Output: 1
  ```
- **LOG10(x)**: Returns the base-10 logarithm of **x**.
  ```
  SELECT LOG10(100); -- Output: 2
  ```

Trigonometric Functions

Trigonometric Functions include computing sine, cosine, tangent, and their inverse functions.

- **SIN(x)**: Returns the sine of **x** (in radians).
  ```
  SELECT SIN(0); -- Output: 0
  ```
- **COS(x)**: Returns the cosine of **x** (in radians).
  ```
  SELECT COS(0); -- Output: 1
  ```
- **TAN(x)**: Returns the tangent of **x** (in radians).
  ```
  SELECT TAN(0); -- Output: 0
  ```

- **ASIN(x)**: Returns the arc sine of **x**.
```
SELECT ASIN(0); -- Output: 0
```
- **ACOS(x)**: Returns the arc cosine of **x**.
```
SELECT ACOS(1); -- Output: 0
```
- **ATAN(x)**: Returns the arc tangent of **x**.
```
SELECT ATAN(0); -- Output: 0
```
- **ATAN2(y, x)**: Returns the arc tangent of **y/x**.
```
SELECT ATAN2(1, 1); -- Output: 0.7853981633974483
```

Random Number Generation

Random Number Generation includes producing random or repeatable pseudo-random numbers.

- **RAND()**: Returns a random floating-point value between 0 and 1.
```
SELECT RAND(); -- Output: Random value between 0 and 1
```
- **RAND(N)**: Returns a repeatable random number if a seed **N** is provided.
```
SELECT RAND(42); -- Output: Same random value for the same seed
```

Sign and Modulus Functions

Sign and Modulus Functions include determining the sign of a number or division remainders.

- **SIGN(x)**: Returns the sign of **x** as -1, 0, or 1.
```
SELECT SIGN(-10); -- Output: -1
SELECT SIGN(0); -- Output: 0
SELECT SIGN(10); -- Output: 1
```
- **MOD(x, y)**: Returns the remainder of **x** divided by **y**.
```
SELECT MOD(10, 3); -- Output: 1
```

Aggregation Functions

Aggregation Functions include calculating summaries such as averages, sums, and counts across data sets.

- **AVG(column)**: Returns the average value of a numeric column.
```
SELECT AVG(salary) FROM employees;
```
- **SUM(column)**: Returns the sum of values in a numeric column.
```
SELECT SUM(salary) FROM employees;
```
- **MIN(column)**: Returns the minimum value in a column.
```
SELECT MIN(salary) FROM employees;
```

- **MAX(column)**: Returns the maximum value in a column.
  ```
  SELECT MAX(salary) FROM employees;
  ```
- **COUNT(column)**: Returns the number of rows in a column.
  ```
  SELECT COUNT(*) FROM employees;
  ```

Bitwise Functions

Bitwise Functions means performing operations at the binary level (AND, OR, shifts, and so on).

- **BIT_COUNT(x)**: Returns the number of bits set to 1 in **x**.
  ```
  SELECT BIT_COUNT(5); -- Output: 2 (5 in binary is 101)
  ```
- **&** (Bitwise AND): Performs a bitwise AND operation.
  ```
  SELECT 5 & 3; -- Output: 1 (5 is 101, 3 is 011; result is 001)
  ```
- **| (Bitwise OR)**: Performs a bitwise OR operation.
  ```
  SELECT 5 | 3; -- Output: 7 (5 is 101, 3 is 011; result is 111)
  ```
- ^ (Bitwise XOR): Performs a bitwise XOR operation.
  ```
  SELECT 5 ^ 3; -- Output: 6 (5 is 101, 3 is 011; result is 110)
  ```
- **<<** (Left Shift): Shifts the bits of **x** to the left by **y** positions.
  ```
  SELECT 1 << 2; -- Output: 4 (1 shifted left by 2 positions)
  ```
- **>>** (Right Shift): Shifts the bits of **x** to the right by **y** positions.
  ```
  SELECT 4 >> 2; -- Output: 1 (4 shifted right by 2 positions)
  ```

Formatting Functions

Formatting Functions means converting numbers into human-readable formatted strings.

- **FORMAT(x, d)**: Formats **x** with **d** decimal places and adds commas as thousand separators.
  ```
  SELECT FORMAT(1234567.89, 2); -- Output: '1,234,567.89'
  ```

Conversion Functions

Conversion Functions include changing data types (for example, string to number).

- **CAST(x AS type)**: Converts **x** to the specified data type.
  ```
  SELECT CAST('10' AS UNSIGNED); -- Output: 10
  ```
- **CONVERT(x, type)**: Similar to **CAST**, converts **x** to the specified data type.
  ```
  SELECT CONVERT('10', UNSIGNED); -- Output: 10
  ```

These numeric functions are essential for performing calculations, data analysis, and formatting in MySQL.

Date Built-in Functions

MySQL provides a variety of built-in date and time functions to manipulate, format, and extract information from date and time values. Here is a list of commonly used date and time functions in MySQL:

Current Date and Time

Current Date and Time includes functions that return the current date, time, or timestamp in various formats.

- **`CURDATE()`**: Returns the current date in **YYYY-MM-DD** format.
  `SELECT CURDATE(); -- Output: Current date (e.g., '2025-03-10')`
- **`CURTIME()`**: Returns the current time in **HH:MM:SS** format.
  `SELECT CURTIME(); -- Output: Current time (e.g., '14:30:45')`
- **`NOW()`**: Returns the current date and time in **YYYY-MM-DD HH:MM:SS** format.
  `SELECT NOW(); -- Output: Current date and time (e.g., '2025-03-10 14:30:45')`
- **`SYSDATE()`**: Similar to **`NOW()`**, but returns the time at which the function executes.
  `SELECT SYSDATE(); -- Output: Current date and time`
- **`UTC_DATE()`**: Returns the current UTC date.
  `SELECT UTC_DATE(); -- Output: Current UTC date (e.g., '2025-03-10')`
- **`UTC_TIME()`**: Returns the current UTC time.
  `SELECT UTC_TIME(); -- Output: Current UTC time (e.g., '14:30:45')`
- **`UTC_TIMESTAMP()`**: Returns the current UTC date and time.
  `SELECT UTC_TIMESTAMP(); -- Output: Current UTC date and time (e.g., '2025-03-10 14:30:45')`

Date and Time Extraction

Date and Time Extraction includes functions that extract specific components (year, month, day, and so on) from date/time values.

- **YEAR(date)**: Extracts the year from a date.
  `SELECT YEAR('2025-10-05'); -- Output: 2025`

- **MONTH(date)**: Extracts the month from a date.
  `SELECT MONTH('2025-10-05'); -- Output: 10`
- **DAY(date)**: Extracts the day of the month from a date.
  `SELECT DAY('2025-10-05'); -- Output: 5`
- **HOUR(time)**: Extracts the hour from a time.
  `SELECT HOUR('14:30:45'); -- Output: 14`
- **MINUTE(time)**: Extracts the minute from a time.
  `SELECT MINUTE('14:30:45'); -- Output: 30`
- **SECOND(time)**: Extracts the second from a time.
  `SELECT SECOND('14:30:45'); -- Output: 45`
- **DAYOFWEEK(date)**: Returns the day of the week (1 = Sunday, 2 = Monday, ..., 7 = Saturday).
  `SELECT DAYOFWEEK('2025-03-10'); -- Output: 2 (Monday)`
- **WEEKDAY(date)**: Returns the day of the week (0 = Monday, 1 = Tuesday, ..., 6 = Sunday).
  `SELECT WEEKDAY('2025-03-10'); -- Output: 0 (Monday)`
- **DAYOFYEAR(date)**: Returns the day of the year (1 to 366).
  `SELECT DAYOFYEAR('2025-03-11'); -- Output: 70`
- **WEEK(date)**: Returns the week number of the year.
  `SELECT WEEK('2025-03-11'); -- Output: 10`
- **QUARTER(date)**: Returns the quarter of the year (1 to 4).
  `SELECT QUARTER('2025-03-11'); -- Output: 1`

Date and Time Arithmetic

Date and Time Arithmetic includes functions that perform calculations with dates and times (addition, subtraction, differences).

- **DATE_ADD(date, INTERVAL expr unit)**: Adds a specified time interval to a date.
  `SELECT DATE_ADD('2025-03-11', INTERVAL 7 DAY); -- Output: '2026-03-18'`
- **DATE_SUB(date, INTERVAL expr unit)**: Subtracts a specified time interval from a date.
  `SELECT DATE_SUB('2025-03-11', INTERVAL 1 MONTH); -- Output: '2025-02-11'`
- **DATEDIFF(date1, date2)**: Returns the number of days between two dates.
  `SELECT DATEDIFF('2025-03-11', '2025-03-05'); -- Output: 6`

- **TIMEDIFF(time1, time2)**: Returns the difference between two times.
  ```
  SELECT TIMEDIFF('14:30:45', '12:00:00'); -- Output: '02:30:45'
  ```
- **TIMESTAMPDIFF(unit, start, end)**: Returns the difference between two timestamps in the specified unit.
  ```
  SELECT TIMESTAMPDIFF(YEAR, '2000-01-01', '2025-03-11'); -- Output: 25
  ```

Date and Time Formatting

Date and Time Formatting includes functions that format date/time values into specific string representations.

- **DATE_FORMAT(date, format)**: Formats a date according to the specified format.
  ```
  SELECT DATE_FORMAT('2025-03-11', '%W, %M %e, %Y'); -- Output: 'Tuesday, March 11, 2025'
  ```
- **TIME_FORMAT(time, format)**: Formats a time according to the specified format.
  ```
  SELECT TIME_FORMAT('14:30:45', '%h:%i %p'); -- Output: '02:30 PM'
  ```

Date and Time Conversion

Date and Time Conversion includes functions that convert between different date/time formats and representations.

- **STR_TO_DATE(str, format): Converts a string to a date based on the specified format.**
  ```
  SELECT STR_TO_DATE('03-10-2025', '%d-%m-%Y'); -- Output: '2025-10-03'
  ```
- **DATE(date)**: Extracts the date part from a datetime expression.
  ```
  SELECT DATE('2025-10-03 14:30:45'); -- Output: '2026-10-03'
  ```
- **TIME(datetime)**: Extracts the time part from a datetime expression.
  ```
  SELECT TIME('2025-10-03 14:30.45'); -- Output: '14:30:45'
  ```

Miscellaneous Functions

Miscellaneous Functions include additional specialized functions for working with dates and times (last day of the month, creating dates/times, Unix timestamp conversion).

- **LAST_DAY(date)**: Returns the last day of the month for the given date.
  ```
  SELECT LAST_DAY('2025-10-05'); -- Output: '2025-10-31'
  ```
- **MAKEDATE(year, dayofyear)**: Creates a date from a year and day of the year.
  ```
  SELECT MAKEDATE(2025, 278); -- Output: '2025-10-05'
  ```

- **MAKETIME(hour, minute, second)**: Creates a time from hour, minute, and second values.

  ```
  SELECT MAKETIME(14, 30, 45); -- Output: '14:30:45'
  ```

- **UNIX_TIMESTAMP([date])**: Returns the Unix timestamp (seconds since '1970-01-01 00:00:00' UTC).

  ```
  SELECT UNIX_TIMESTAMP('2025-10-05 14:30:45'); -- Output:
  1759909845
  ```

- **FROM_UNIXTIME(unix_timestamp)**: Converts a Unix timestamp to a datetime value.

  ```
  SELECT FROM_UNIXTIME(1759909845); -- Output: '2025-10-05
  14:30:45'
  ```

These date and time functions are essential for working with temporal data in MySQL.

Aggregate Built-in Functions

MySQL provides a variety of **aggregate functions** that allow you to perform calculations on a set of values and return a single value. These functions are commonly used with the **GROUP BY** clause to group rows and perform calculations on each group. Here is a list of commonly used aggregate functions in MySQL:

Basic Aggregate Functions

Basic Aggregate Functions include functions that perform calculations on sets of values to return single summary values.

- **COUNT(expression)**: Returns the number of rows that match the specified condition.

  ```
  SELECT COUNT(*) FROM employees; -- Counts all rows in the table
        SELECT COUNT(salary) FROM employees WHERE salary > 50000;
        -- Counts rows where salary > 50000
  ```

- **SUM(expression)**: Returns the sum of values in a numeric column.

  ```
  SELECT SUM(salary) FROM employees; -- Sum of all salaries
  ```

- **AVG(expression)**: Returns the average value of a numeric column.

  ```
  SELECT AVG(salary) FROM employees; -- Average salary
  ```

- **MIN(expression)**: Returns the minimum value in a column.

  ```
  SELECT MIN(salary) FROM; -- Minimum salary
  ```

- **MAX(expression)**: Returns the maximum value in a column.

  ```
  SELECT MAX(salary) FROM employees; -- Maximum salary
  ```

Grouping Data with GROUP BY

Aggregate functions are often used with the **GROUP BY** clause to group rows and perform calculations on each group.

- Example: Calculate the total salary for each department.

```
SELECT department_id, SUM(salary)
FROM employees
      GROUP BY department_id;
```

- Example: Count the number of employees in each department.

```
SELECT department_id, COUNT(*)
FROM employees
      GROUP BY department_id;
```

Filtering Groups with HAVING

The **HAVING** clause is used to filter groups after aggregation. It is similar to **WHERE**, but it works on aggregated results.

Example: Find departments with an average salary greater than 50000.

```
SELECT department_id, AVG(salary)
FROM employees
GROUP BY department_id
HAVING AVG(salary) > 50000;
```

Advanced Aggregate Functions

- **GROUP_CONCAT(expression)**: Concatenates values from multiple rows into a single string.

```
SELECT department_id, GROUP_CONCAT(first_name)
FROM employees
      GROUP BY department_id;
```

- **STD(expression)**: Returns the standard deviation of a numeric column.

```
SELECT STD(salary) FROM employees; -- Standard deviation of
salaries
```

- **VARIANCE(expression)**: Returns the variance of a numeric column.

```
SELECT VARIANCE(salary) FROM employees; -- Variance of salaries
```

Handling NULL Values

Aggregate functions ignore **NULL** values by default. For example:

- **COUNT(column)** counts only non-NULL values.
- **SUM(column)** ignores NULL values.

To include **NULL** values, you can use **IFNULL** or **COALESCE**:

```
SELECT AVG(IFNULL(salary, 0)) FROM employees; -- Treats NULL as 0
```

Combining Aggregate Functions

You can combine multiple aggregate functions in a single query.

Example: Calculate the total, average, minimum, and maximum salary for each department.

```
SELECT department_id,
       SUM(salary) AS total_salary,
       AVG(salary) AS avg_salary,
       MIN(salary) AS min_salary,
       MAX(salary) AS max_salary
FROM employees
GROUP BY department_id;
```

Using Aggregate Functions with DISTINCT

You can use **DISTINCT** with aggregate functions to perform calculations on unique values.

- Example: Count the number of unique departments.
  ```
  SELECT COUNT(DISTINCT department_id) FROM employees;
  ```
- Example: Calculate the average of unique salaries.
  ```
  SELECT AVG(DISTINCT salary) FROM employees;
  ```

Examples of Common Use Cases

1. **Count the total number of employees:**
   ```
   SELECT COUNT(*) FROM employees;
   ```
2. **Find the highest salary in the company:**
   ```
   SELECT MAX(salary) FROM employees;
   ```
3. **Calculate the total salary expense for each department:**
   ```
   SELECT department_id, SUM(salary)
   FROM employees
         GROUP BY department_id;
   ```
4. **Find departments with more than 10 employees:**
   ```
   SELECT department_id, COUNT(*)
   FROM employees
   GROUP BY department_id
         HAVING COUNT(*) > 10;
   ```

5. **List all employees in each department as a comma-separated string:**

```
SELECT department_id, GROUP_CONCAT(first_name)
FROM employees
      GROUP BY department_id;
```

Notes on Aggregate Functions

- Aggregate functions are often used with **GROUP BY** to group rows and perform calculations on each group.
- The **HAVING** clause is used to filter groups after aggregation.
- Aggregate functions ignore **NULL** values by default.
- You can use **DISTINCT** with aggregate functions to work with unique values.

These functions are essential for summarizing and analyzing data in MySQL.

Practical Exercise

Here is a practical exercise that builds on the previous **Employee Management System** and incorporates the MySQL topics of this lesson. This exercise will guide you through using **String**, **Numeric**, **Date**, and **Aggregate** built-in functions in MySQL to manipulate and analyze data.

Exercise: Analyzing Employee Data

Step 1: Use the Existing Database

Use the **employee_management_advanced** database created in the previous exercise.

```
USE employee_management_advanced;
```

Step 2: Insert Additional Records

Insert additional records into the employees table to make the queries more meaningful.

```
INSERT INTO employees (name, department_id, salary, join_date,
email) VALUES
('Liam Johnson', 2, 72000.00, '2024-08-01', 'liam.johnson@
example.com'),
('Mia Martinez', 3, 59000.00, '2024-09-15', 'mia.martinez@
example.com'),
('Noah Garcia', 1, 54000.00, '2024-10-10', 'noah.garcia@
example.com'),
```

```
('Olivia Brown', 2, 68000.00, '2024-11-20', 'olivia.brown@
example.com'),
('William Davis', 1, 55000.00, '2024-12-05', 'william.davis@
example.com');
```

Step 3: String Built-in Functions

Use string functions to manipulate employee names and emails:

- Retrieve employee names in uppercase.
- Retrieve the first 3 characters of employee names.
- Retrieve employee emails and extract the domain part (text after @).

Here is the query:

```
-- Uppercase names
SELECT UPPER(name) AS uppercase_name FROM employees;

-- First 3 characters of names
SELECT LEFT(name, 3) AS name_prefix FROM employees;

-- Extract domain from email
SELECT SUBSTRING(email, LOCATE('@', email) + 1) AS email_domain
FROM employees;
```

Step 4: Numeric Built-in Functions

Use numeric functions to analyze employee salaries:

- Retrieve the rounded salary (to the nearest thousand).
- Retrieve the square root of the salary.
- Retrieve the absolute difference between the salary and 60000.

Here is the query:

```
-- Rounded salary
SELECT ROUND(salary, -3) AS rounded_salary FROM employees;

-- Square root of salary
SELECT SQRT(salary) AS salary_sqrt FROM employees;

-- Absolute difference from 60000
SELECT ABS(salary - 60000) AS salary_diff FROM employees;
```

Step 5: Date Built-in Functions

Use date functions to analyze employee join dates:

- Retrieve the year and month of the join date.
- Retrieve the number of days since each employee joined.
- Retrieve the join date in the format DD-Mon-YYYY.

Here is the query:

```
-- Year and month of join date
SELECT YEAR(join_date) AS join_year, MONTH(join_date) AS join_
month FROM employees;

-- Days since joining
SELECT DATEDIFF(CURRENT_DATE, join_date) AS days_since_joining
FROM employees;

-- Join date in DD-Mon-YYYY format
SELECT DATE_FORMAT(join_date, '%d-%b-%Y') AS formatted_join_date
FROM employees;
```

Step 6: Aggregate Built-in Functions

Use aggregate functions to analyze employee data:

- Retrieve the total salary expenditure for the company.
- Retrieve the average salary in the IT department.
- Retrieve the highest and lowest salary in the HR department.
- Retrieve the number of employees in each department.

Here is the query:

```
-- Total salary expenditure
SELECT SUM(salary) AS total_salary_expenditure FROM employees;

-- Average salary in IT department
SELECT AVG(salary) AS avg_salary_it FROM employees WHERE
department_id = 2;

-- Highest and lowest salary in HR department
SELECT MAX(salary) AS max_salary_hr, MIN(salary) AS min_salary_hr
FROM employees
WHERE department_id = 1;

-- Number of employees in each department
```

```
SELECT department_id, COUNT(*) AS employee_count
FROM employees
GROUP BY department_id;
```

Step 7: Combining Functions

Combine multiple functions to create advanced queries:

- Retrieve the average salary for employees who joined in the last 6 months.
- Retrieve the total salary expenditure for employees whose names start with J.

Here is the query:

```
-- Average salary for employees who joined in the last 6 months
SELECT AVG(salary) AS avg_salary_last_6_months
FROM employees
WHERE join_date >= DATE_SUB(CURRENT_DATE, INTERVAL 6 MONTH);

-- Total salary expenditure for employees whose names start with
'J'
SELECT SUM(salary) AS total_salary_j_names
FROM employees
WHERE name LIKE 'J%';
```

Step 8: Verify Data

Retrieve all records from the employees table to verify the results of your queries.

```
SELECT * FROM employees;
```

Final Queries

```
USE employee_management_advanced;
INSERT INTO employees (name, department_id, salary, join_date,
email) VALUES
('Liam Johnson', 2, 72000.00, '2024-08-01', 'liam.johnson@
example.com'),
('Mia Martinez', 3, 59000.00, '2024-09-15', 'mia.martinez@
example.com'),
('Noah Garcia', 1, 54000.00, '2024-10-10', 'noah.garcia@
example.com'),
('Olivia Brown', 2, 68000.00, '2024-11-20', 'olivia.brown@
example.com'),
('William Davis', 1, 55000.00, '2024-12-05', 'william.davis@
example.com');

-- Uppercase names
SELECT UPPER(name) AS uppercase_name FROM employees;
```

```
-- First 3 characters of names
SELECT LEFT(name, 3) AS name_prefix FROM employees;

-- Extract domain from email
SELECT SUBSTRING(email, LOCATE('@', email) + 1) AS email_domain
FROM employees;

-- Rounded salary
SELECT ROUND(salary, -3) AS rounded_salary FROM employees;

-- Square root of salary
SELECT SQRT(salary) AS salary_sqrt FROM employees;

-- Absolute difference from 60000
SELECT ABS(salary - 60000) AS salary_diff FROM employees;

-- Year and month of join date
SELECT YEAR(join_date) AS join_year, MONTH(join_date) AS join_
month FROM employees;

-- Days since joining
SELECT DATEDIFF(CURRENT_DATE, join_date) AS days_since_joining
FROM employees;

-- Join date in DD-Mon-YYYY format
SELECT DATE_FORMAT(join_date, '%d-%b-%Y') AS formatted_join_date
FROM employees;

-- Total salary expenditure
SELECT SUM(salary) AS total_salary_expenditure FROM employees;

-- Average salary in IT department
SELECT AVG(salary) AS avg_salary_it FROM employees WHERE
department_id = 2;

-- Highest and lowest salary in HR department
SELECT MAX(salary) AS max_salary_hr, MIN(salary) AS min_salary_hr
FROM employees
WHERE department_id = 1;

-- Number of employees in each department
SELECT department_id, COUNT(*) AS employee_count
FROM employees
GROUP BY department_id;

-- Average salary for employees who joined in the last 6 months
```

```
SELECT AVG(salary) AS avg_salary_last_6_months
FROM employees
WHERE join_date >= DATE_SUB(CURRENT_DATE, INTERVAL 6 MONTH);

-- Total salary expenditure for employees whose names start with
'J'
SELECT SUM(salary) AS total_salary_j_names
FROM employees
WHERE name LIKE 'J%';

SELECT * FROM employees;
```

Expected Output

After completing the exercise, you should have:

- Used **String Functions** (**UPPER, LEFT, SUBSTRING, LOCATE**) to manipulate text data.
- Used **Numeric Functions** (**ROUND, SQRT, ABS**) to analyze numeric data.
- Used **Date Functions** (**YEAR, MONTH, DATEDIFF, DATE_FORMAT**) to analyze date data.
- Used **Aggregate Functions** (**SUM, AVG, MAX, MIN, COUNT**) to summarize data.
- Combined multiple functions to create advanced queries.
- Verified the results by querying the employees table.

This exercise covers all the topics of this lesson and provides hands-on practice with MySQL built-in functions.

Conclusion

We are now familiar with the built-in functions in MySQL. String Functions such as **CONCAT()** and **SUBSTRING()** enable efficient text manipulation, while Numeric Functions such as **ROUND()** and **POWER()** simplify mathematical operations. Date Functions such as **NOW()** and **DATE_ADD()** facilitate easy handling of date and time values, and Aggregate Functions such as **SUM()** and **AVG()** are essential for summarizing and analyzing data. Together, these built-in functions provide powerful tools for querying, processing, and managing data effectively in MySQL.

In the next chapter, we will see the statements in MySQL with examples.

Points to Remember

- String Functions such as **`CONCAT()`**, **`SUBSTRING()`**, and **`TRIM()`** are essential for manipulating and processing text data efficiently.
- Numeric Functions such as **`ROUND()`**, **`ABS()`**, and **`POWER()`** help perform mathematical operations and calculations on numeric data.
- Date Functions such as **`NOW()`**, **`DATE_ADD()`**, and **`DATEDIFF()`** simplify working with date and time values, enabling easy date manipulation and extraction.
- Aggregate Functions such as **`SUM()`**, **`AVG()`**, and **`COUNT()`** are crucial for summarizing and analyzing data, often used with **`GROUP BY`** for grouped calculations.
- Functions such as **`LENGTH()`** (for strings) and **`DATEDIFF()`** (for dates) provide insights into data properties, such as string length or date differences.
- Combining these functions in SQL queries allows for powerful data manipulation, transformation, and analysis, making MySQL a versatile tool for database management.

Multiple Choice Questions

1. Which function is used to extract a portion of a string in MySQL?
   a. `CONCAT()`
   b. `SUBSTRING()`
   c. `TRIM()`
   d. `REPLACE()`
2. What does the ROUND(3.14159, 2) function return?
   a. 3.14
   b. 3.15
   c. 3.1
   d. 3.141
3. Which function returns the current date and time in MySQL?
   a. `CURDATE()`
   b. `CURTIME()`
   c. `NOW()`
   d. `DATE()`

4. What is the result of `CEIL(3.2)`
    a. 3
    b. 3.2
    c. 4
    d. 3.5
5. What will `CHAR_LENGTH('Hello')` return?
    a. 5
    b. 6
    c. 4
    d. 7
6. What does `INSTR('Hello World', 'World')` return?
    a. 6
    b. 7
    c. 5
    d. 4

Answer

1. b
2. a
3. c
4. c
5. a
6. b

Questions

1. How would you extract the first 5 characters from the string "Hello World" using a MySQL function?
2. How would you calculate the square root of 25 in MySQL?
3. Write a MySQL query to generate a random number between 0 and 1.

4. How would you get the current date and time in MySQL?
5. What MySQL function would you use to extract the year from the date "2025-03-25"?
6. How would you concatenate all employee names into a single string, separated by commas in MySQL?
7. Write a query to calculate the total salary of all employees in the employees table.

Key Terms

- **String Manipulation**: Refers to functions such as `CONCAT()`, `SUBSTRING()`, and `TRIM()` used for processing and modifying text data.
- **Mathematical Operations**: Involves numeric functions such as `ROUND()`, `ABS()`, and `POWER()` for performing calculations on numbers.
- **Date and Time Handling**: Includes functions such as `NOW()`, `DATE_ADD()`, and `DATEDIFF()` for managing and manipulating date and time values.
- **Aggregation**: Refers to functions such as `SUM()`, `AVG()`, and `COUNT()` used to summarize and analyze data sets.
- **Data Extraction**: Involves functions such as `DAY()`, `MONTH()`, and `YEAR()` to extract specific parts of date or string values.
- **Data Transformation**: The process of converting or formatting data using functions such as `DATE_FORMAT()` or `UPPER()`.
- **Grouping and Summarization**: The use of aggregate functions with GROUP BY to perform calculations on grouped data, such as finding totals or averages per category.

CHAPTER 6
MySQL Statements

Introduction

The chapter covers some key statements in MySQL with examples to order, update, drop, delete, and perform other operations on the records. We will also understand the CASE Statement. The differences between drop and delete are also discussed, with examples to easily drop a table and a database.

Structure

In this chapter, we will discuss the following topics:

- **ORDER BY** Statement in MySQL
- **CASE** Statement in MySQL
- **UPDATE** Statement in MySQL
- **DELETE** Statement in MySQL
- **DROP TABLE** Statement in MySQL
- **DROP DATABASE** Statement in MySQL
- Practical Exercise

ORDER BY Statement

The **ORDER BY** statement in MySQL is used to sort the result set of a query by one or more columns. It can sort the data in ascending (default) or descending order. Here is the basic syntax:

```
SELECT column1, column2, ...
FROM table_name
ORDER BY column1 [ASC|DESC], column2 [ASC|DESC], ...;
```

Key Points of ORDER BY Statement

- **Sorting Order**:
  - **ASC** (ascending): Sorts the result set in ascending order (default if not specified).
  - **DESC** (descending): Sorts the result set in descending order.
- **Sorting by Multiple Columns:**

  You can sort by multiple columns by specifying them in a comma-separated list. The sorting is applied in the order the columns are listed.
- **Numeric and String Sorting:**
  - Numeric columns are sorted by their numeric value.
  - String columns are sorted alphabetically.
- **NULL Values**: By default, **NULL** values are considered the lowest possible values and appear first when sorting in ascending order.

Examples of ORDER BY

- ## Basic ORDER BY

  Sort the **employees** table by the **last_name** column in ascending order:

```
SELECT first_name, last_name
FROM employees
ORDER BY last_name ASC;
```

- ## Sorting in OrderDescending

  Sorting in Descending Order means arranging query results from highest to lowest values based on a specified column.

  Here, **ORDER BY price DESC** means sorting products by their price from the most expensive to the least expensive.

```
SELECT product_name, price
FROM products
ORDER BY price DESC;
```

  Sort the **products** table by the **price** column in descending order:

- ## Sorting by Multiple Columns

  Sort the **orders** table first by **order_date** in ascending order, and then by **total_amount** in descending order:

```
SELECT order_id, order_date, total_amount
```

```
FROM orders
ORDER BY order_date ASC, total_amount DESC;
```

- ## Sorting by Column Position

  You can also sort by the position of the column in the **SELECT** statement (instead of the column name). For example, sort by the second column (**last_name**):

  ```
  SELECT first_name, last_name
  FROM employees
  ORDER BY 2 ASC;
  ```

- ## Sorting with NULL Values

  Sort the **customers** table by the **city** column, with **NULL** values appearing last:

  ```
  SELECT customer_name, city
  FROM customers
  ORDER BY city IS NULL, city ASC;
  ```

Notes:

- *The **ORDER BY** clause is executed after the **SELECT** statement, so you can use aliases defined in the **SELECT** statement for sorting.*
- *Sorting large datasets can be resource-intensive, so ensure proper indexing on columns used in **ORDER BY** for better performance.*

CASE Statement

The **CASE** statement in MySQL is a conditional expression that allows you to perform conditional logic within SQL queries. It is similar to the **IF-THEN-ELSE** logic in programming languages. The **CASE** statement can be used in **SELECT, UPDATE, INSERT**, and **DELETE** statements, as well as in **ORDER BY** and **WHERE** clauses.

Syntax of CASE Statement

There are two forms of the **CASE** statement in MySQL. Let us see the syntaxes as well:

Simple CASE Statement

This form compares a single expression to a set of values.

```
CASE expression
    WHEN value1 THEN result1
    WHEN value2 THEN result2
    ...
    ELSE default_result
END
```

Searched CASE Statement

This form evaluates multiple conditions.

```
CASE
    WHEN condition1 THEN result1
    WHEN condition2 THEN result2
    ...
    ELSE default_result
END
```

Key Points of CASE Statement

- The **CASE** statement evaluates conditions in the order they are written and returns the result for the first condition that evaluates to **TRUE**.
- If no condition is met, the **ELSE** clause is executed. If no **ELSE** clause is provided, the **CASE** statement returns **NULL**.
- The **CASE** statement can be used in:
  - **SELECT** clauses to create calculated columns.
  - **WHERE** clauses to filter data conditionally.
  - **ORDER BY** clauses to sort data conditionally.
  - **UPDATE** and **INSERT** statements to set values conditionally.

Examples of the CASE Statement

Simple CASE Statement

Classify products based on their price range:

```
SELECT product_name, price,
    CASE
        WHEN price < 20 THEN 'Low'
        WHEN price BETWEEN 20 AND 50 THEN 'Medium'
        ELSE 'High'
    END AS price_category
FROM products;
```

Searched CASE Statement

Assign a grade based on a student's score:

```
SELECT student_name, score,
    CASE
        WHEN score >= 90 THEN 'A'
```

```
        WHEN score >= 80 THEN 'B'
        WHEN score >= 70 THEN 'C'
        WHEN score >= 60 THEN 'D'
        ELSE 'F'
    END AS grade
FROM students;
```

Using CASE in ORDER BY

Sort employees by job title, but prioritize managers:

```
SELECT employee_name, job_title
FROM employees
ORDER BY
    CASE
        WHEN job_title = 'Manager' THEN 1
        ELSE 2
    END;
```

Using CASE in UPDATE

Update the status of orders based on their total amount:

```
UPDATE orders
SET status =
    CASE
        WHEN total_amount > 1000 THEN 'High Priority'
        ELSE 'Normal'
    END;
```

Using CASE in WHERE

Filter products based on a dynamic condition:

```
SELECT product_name, price
FROM products
WHERE
    CASE
        WHEN price < 50 THEN 1
        ELSE 0
    END = 1;
```

Notes:

- *The **CASE** statement is very flexible and can be nested if needed.*
- *It is a powerful tool for transforming or categorizing data directly within SQL queries.*
- *Always ensure that the **CASE** statement is properly closed with an **END**.*

UPDATE Statement

The **UPDATE** statement in MySQL is used to modify existing records in a table. It allows you to change the values of one or more columns in one or more rows based on specified conditions.

Syntax of the UPDATE Statement

Here is the basic syntax:

```
UPDATE table_name
SET column1 = value1, column2 = value2, ...
WHERE condition;
```

Key Points of the UPDATE Statement:

- **SET** Clause:
  - Specifies the columns to be updated and their new values.
  - You can update multiple columns in a single **UPDATE** statement.
- **WHERE** Clause:
  - Specifies the condition(s) that determine which rows will be updated.
  - If the **WHERE** clause is omitted, **all rows** in the table will be updated.
- **Updating Multiple Rows**:
  - If the **WHERE** condition matches multiple rows, all those rows will be updated.
- **Limiting Updates**:
  - You can use the **LIMIT** clause to restrict the number of rows updated.
- **Updating with Subqueries**:
  - You can use subqueries in the **SET** or **WHERE** clauses to update rows based on values from another table.

Examples of the UPDATE Statement

Basic UPDATE

Update the **email** column for a specific user in the **users** table:

```
UPDATE users
SET email = 'new_email@example.com'
WHERE user_id = 1;
```

Updating Multiple Columns

Update both the **salary** and **department** columns for an employee:

```
UPDATE employees
SET salary = 60000, department = 'Marketing'
WHERE employee_id = 5;
```

Updating All Rows

Increase the price of all products by 10%:

```
UPDATE products
SET price = price * 1.10;
```

Updating with a Condition

Update the status of orders that are older than 30 days:

```
UPDATE orders
SET status = 'Archived'
WHERE order_date < NOW() - INTERVAL 30 DAY;
```

Updating with a LIMIT

Update the status of only the first 5 pending orders:

```
UPDATE orders
SET status = 'Processing'
WHERE status = 'Pending'
LIMIT 5;
```

Updating with a Subquery

Update the **salary** column for employees based on their performance rating from another table:

```
UPDATE employees e
SET e.salary = e.salary * 1.15
WHERE e.employee_id IN (
    SELECT employee_id
    FROM performance_reviews
    WHERE rating = 'Excellent'
);
```

Updating with CASE

Conditionally update the **discount** column based on the order amount:

```
UPDATE orders
SET discount =
    CASE
        WHEN total_amount > 1000 THEN 0.10
        WHEN total_amount > 500 THEN 0.05
        ELSE 0
    END;
```

Notes:

- *Always use a* ***WHERE*** *clause unless you intend to update all rows in the table.*
- *Be cautious when updating data, as it cannot be undone unless you are using transactions.*
- *Test your* ***UPDATE*** *statement with a* ***SELECT*** *query first to ensure it affects the correct rows.*

DELETE Statement

The **DELETE** statement in MySQL is used to remove one or more rows from a table. It allows you to delete records based on specified conditions. If no condition is provided, **all rows** in the table will be deleted. Here is the basic syntax:

```
DELETE FROM table_name
WHERE condition;
```

Key Points of the DELETE Statement

- **WHERE** Clause:
    - Specifies the condition(s) that determine which rows will be deleted.
    - If the **WHERE** clause is omitted, **all rows** in the table will be deleted.
- **Deleting Specific Rows**: Use the **WHERE** clause to delete only the rows that meet the specified condition(s).
- **Deleting All Rows**: If you omit the **WHERE** clause, all rows in the table will be deleted. This is equivalent to truncating the table, but unlike **TRUNCATE TABLE**, **DELETE** can be rolled back if used within a transaction.
- **Limiting Deletions**: You can use the **LIMIT** clause to restrict the number of rows deleted.
- **Deleting with Joins**: You can use **DELETE** with **JOIN** to delete rows from one table based on conditions involving another table.

Examples of the `DELETE` Statement

Let us see some examples of the **`DELETE`** Statement in MySQL:

Basic DELETE

Delete a specific user from the **`users`** table:

```
DELETE FROM users
WHERE user_id = 1;
```

Deleting with a Condition

Delete all orders that are older than 30 days:

```
DELETE FROM orders
WHERE order_date < NOW() - INTERVAL 30 DAY;
```

Deleting All Rows

Delete all rows from the **`logs`** table:

```
DELETE FROM logs;
```

Deleting with a `LIMIT`

Delete only the first 5 rows from the **`temp_data`** table:

```
DELETE FROM temp_data
LIMIT 5;
```

Deleting with a Subquery

Delete all employees who have not completed their probation:

```
DELETE FROM employees
WHERE employee_id IN (
    SELECT employee_id
    FROM probation_reviews
    WHERE status = 'Failed'
);
```

Deleting with `JOIN`

Delete all orders placed by a specific customer using a **`JOIN`**:

```
DELETE o
FROM orders o
```

```
JOIN customers c ON o.customer_id = c.customer_id
WHERE c.customer_name = 'John Doe';
```

Deleting with ORDER BY and LIMIT

Delete the 10 oldest records from the **logs** table:

```
DELETE FROM logs
ORDER BY log_date ASC
LIMIT 10;
```

Notes:

- **Backup Data**: *Always ensure you have a backup of your data before performing a **DELETE** operation, especially if you are deleting many rows.*
- **Transactions**: *Use transactions (**BEGIN, COMMIT, ROLLBACK**) to ensure data integrity when performing deletions.*
- **Performance**: *Deleting many rows can be slow and resource-intensive. Consider using **TRUNCATE TABLE** if you need to delete all rows from a table, as it is faster and uses fewer system resources.*

Difference Between DELETE and TRUNCATE

Feature	DELETE	TRUNCATE
Removes	Specific rows or all rows	All rows
Condition	Can use **WHERE** clause	No **WHERE** clause
Speed	Slower (logs individual row deletions)	Faster (deallocates entire table)
Rollback	Can be rolled back	Cannot be rolled back
Auto-Increment	Does not reset auto-increment value	Resets auto-increment value

Table 6.1: *Differences between DELETE and TRUNCATE*

DROP TABLE Statement

The **DROP TABLE** statement in MySQL is used to delete an entire table, including its structure, data, indexes, triggers, and constraints. Once a table is dropped, it cannot be recovered unless you have a backup.

Note: *The drop table deletes the entire table. Use it with caution.*

Syntax of DROP TABLE Statement

Here is the basic syntax:

```
DROP TABLE [IF EXISTS] table_name;
```

Key Points of `DROP TABLE` Statement:

- **Permanent Deletion**: The `DROP TABLE` statement removes the table and all its associated data and metadata permanently.
- `IF EXISTS` Clause: The `IF EXISTS` clause prevents an error from being thrown if the table does not exist. This is useful for avoiding errors in scripts.
- **Multiple Tables**: You can drop multiple tables in a single `DROP TABLE` statement by separating the table names with commas.
- **Dependencies**: If the table is referenced by foreign keys in other tables, the `DROP TABLE` statement will fail unless the referencing tables are also dropped or the foreign key constraints are removed.
- **Permissions**: You must have the `DROP` privilege on the table to execute this statement.

Examples of `DROP TABLE` Statement

Basic `DROP TABLE`

Drop a single table:

```
DROP TABLE employees;
```

Using `IF EXISTS`

Drop a table only if it exists:

```
DROP TABLE IF EXISTS temp_data;
```

Dropping Multiple Tables

Drop multiple tables in a single statement:

```
DROP TABLE table1, table2, table3;
```

Dropping a Table with Foreign Key Constraints

If the table is referenced by foreign keys, you must either:

- Drop the referencing tables first, or
- Remove the foreign key constraints.

For example:

```
-- Drop the referencing table first
DROP TABLE orders;
```

```
-- Then drop the referenced table
DROP TABLE customers;
```

Notes:

- **Backup Data**: *Always ensure you have a backup of your data before dropping a table, as this operation cannot be undone.*
- **Dependencies**: *Be cautious when dropping tables that are referenced by other tables or have dependencies (for example, views, stored procedures).*
- **Performance**: *Dropping a table is a quick operation, but it permanently removes all data and structure.*

Difference Between `DROP TABLE`, `DELETE`, and `TRUNCATE`

Feature	`DROP TABLE`	`DELETE`	`TRUNCATE`
Removes	Entire table (structure and data)	Specific rows or all rows	All rows
Structure	Deletes table structure	Keeps table structure	Keeps table structure
Auto-Increment	Resets auto-increment value	Does not reset auto-increment value	Resets auto-increment value
Speed	Fast	Slower (logs individual deletions)	Fast (deallocates entire table)
Rollback	Cannot be rolled back	Can be rolled back	Cannot be rolled back
Permissions	Requires `DROP` privilege	Requires `DELETE` privilege	Requires `DROP` privilege

Table 6.2: *Differences between DROP TABLE, DELETE, and TRUNCATE*

`DROP DATABASE` Statement

The `DROP DATABASE` statement in MySQL is used to delete an entire database, including all its tables, data, indexes, triggers, and other associated objects. Once a database is dropped, it cannot be recovered unless you have a backup.

Note: *The drop database deletes the entire database. Use it with caution.*

Syntax of `DROP DATABASE` Statement

Here is the basic syntax:

```
DROP DATABASE [IF EXISTS] database_name;
```

Key Points of DROP DATABASE Statement

- **Permanent Deletion**: The **`DROP DATABASE`** statement removes the entire database and all its contents permanently.
- **`IF EXISTS`** Clause: The **`IF EXISTS`** clause prevents an error from being thrown if the database does not exist. This is useful for avoiding errors in scripts.
- **Permissions:** You must have the **`DROP`** privilege on the database to execute this statement.
- **Dependencies**: Dropping a database will also remove all objects within it, such as tables, views, stored procedures, and triggers.
- **Backup**: Always ensure you have a backup of your database before dropping it, as this operation cannot be undone.

Examples of `DROP DATABASE` Statement

Let us see some examples of the **`DROP DATABASE`** Statement in MySQL:

Basic `DROP DATABASE`

Drop a database:

```
DROP DATABASE my_database;
```

Using `IF EXISTS`

Drop a database only if it exists:

```
DROP DATABASE IF EXISTS my_database;
```

Notes:

- ***Backup Data**: Always ensure you have a backup of your database before dropping it, as this operation is irreversible.*
- ***Permissions**: You need the **`DROP`** privilege to execute this statement.*
- ***Dependencies**: Dropping a database will remove all objects within it, so ensure no critical data or objects are lost.*

Difference Between `DROP DATABASE`, `DROP TABLE`, and `TRUNCATE`

Feature	`DROP DATABASE`	`DROP TABLE`	`TRUNCATE`
Removes	Entire database (all tables and data)	Entire table (structure and data)	All rows in a table

Structure	Deletes database and all objects	Deletes table structure	Keeps table structure
Auto-Increment	Resets auto-increment value	Resets auto-increment value	Resets auto-increment value
Speed	Fast	Fast	Fast (deallocates entire table)
Rollback	Cannot be rolled back	Cannot be rolled back	Cannot be rolled back
Permissions	Requires **DROP** privilege	Requires **DROP** privilege	Requires **DROP** privilege

Table 6.3: *Differences between DROP DATABASE, DROP TABLE, and TRUNCATE*

Practical Exercise

Here is a practical exercise that builds on the previous **Employee Management System** and incorporates the MySQL topics of this lesson. This exercise will guide you through sorting data, using conditional logic, updating and deleting records, and dropping tables and databases.

Exercise: Managing Employee Data

Step 1: Use the Existing Database

Use the **employee_management_advanced** database created in the previous exercise:

```
USE employee_management_advanced;
```

Step 2: ORDER BY Statement

Use the ORDER BY statement to sort employee data:

- Retrieve all employees sorted by their **salary** in descending order.
- Retrieve all employees sorted by their **join_date** in ascending order.

Here it is:

```
-- Sort by salary (descending)
SELECT * FROM employees
ORDER BY salary DESC;

-- Sort by join_date (ascending)
SELECT * FROM employees
ORDER BY join_date ASC;
```

Step 3: CASE Statement

Use the **CASE** statement to categorize employees based on their salary:

- If the **salary** is greater than 70000, label them as **High**.
- If the **salary** is between 50000 and 70000, label them as **Medium.**
- If the **salary** is less than 50000, label them as **Low**.

Here it is:

```
SELECT name, salary,
    CASE
        WHEN salary > 70000 THEN 'High'
        WHEN salary BETWEEN 50000 AND 70000 THEN 'Medium'
        ELSE 'Low'
    END AS salary_category
FROM employees;
```

Step 4: UPDATE Statement

Use the **UPDATE** statement to modify employee data:

- Increase the salary of employees in the IT department (**department_id = 2**) by 10%.
- Update the email of John Doe to john.doe@newdomain.com.

Here it is:

```
-- Increase IT department salaries by 10%
UPDATE employees
SET salary = salary * 1.10
WHERE department_id = 2;

-- Update John Doe's email
UPDATE employees
SET email = 'john.doe@newdomain.com'
WHERE name = 'John Doe';
```

Step 5: DELETE Statement

Use the **DELETE** statement to remove employee data:

Delete employees who joined before **2024-01-01**.

```
DELETE FROM employees
WHERE join_date < '2024-01-01';
```

Step 6: Verify Data

Retrieve all records from the employees table to verify the updates and deletions:

```
SELECT * FROM employees;
```

Step 7: `DROP TABLE` Statement

Drop the departments table. Before dropping, ensure that the **`employees`** table no longer depends on it by removing the foreign key constraint:

```
-- Remove foreign key constraint
ALTER TABLE employees DROP FOREIGN KEY employees_ibfk_1;

-- Drop departments table
DROP TABLE departments;
```

Note: *Using the **`DROP TABLE`** statement will delete the table and its data. Backup the table by following our Lesson: Backup and Restore.*

Step 8: `DROP DATABASE` Statement

Drop the **`employee_management_advanced`** database:

```
DROP DATABASE employee_management_advanced;
```

Note: *Using the **`DROP DATABASE`** statement will delete the database and its data. Backup the database by following our Lesson: Backup and Restore.*

Final Queries

```
USE employee_management_advanced;

-- Sort by salary (descending)
SELECT * FROM employees
ORDER BY salary DESC;

-- Sort by join_date (ascending)
SELECT * FROM employees
ORDER BY join_date ASC;

SELECT name, salary,
    CASE
        WHEN salary > 70000 THEN 'High'
        WHEN salary BETWEEN 50000 AND 70000 THEN 'Medium'
        ELSE 'Low'
    END AS salary_category
FROM employees;
```

```
-- Increase IT department salaries by 10%
UPDATE employees
SET salary = salary * 1.10
WHERE department_id = 2;

-- Update John Doe's email
UPDATE employees
SET email = 'john.doe@newdomain.com'
WHERE name = 'John Doe';

DELETE FROM employees
WHERE join_date < '2024-01-01';

SELECT * FROM employees;

-- Remove foreign key constraint
ALTER TABLE employees DROP FOREIGN KEY employees_ibfk_1;

-- Drop departments table
DROP TABLE departments;

DROP DATABASE employee_management_advanced;
```

Expected Output

After completing the exercise, you should have:

- Used the **ORDER BY** statement to sort employee data.
- Used the **CASE** statement to categorize employees based on their salary.
- Used the **UPDATE** statement to modify employee data.
- Used the **DELETE** statement to remove employee data.
- Dropped the **departments** table after removing its dependency.
- Dropped the **employee_management_advanced** database.
- Verified the results at each step by querying the **employees** table.

This exercise covers all the topics of this lesson and provides hands-on practice with MySQL data manipulation and management.

Conclusion

We are now familiar with statements in MySQL. MySQL provides powerful statements such as ORDER BY for sorting data, CASE for conditional logic, and UPDATE for modifying records. The DELETE statement allows for removing specific rows, while

DROP TABLE and DROP DATABASE are used to permanently delete tables and databases, respectively.

These statements are essential for managing and manipulating data effectively. However, caution is advised, especially with UPDATE, DELETE, DROP TABLE, and DROP DATABASE, as they can lead to irreversible data loss if misused. The proper use of these commands ensures efficient database management and data integrity.

In the next chapter, we will learn how to create joins in MySQL.

Points to Remember

- The **`CASE`** statement is used for conditional logic in **`SELECT, WHERE`**, or **`ORDER BY`** clauses.
- Always use a **`WHERE`** clause to avoid updating all rows unintentionally.
- Consider backing up data before running a DELETE operation.
- This **`DROP TABLE`** permanently deletes the table and its data; use it cautiously.
- This **`DROP DATABASE`** permanently deletes the entire database and all its content; use it cautiously.
- Backup the database before dropping it to prevent irreversible data loss.

Multiple Choice Questions

1. Which of the following queries deletes all rows from the employees table?
   a. `DELETE FROM` employees `WHERE` employee_id = 101;
   b. `DELETE FROM` employees;
   c. `DROP TABLE` employees;
   d. `TRUNCATE TABLE` employees;
2. What is the difference between `DROP TABLE` and `DELETE FROM` in MySQL?
   a. `DROP TABLE` removes the table structure and data, while `DELETE FROM` only removes data.
   b. `DROP TABLE` only removes data, while `DELETE FROM` removes the table structure and data.
   c. Both `DROP TABLE` and `DELETE FROM` remove only data.
   d. Both `DROP TABLE` and `DELETE FROM` remove the table structure and data.

3. Which of the following queries updates the status column to "`Inactive`" for all employees in the "`Sales`" department?

    a. `UPDATE employees SET status = 'Inactive';`

    b. `UPDATE employees SET status = 'Inactive' WHERE department = 'Sales';`

    c. `UPDATE employees SET status = 'Sales' WHERE department = 'Inactive';`

    d. `UPDATE employees SET department = 'Sales' WHERE status = 'Inactive';`

4. What is the purpose of the `WHERE` clause in a `DELETE` statement?

    a. To specify the database to delete.

    b. To specify which columns to delete.

    c. To specify the table to delete.

    d. To specify which rows to delete.

5. What happens if you execute the following query: `DROP TABLE` customers;?

    a. The customers table and its structure are permanently deleted.

    b. Only the data in the customers table is deleted.

    c. The customers table is renamed.

    d. The customers table is moved to another database.

Answer

1. b
2. a
3. b
4. d
5. a

Questions

1. How can you update multiple columns in a single **`UPDATE`** query?
2. What happens to the data and structure of a table when you use the **`DROP TABLE`** statement?
3. Write a query to drop a table named **`temp_data`**.
4. What happens to the data and structure of a table when you use the **`DROP TABLE`** statement?
5. Write a query to drop a database named **`old_records`**.
6. What precautions should you take before executing a **`DROP DATABASE`** command?

Key Terms

- **`ORDER BY` statement:** Sorts query results.
- **`CASE` statement:** It implements conditional logic.
- **`UPDATE` statement:** Modifies existing records.
- **`DELETE` statement:** Removes records from a table.
- **`DROP TABLE` statement:** Deletes a table and its data.
- **`DROP DATABASE` statement:** Deletes an entire database.

CHAPTER 7
MySQL Joins

Introduction

The chapter covers the role of Joins and how multiple tables can be joined in MySQL. Joins in MySQL are powerful tools used to combine data from two or more tables based on a related column, enabling efficient querying of relational databases. Let us understand Joins and its types, such as INNER, LEFT, RIGHT, CROSS, and so on, with query examples.

Structure

In this chapter, we will discuss the following topics:

- Joins in MySQL
- `INNER` Joins in MySQL
- `LEFT` Join in MySQL
- `RIGHT` Join in MySQL
- `CROSS` Join in MySQL
- `FULL` Join in MySQL
- Optimize the performance of Joins in MySQL
- Practical Exercise

Joins in MySQL

Joins in MySQL are used to combine rows from two or more tables based on a related column between them. They are essential for querying data from multiple tables in a relational database. The most common types of joins are:

1. `INNER JOIN`
2. `LEFT JOIN` (or LEFT OUTER JOIN)
3. `RIGHT JOIN` (or RIGHT OUTER JOIN)

4. **CROSS JOIN**
5. **FULL JOIN** (or FULL OUTER JOIN)
6. **SELF-JOIN**

Note: *Use table aliases to simplify queries when working with multiple tables.*

Be cautious with NULL values in join conditions, as they can affect the results.

INNER Joins

In MySQL, an **INNER JOIN** is used to combine rows from two or more tables based on a related column between them. It returns only the rows where there is a match in both tables. If there is no match, the rows are not included in the result set.

Syntax of INNER JOIN

```
SELECT columns
FROM table1
INNER JOIN table2
ON table1.column_name = table2.column_name;
```

Above:

- **table1** and **table2** are the tables you want to join.
- **column_name** is the common column between the two tables.
- **ON** specifies the condition for the join.

Example of INNER JOIN

Suppose you have two tables: **customers** and **orders**.

Table: customers

customer_id	name	email
1	John Doe	john@example.com
2	Jane Smith	jane@example.com
3	Alice	alice@example.com

Table 7.1: *Records of the customers table*

Table: orders

order_id	customer_id	order_date
101	1	2024-10-01

102	2	2024-10-02
103	3	2024-10-03

Table 7.2: *Records of the orders table*

To retrieve the customer name and their corresponding order details, you can use an **`INNER JOIN`**:

```
SELECT customers.name, orders.order_id, orders.order_date
FROM customers
INNER JOIN orders
ON customers.customer_id = orders.customer_id;
```

Result:

name	order_id	order_date
John Doe	101	2024-10-01
Jane Smith	102	2024-10-02
Alice	103	2024-10-03

Table 7.3: *Output of the inner join*

Key Points of `INNER JOIN`:

- **Matching Rows Only**: **`INNER JOIN`** returns only the rows where there is a match in both tables.
- **No NULLs**: If there is no match, the row is excluded from the result set.
- **Multiple Tables**: You can join more than two tables using multiple **`INNER JOIN`** clauses.

Example of `INNER JOIN` with Multiple Tables

If you have a third table **`products`** and want to include product details in the result:

Table: `products`

product_id	order_id	product_name
1001	101	Laptop
1002	102	Smartphone
1003	103	Tablet

Table 7.4: *Records of the products table*

The following is the query:

```
SELECT customers.name, orders.order_id, orders.order_date,
products.product_name
FROM customers
```

```
INNER JOIN orders ON customers.customer_id = orders.customer_id
INNER JOIN products ON orders.order_id = products.order_id;
```

Result:

name	order_id	order_date	product_name
John Doe	101	2024-10-01	Laptop
Jane Smith	102	2024-10-02	Smartphone
Alice	103	2024-10-03	Tablet

Table 7.5: *Output of the inner join*

This is how **INNER JOIN** works in MySQL. It is one of the most commonly used joins in SQL queries.

LEFT Join

In MySQL, a **LEFT JOIN** (or **LEFT OUTER JOIN**) is used to fetch all rows from the left table (table1), along with the corresponding matching rows from the right table (table2). When no matching records are found in the right table, the result will still display the rows from the left table, with NULL values populating the columns from the right table."

Syntax of LEFT JOIN

```
SELECT columns
FROM table1
LEFT JOIN table2
ON table1.column_name = table2.column_name;
```

Above:

- **table1** is the left table.
- **table2** is the right table.
- **column_name** is the common column used to join the tables.
- **ON** specifies the condition for the join.

Example of LEFT JOIN

Suppose you have two tables: **customers** and **orders**.

Table: customers

customer_id	name	email
1	John Doe	john@example.com

2	Jane Smith	jane@example.com
3	Alice	alice@example.com
4	Bob	bob@example.com

Table 7.6: *Records of the customers table*

Table: `orders`

order_id	customer_id	order_date
101	1	2024-10-01
102	2	2024-10-02
103	3	2024-10-03

Table 7.7: *Records of the orders table*

To retrieve all customers and their orders (if any), you can use a **`LEFT JOIN`**:

```
SELECT customers.name, orders.order_id, orders.order_date
FROM customers
LEFT JOIN orders
ON customers.customer_id = orders.customer_id;
```

Result:

name	order_id	order_date
John Doe	101	2024-10-01
Jane Smith	102	2024-10-02
Alice	103	2024-10-03
Bob	NULL	NULL

Table 7.8: *Output of left join*

Explanation

- **`John Doe`**, **`Jane Smith`**, and **`Alice`** have matching orders in the **`orders`** table, so their order details are included.
- **`Bob`** does not have any orders, so the columns from the **`orders`** table (**`order_id`** and **`order_date`**) are filled with **`NULL`**.

Key Points of `LEFT JOIN`:

- **All Rows from Left Table**: A **`LEFT JOIN`** returns all rows from the left table, even if there are no matching rows in the right table.
- **NULL for Non-Matching Rows**: When no matching record exists in the right table, the output will display NULL values in its columns.

- **Use Cases**: **LEFT JOIN** is useful when you want to include all records from one table and only the matching records from another table (for example, finding customers with or without orders).

Example of LEFT JOIN with Filtering

You can also add a **WHERE** clause to filter the results. For example, to find customers who have not placed any orders:

```
SELECT customers.name, orders.order_id, orders.order_date
FROM customers
LEFT JOIN orders
ON customers.customer_id = orders.customer_id
WHERE orders.order_id IS NULL;
```

Result:

name	order_id	order_date
Bob	NULL	NULL

***Table 7.9**: Output of left join with filtering*

This query returns only the customers who have no orders.

Example of LEFT JOIN with Multiple Tables

If you have a third table, such as **products**, you can extend the **LEFT JOIN**:

Table: products

product_id	order_id	product_name
1001	101	Laptop
1002	102	Smartphone
1003	103	Tablet

***Table 7.10**: Records of the products table*

The following is the query:

```
SELECT customers.name, orders.order_id, orders.order_date,
products.product_name
FROM customers
LEFT JOIN orders ON customers.customer_id = orders.customer_id
LEFT JOIN products ON orders.order_id = products.order_id;
```

Result:

name	order_id	order_date	product_name
John Doe	101	2024-10-01	Laptop
Jane Smith	102	2024-10-02	Smartphone
Alice	103	2024-10-03	Tablet
Bob	NULL	NULL	NULL

Table 7.11: *Output of left join*

This query retrieves all customers, their orders (if any), and the corresponding product details (if any). If there is no match, **`NULL`** values are returned for the missing data.

Summary

- Use **`LEFT JOIN`** when you want to include all records from the left table and only matching records from the right table.
- Non-matching rows from the right table will have **`NULL`** values in the result.
- It is commonly used for queries where you need to find records with optional relationships (for example, customers with or without orders).

RIGHT Join

In MySQL, a **`RIGHT JOIN`** (or **`RIGHT OUTER JOIN`**) is used to retrieve all records from the right table (**`table2`**) and the matched records from the left table (**`table1`**). If there is no match in the left table, the result will still include the rows from the right table, but with **`NULL`** values for the columns from the left table.

Syntax of RIGHT JOIN

```
SELECT columns
FROM table1
RIGHT JOIN table2
ON table1.column_name = table2.column_name;
```

Above:

- **`table1`** is the left table.
- **`table2`** is the right table.
- **`column_name`** is the common column used to join the tables.
- **`ON`** specifies the condition for the join.

Example

Suppose you have two tables: **customers** and **orders**.

Table: customers

customer_id	name	email
1	John Doe	john@example.com
2	Jane Smith	jane@example.com
3	Alice	alice@example.com

Table 7.12: *Records of the customers table*

Table: orders

order_id	customer_id	order_date
101	1	2024-10-01
102	2	2024-10-02
103	3	2024-10-03
104	4	2024-10-04

Table 7.13: *Records of the orders table*

To retrieve all orders and their corresponding customer details (if any), use a **RIGHT JOIN**:

```
SELECT customers.name, orders.order_id, orders.order_date
FROM customers
RIGHT JOIN orders
ON customers.customer_id = orders.customer_id;
```

Result

name	order_id	order_date
John Doe	101	2024-10-01
Jane Smith	102	2024-10-02
Alice	103	2024-10-03
NULL	104	2024-10-04

Table 7.14: *Output of right join*

Explanation

- **John Doe**, **Jane Smith**, and **Alice** have matching customer records in the **customers** table, so their details are included.
- The order with **order_id = 104** does not have a matching customer in the

customers table, so the columns from the **customers** table (**name**) are filled with **NULL**.

Key Points of RIGHT JOIN:

- **All Rows from Right Table**: A **RIGHT JOIN** returns all rows from the right table, even if there are no matching rows in the left table.
- **NULL for Non-Matching Rows**: If there is no match in the left table, the result will include **NULL** values for the columns from the left table.
- **Use Cases**: **RIGHT JOIN** is useful when you want to include all records from the right table and only the matching records from the left table (for example, finding orders with or without customer details).

Example of RIGHT JOIN with Filtering

You can also add a **WHERE** clause to filter the results. For example, to find orders that do not have a corresponding customer:

```
SELECT customers.name, orders.order_id, orders.order_date
FROM customers
RIGHT JOIN orders
ON customers.customer_id = orders.customer_id
WHERE customers.customer_id IS NULL;
```

Result:

name	order_id	order_date
NULL	104	2024-10-04

***Table 7.15:** Output of right join with filtering*

This query returns only the orders that do not have a matching customer.

Example of RIGHT JOIN with Multiple Tables

If you have a third table, such as **products**, you can extend the **RIGHT JOIN**:

Table: products

product_id	order_id	product_name
1001	101	Laptop
1002	102	Smartphone
1003	103	Tablet
1004	104	Monitor

***Table 7.16:** Records of the products table*

The following is the query:

```
SELECT customers.name, orders.order_id, orders.order_date,
products.product_name
FROM customers
RIGHT JOIN orders ON customers.customer_id = orders.customer_id
RIGHT JOIN products ON orders.order_id = products.order_id;
```

Result:

name	order_id	order_date	product_name
John Doe	101	2024-10-01	Laptop
Jane Smith	102	2024-10-02	Smartphone
Alice	103	2024-10-03	Tablet
NULL	104	2024-10-04	Monitor

Table 7.17: *Output of right join*

This query retrieves all products, their corresponding orders (if any), and the corresponding customer details (if any). If there is no match, **NULL** values are returned for the missing data.

Summary

- Use **`RIGHT JOIN`** when you want to include all records from the right table and only matching records from the left table.
- Non-matching rows from the left table will have **`NULL`** values in the result.
- It is commonly used for queries where you need to find records with optional relationships (for example, orders with or without customer details).

CROSS Join

In MySQL, a **`CROSS JOIN`** is used to combine every row from the first table with every row from the second table. A Cartesian product is produced of the two tables that returns all combinations of rows from both tables. Unlike **`INNER JOIN`**, **`LEFT JOIN`**, or **`RIGHT JOIN`**, a **`CROSS JOIN`** does not require a condition to match rows between the tables.

Syntax of CROSS JOIN

```
SELECT columns
FROM table1
CROSS JOIN table2;
```

On the other hand, you can achieve the same result by using a comma (,) between the tables without specifying **CROSS JOIN**:

```
SELECT columns
FROM table1, table2;
```

Example of CROSS JOIN

Suppose you have two tables: **colors** and **sizes**.

Table: colors

color_id	color_name
1	Red
2	Blue
3	Green

Table 7.18: *Records of the colors table*

Table: sizes

size_id	size_name
S	Small
M	Medium
L	Large

Table 7.19: *Records of the sizes table*

To retrieve all possible combinations of colors and sizes, you can use a **CROSS JOIN**:

```
SELECT colors.color_name, sizes.size_name
FROM colors
CROSS JOIN sizes;
```

Result:

color_name	size_name
Red	Small
Red	Medium
Red	Large
Blue	Small
Blue	Medium
Blue	Large
Green	Small

Green	Medium
Green	Large

Table 7.20: *Output of cross join*

Explanation

- The **CROSS JOIN** combines each row from the **colors** table with every row from the **sizes** table.
- Since there are 3 colors and 3 sizes, the result contains **3×3=9 rows**.

Key Points of CROSS JOIN:

- **Cartesian Product**: A **CROSS JOIN** returns the Cartesian product of the two tables, meaning it combines every row from the first table with every row from the second table.
- **No Join Condition**: Unlike other joins, a **CROSS JOIN** does not require an **ON** or **USING** clause.
- **Use Cases**: **CROSS JOIN** is useful to generate all possible combinations of rows from two tables (for example, generating a matrix of options).

Example of CROSS JOIN with Filtering

You can add a **WHERE** clause to filter the results of a **CROSS JOIN**. For example, to retrieve only combinations where the color is "**Red**":

```
SELECT colors.color_name, sizes.size_name
FROM colors
CROSS JOIN sizes
WHERE colors.color_name = 'Red';
```

Result:

color_name	**size_name**
Red	Small
Red	Medium
Red	Large

Table 7.21: *Output of cross join*

Example of CROSS JOIN with Multiple Tables

If you have more than two tables, you can perform a **CROSS JOIN** across all of them. For example, suppose you have a third table **materials**:

Table: `materials`

material_id	material_name
1	Cotton
2	Polyester

Table 7.22: *Records of the materials table*

To retrieve all combinations of colors, sizes, and materials:

```
SELECT colors.color_name, sizes.size_name, materials.material_
name
FROM colors
CROSS JOIN sizes
CROSS JOIN materials;
```

Result:

color_name	size_name	material_name
Red	Small	Cotton
Red	Small	Polyester
Red	Medium	Cotton
Red	Medium	Polyester
Red	Large	Cotton
Red	Large	Polyester
Blue	Small	Cotton
Blue	Small	Polyester
Blue	Medium	Cotton
Blue	Medium	Polyester
Blue	Large	Cotton
Blue	Large	Polyester
Green	Small	Cotton
Green	Small	Polyester
Green	Medium	Cotton
Green	Medium	Polyester
Green	Large	Cotton
Green	Large	Polyester

Table 7.23: *Output of cross join*

Explanation

- The result contains **3 colors×3 sizes×2 materials=18 rows.**
- Each row represents a unique combination of color, size, and material.

Summary

- Use **CROSS JOIN** to generate all possible combinations of rows from two or more tables.
- It does not require a join condition and returns the Cartesian product of the tables.
- Be cautious with large tables, as the result can grow exponentially and consume significant resources.

FULL Join

In MySQL, a **FULL JOIN** (or **FULL OUTER JOIN**) is used to retrieve all records from both tables, including matching records and non-matching records from either table. When there is no corresponding match between rows, the resulting output will display **NULL** values in the columns from the table that does not have a matching row.

However, **MySQL does not natively support FULL JOIN**. To achieve the same result, you can use a combination of **LEFT JOIN** and **RIGHT JOIN** with the **UNION** operator.

Simulating FULL JOIN in MySQL

To simulate a **FULL JOIN** in MySQL, you can use the following approach:

```
SELECT columns
FROM table1
LEFT JOIN table2 ON table1.column_name = table2.column_name
UNION
SELECT columns
FROM table1
RIGHT JOIN table2 ON table1.column_name = table2.column_name;
```

Above:

- **LEFT JOIN** retrieves all records from **table1** and matching records from **table2**.
- **RIGHT JOIN** retrieves all records from **table2** and matching records from **table1**.
- **UNION** combines the results of both queries and removes duplicates.

Example

Suppose you have two tables: **`customers`** and **`orders`**.

Table: `customers`

customer_id	name	email
1	John Doe	john@example.com
2	Jane Smith	jane@example.com
3	Alice	alice@example.com
4	Bob	bob@example.com

***Table 7.24:** Records of the customers table*

Table: `orders`

order_id	customer_id	order_date
101	1	2024-10-01
102	2	2024-10-02
103	3	2024-10-03
104	5	2024-10-04

***Table 7.25:** Records of the orders table*

To retrieve all customers and all orders, including unmatched records from both tables, you can simulate a **`FULL JOIN`**:

```
SELECT customers.customer_id, customers.name, orders.order_id,
orders.order_date
FROM customers
LEFT JOIN orders ON customers.customer_id = orders.customer_id
UNION
SELECT customers.customer_id, customers.name, orders.order_id,
orders.order_date
FROM customers
RIGHT JOIN orders ON customers.customer_id = orders.customer_id;
```

Result:

customer_id	name	order_id	order_date
1	John Doe	101	2024-10-01
2	Jane Smith	102	2024-10-02
3	Alice	103	2024-10-03

4	Bob	NULL	NULL
NULL	NULL	104	2024-10-04

Table 7.26: *Output of Full Join*

Explanation

- **John Doe**, **Jane Smith**, and **Alice** have matching records in both tables, so their details are included.
- **Bob** does not have any orders, so the columns from the **orders** table (**order_id** and **order_date**) are filled with **NULL**.
- The order with **order_id = 104** does not have a matching customer, so the columns from the **customers** table (**customer_id** and **name**) are filled with **NULL**.

Key Points:

- **Combination of LEFT and RIGHT JOIN**: A **FULL JOIN** is simulated using **LEFT JOIN, RIGHT JOIN,** and **UNION.**
- **Includes All Records**: It retrieves all records from both tables, including unmatched rows.
- **NULL for Non-Matching Rows**: If there is no match, the result includes **NULL** values for the missing data.

Example with Filtering

You can add a **WHERE** clause to filter the results. For example, to find customers without orders or orders without customers:

```
SELECT customers.customer_id, customers.name, orders.order_id,
orders.order_date
FROM customers
LEFT JOIN orders ON customers.customer_id = orders.customer_id
WHERE orders.order_id IS NULL
UNION
SELECT customers.customer_id, customers.name, orders.order_id,
orders.order_date
FROM customers
RIGHT JOIN orders ON customers.customer_id = orders.customer_id
WHERE customers.customer_id IS NULL;
```

Result:

customer_id	name	order_id	order_date
4	Bob	NULL	NULL
NULL	NULL	104	2024-10-04

Table 7.27: *Output of full join with filtering*

This query returns only the unmatched records from both tables.

Summary

- MySQL does not natively support **`FULL JOIN`**, but you can simulate it using **`LEFT JOIN, RIGHT JOIN`**, and **`UNION`**.
- A **`FULL JOIN`** retrieves all records from both tables, including unmatched rows.
- Use this approach when you need to combine data from two tables and include all records, even if there are no matches.

Optimize the Performance of Joins in MySQL

Optimizing the performance of joins in MySQL is crucial, especially when dealing with large datasets or complex queries. Here are some strategies to improve join performance:

Use Indexes

Why? Indexes speed up the retrieval of rows by creating a quick lookup mechanism.

How? Ensure that the columns used in join conditions (for example, ON table1.column = table2.column) are indexed.

Example:

```
CREATE INDEX idx_column ON table1(column);
CREATE INDEX idx_column ON table2(column);
```

Note: *Indexes in MySQL are covered in the next lesson.*

Choose the Right Join Type

- **Why?** Using the appropriate join type (INNER JOIN, LEFT JOIN, and so on) can reduce unnecessary data processing.
- **How?** Use INNER JOIN when you only need matching rows, and avoid CROSS JOIN unless necessary.

Limit the Number of Rows

- **Why?** Joins perform better when working with smaller datasets.
- **How?** Use WHERE clauses to filter rows before joining tables.

- **Example:**

```
SELECT *
FROM table1
INNER JOIN table2
ON table1.column = table2.column
WHERE table1.column = 'value';
```

Avoid Nested Joins

- **Why?** Deeply nested joins can be inefficient and hard to optimize.
- **How?** Simplify queries by breaking them into smaller, manageable parts.

By applying these strategies, you can significantly improve the performance of joins in MySQL.

Select Only Necessary Columns

- **Why**? Retrieving only required columns reduces data transfer and memory usage
- **How**? Replace **SELECT *** with specific column names

Let us see an example:

```
SELECT t1.id, t1.name, t2.order_date
FROM customers t1
JOIN orders t2 ON t1.id = t2.customer_id
```

Monitor and Analyze Join Performance

- **Why?** Helps identify bottlenecks in real-world usage
- **How:** Use **EXPLAIN ANALYZE** and MySQL's performance schema

Let us see an example:

```
EXPLAIN ANALYZE
SELECT * FROM table1 JOIN table2 ON table1.id = table2.id;
```

Practical Exercise

Here is a practical exercise that builds on the previous **Employee Management System** and incorporates the MySQL topics of this lesson. This exercise will guide you through using **INNER JOIN**, **LEFT JOIN**, **RIGHT JOIN**, **CROSS JOIN**, and **FULL JOIN** to combine and analyze data from multiple tables.

Note: *We dropped the database and tables in the previous Lesson 6. Therefore, we are creating a new database and tables for this lesson.*

Exercise: Joining Employee and Department Data

Step 1: Create a New Database

Create a new database named **`employee_management_joins`**.

```
CREATE DATABASE employee_management_joins;
USE employee_management_joins;
```

Step 2: Create Tables

Create two tables:

- **departments**: Stores department details.
  - `department_id` (INT, Primary Key, Auto Increment)
  - `department_name` (VARCHAR(50), Unique, Not Null)
- **employees**: Stores employee details.
  - `id` (INT, Primary Key, Auto Increment)
  - `name` (VARCHAR(50), Not Null
  - `department_id` (INT, Foreign Key referencing departments. department_id)
  - `salary` (DECIMAL(10, 2), Not Null

Here is the query:

```
CREATE TABLE departments (
    department_id INT PRIMARY KEY AUTO_INCREMENT,
    department_name VARCHAR(50) NOT NULL UNIQUE
);

CREATE TABLE employees (
    id INT PRIMARY KEY AUTO_INCREMENT,
    name VARCHAR(50) NOT NULL,
    department_id INT,
    salary DECIMAL(10, 2) NOT NULL,
    FOREIGN KEY (department_id) REFERENCES departments
(department_id)
);
```

Step 3: Insert Records

Insert records into the departments and **employees** tables:

```
-- Insert departments
INSERT INTO departments (department_name) VALUES
('HR'),
('IT'),
('Finance'),
('Marketing');

-- Insert employees
INSERT INTO employees (name, department_id, salary) VALUES
('John Doe', 1, 50000.00),
('Jane Smith', 2, 60000.00),
('Alice Johnson', 3, 55000.00),
('Bob Brown', 2, 62000.00),
('Charlie Davis', 1, 48000.00),
('Eva Green', NULL, 58000.00); -- Employee without a department
```

Step 4: `INNER JOIN`

Use **`INNER JOIN`** to retrieve employees along with their department names. Only employees with a valid department will be included.

```
SELECT e.id, e.name, e.salary, d.department_name
FROM employees e
INNER JOIN departments d ON e.department_id = d.department_id;
```

Step 5: `LEFT JOIN`

Use **`LEFT JOIN`** to retrieve all employees and their department names. Employees without a department will also be included.

```
SELECT e.id, e.name, e.salary, d.department_name
FROM employees e
LEFT JOIN departments d ON e.department_id = d.department_id;
```

Step 6: `RIGHT JOIN`

Use **`RIGHT JOIN`** to retrieve all departments and their employees. Departments without employees will also be included.

```
SELECT e.id, e.name, e.salary, d.department_name
FROM employees e
RIGHT JOIN departments d ON e.department_id = d.department_id;
```

Step 7: `CROSS JOIN`

Use CROSS JOIN to retrieve all possible combinations of **`employees`** and **`departments`**.

```
SELECT e.id, e.name, e.salary, d.department_name
FROM employees e
CROSS JOIN departments d;
```

Step 8: `FULL JOIN`

MySQL does not support **`FULL JOIN`** directly, but you can simulate it using a combination of **`LEFT JOIN`** and **`RIGHT JOIN`** with **`UNION`**.

```
SELECT e.id, e.name, e.salary, d.department_name
FROM employees e
LEFT JOIN departments d ON e.department_id = d.department_id
UNION
SELECT e.id, e.name, e.salary, d.department_name
FROM employees e
RIGHT JOIN departments d ON e.department_id = d.department_id;
```

Step 9: Verify Data

Retrieve all records from the **`departments`** and **`employees`** tables to verify the results of your joins.

```
SELECT * FROM departments;
SELECT * FROM employees;
```

Final Queries

```
CREATE DATABASE employee_management_joins;
USE employee_management_joins;

CREATE TABLE departments (
    department_id INT PRIMARY KEY AUTO_INCREMENT,
    department_name VARCHAR(50) NOT NULL UNIQUE
);

CREATE TABLE employees (
    id INT PRIMARY KEY AUTO_INCREMENT,
    name VARCHAR(50) NOT NULL,
    department_id INT,
    salary DECIMAL(10, 2) NOT NULL,
    FOREIGN KEY (department_id) REFERENCES departments
(department_id)
```

```
);

-- Insert departments
INSERT INTO departments (department_name) VALUES
('HR'),
('IT'),
('Finance'),
('Marketing');

-- Insert employees
INSERT INTO employees (name, department_id, salary) VALUES
('John Doe', 1, 50000.00),
('Jane Smith', 2, 60000.00),
('Alice Johnson', 3, 55000.00),
('Bob Brown', 2, 62000.00),
('Charlie Davis', 1, 48000.00),
('Eva Green', NULL, 58000.00); -- Employee without a department

SELECT e.id, e.name, e.salary, d.department_name
FROM employees e
INNER JOIN departments d ON e.department_id = d.department_id;

SELECT e.id, e.name, e.salary, d.department_name
FROM employees e
LEFT JOIN departments d ON e.department_id = d.department_id;

SELECT e.id, e.name, e.salary, d.department_name
FROM employees e
RIGHT JOIN departments d ON e.department_id = d.department_id;

SELECT e.id, e.name, e.salary, d.department_name
FROM employees e
CROSS JOIN departments d;

SELECT e.id, e.name, e.salary, d.department_name
FROM employees e
LEFT JOIN departments d ON e.department_id = d.department_id
UNION
SELECT e.id, e.name, e.salary, d.department_name
FROM employees e
RIGHT JOIN departments d ON e.department_id = d.department_id;

SELECT * FROM departments;
SELECT * FROM employees;
```

Expected Output

After completing the exercise, you should have:

- Used **INNER JOIN** to retrieve employees with valid departments.
- Used **LEFT JOIN** to retrieve all employees, including those without departments.
- Used **RIGHT JOIN** to retrieve all departments, including those without employees.
- Used **CROSS JOIN** to retrieve all possible combinations of employees and departments.
- Simulated **FULL JOIN** using UNION to retrieve all employees and departments.
- Verified the results by querying the **departments** and **employees** tables.

This exercise covers all the topics of this lesson and provides hands-on practice with MySQL joins.

Conclusion

By now, we have a good understanding of the various types of Joins in MySQL. The widely used ones are INNER JOIN, which retrieves only rows with matching values; LEFT JOIN and RIGHT JOIN, which return all rows from one table and matching rows from the other table; CROSS JOIN, which generates a Cartesian product of rows from both tables; and FULL JOIN, which merges data from both tables while including unmatched rows.

We saw how these joins are essential for retrieving and analyzing data across multiple tables in a database. In the next chapter, we will see what indexes are in MySQL.

Points to Remember

- The **INNER JOIN** returns only rows with matching values in both tables.
- The **LEFT JOIN** returns all rows from the left table and matched rows from the right table.
- The **RIGHT JOIN** returns all rows from the right table and matched rows from the left table.
- The **CROSS JOIN** returns the Cartesian product of both tables (all possible combinations).
- The **FULL JOIN** combines results from both tables, including unmatched rows.
- Joins can be resource-intensive, especially with large datasets. Use indexes on join columns to optimize performance.

Multiple Choice Questions

1. What does an `INNER JOIN` return?
   a. All rows from both tables
   b. Only rows with matching values in both tables
   c. All rows from the left table and matching rows from the right table
   d. All rows from the right table and matching rows from the left table
2. Which join returns all rows from the left table and matching rows from the right table, with NULL for non-matching rows?
   a. `INNER JOIN`
   b. `LEFT JOIN`
   c. `RIGHT JOIN`
   d. `CROSS JOIN`
3. What is the result of a `CROSS JOIN`?
   a. Only matching rows from both tables
   b. All rows from the left table and matching rows from the right table
   c. The Cartesian product of both tables
   d. All rows from the right table and matching rows from the left table
4. How can you simulate a `FULL JOIN` in MySQL?
   a. Use `UNION` of `LEFT JOIN` and `RIGHT JOIN`
   b. Use `INNER JOIN` with a `WHERE` clause
   c. Use `CROSS JOIN` with a `WHERE` clause
   d. Use `LEFT JOIN` with a `WHERE` clause
5. Which join type is used to combine each row of the first table with each row of the second table?
   a. `INNER JOIN`
   b. `LEFT JOIN`
   c. `RIGHT JOIN`
   d. `CROSS JOIN`

6. What is the purpose of using aliases in join queries?
    a. To rename tables permanently
    b. To simplify the query and make it more readable
    c. To exclude certain columns from the result
    d. To filter out duplicate rows

Answers

1. b
2. b
3. c
4. a
5. d
6. b

Questions

1. What is the purpose of using joins in MySQL?
2. Explain the difference between `INNER JOIN` and `LEFT JOIN`.
3. How does a `RIGHT JOIN` differ from a `LEFT JOIN`?
4. What is the difference between `INNER JOIN` and `FULL JOIN`?
5. What is a `CROSS JOIN`, and when would you use it?
6. How can you optimize the performance of joins in MySQL?

Key Terms

- **`INNER JOIN`**: Returns only rows with matching values in both tables.
- **`LEFT JOIN`**: Returns all rows from the left table and matched rows from the right table.
- **`RIGHT JOIN`**: Returns all rows from the right table and matched rows from the left table.
- **`CROSS JOIN`**: Returns the Cartesian product of both tables (all possible combinations).
- **`FULL JOIN`**: Returns all rows when there is a match in either table (requires **`UNION`**).

Chapter 8
MySQL Indexes

Introduction

This chapter covers indexes in MySQL and their purpose. Indexes enhance the data retrieval operations. We will also learn how to create indexes. With that, some other operations, such as displaying and dropping indexes, will also be covered. The concept of unique and clustered indexes, with examples, will be discussed in the later part of the chapter.

Structure

In this chapter, we will discuss the following topics:

- Indexes in MySQL
- Create Indexes in MySQL
- Show Indexes in MySQL
- Drop Indexes in MySQL
- Unique Index in MySQL
- Clustered Index in MySQL
- Practical Exercise

Indexes in MySQL

In MySQL, indexes are data structures that improve the speed of data retrieval operations on database tables. They work similarly to an index in a book, allowing the database to find and access specific rows much faster than scanning the entire table. Indexes are particularly useful for speeding up queries that involve filtering, sorting, or joining data.

Key Concepts of Indexes in MySQL:

- **Purpose:**
    - Indexes speed up **SELECT** queries by providing quick access to rows.

  - They are especially useful for large tables where searching without an index would require a full table scan.
- **Types of Indexes:**
  - **Primary Key Index**: Automatically created when you define a primary key. Ensures uniqueness and fast access to the row.
  - **Unique Index**: Ensures that all values in the indexed column(s) are unique.
  - **Index (or Key)**: A general-purpose index that improves query performance.
  - **Full-Text Index**: Used for full-text searches on text-based columns.
  - **Spatial Index**: Used for spatial data types (for example, geometry).
  - **Composite Index**: An index on multiple columns.
- **How Indexes Work:**
  - Indexes store a sorted copy of the indexed column(s) along with pointers to the actual rows in the table.
  - When a query is executed, MySQL uses the index to locate the relevant rows quickly instead of scanning the entire table.
- **Creating Indexes:**
  - Indexes can be created when defining a table or added later using **`CREATE INDEX`**.
  - Example:

```
CREATE INDEX idx_name ON table_name (column_name);
```

- **When to Use Indexes**:
  - Columns frequently used in **`WHERE`** clauses.
  - Columns used in **`JOIN`** conditions.
  - Columns used for sorting (**`ORDER BY`**) or grouping (**`GROUP BY`**).
- **Trade-offs**:
  - **Storage**: Indexes consume additional disk space.
  - **Write Performance**: Indexes slow down **`INSERT`**, **`UPDATE`**, and **`DELETE`** operations because the index must be updated whenever the data changes.
- **Managing Indexes**:
  - Use **`SHOW INDEX FROM table_name`** to view indexes on a table.
  - Use **`DROP INDEX`** to remove an index:

```
DROP INDEX idx_name ON table_name;
```

Example of Indexes in MySQL

Let us see an example of indexes in MySQL:

```
-- Create a table
CREATE TABLE users (
    id INT PRIMARY KEY,
    username VARCHAR(50),
    email VARCHAR(100)
);

-- Add an index on the email column
CREATE INDEX idx_email ON users (email);

-- Query using the indexed column
SELECT * FROM users WHERE email = 'example@example.com';
```

In this example, the **idx_email** index speeds up the query that filters by the email column.

Best Practices of Indexes

Here are some best practices of indexes in MySQL:

- Avoid over-indexing, as too many indexes can degrade write performance.
- Use composite indexes for queries that filter or sort by multiple columns.
- Regularly analyze and optimize indexes based on query patterns.
- Implement partial indexes for large tables
- Use descending indexes for DESC sorting operations
- Regularly monitor and remove unused indexes
- Balance index benefits against storage and maintenance costs

By using indexes effectively, you can significantly improve the performance of your MySQL database.

Let us now see how indexes work in detail, beginning with creating indexes.

Create Indexes

In MySQL, you can create indexes to improve the performance of queries. Indexes can be created when defining a table or added later using the **CREATE INDEX** statement. The following are examples of how to create different types of indexes in MySQL:

Example to Create Indexes

1. Creating Indexes When Defining a Table

You can define indexes directly in the **CREATE TABLE** statement.

Example:

```
CREATE TABLE users (
    id INT PRIMARY KEY,                    -- Primary key index
(automatically created)
    username VARCHAR(50) NOT NULL,
    email VARCHAR(100) NOT NULL,
    age INT,
    INDEX idx_username (username),         -- Single-column index
    UNIQUE INDEX idx_email (email),        -- Unique index
    INDEX idx_age_email (age, email)      -- Composite index
(multiple columns)
);
```

2. Adding Indexes to an Existing Table

You can add indexes to an existing table using the **CREATE INDEX** statement.

Syntax:

```
CREATE [UNIQUE|FULLTEXT|SPATIAL] INDEX index_name
ON table_name (column1, column2, ...);
```

Examples:

- **Single-Column Index**:
  `CREATE INDEX idx_username ON users (username);`
- **Unique Index**:
  `CREATE UNIQUE INDEX idx_email ON users (email);`
- **Composite Index (on multiple columns)**:
  `CREATE INDEX idx_age_email ON users (age, email);`
- **Full-Text Index (for text-based searches)**:

  `CREATE FULLTEXT INDEX idx_description ON products (description);`

3. Creating a Primary Key Index

A primary key index is automatically created when you define a primary key. If the table already exists, you can add a primary key using the **ALTER TABLE** statement.

Example:

```
ALTER TABLE users ADD PRIMARY KEY (id);
```

4. Creating a Spatial Index

Spatial indexes are used for spatial data types such as **GEOMETRY**.

Example:

```
CREATE TABLE locations (
    id INT PRIMARY KEY,
    name VARCHAR(100),
    coordinates GEOMETRY NOT NULL,
    SPATIAL INDEX idx_coordinates (coordinates)
);
```

Best Practices for Creating Indexes

Here are some best practices you can follow for creating indexes in MySQL:

- **Index Columns Used in WHERE, JOIN, ORDER BY, and GROUP BY Clauses**: Indexes are most useful for columns frequently used in filtering, sorting, or joining.
- **Avoid Over-Indexing**: Too many indexes can slow down **INSERT, UPDATE,** and **DELETE** operations.
- **Use Composite Indexes for Multiple Columns**:
- If queries often filter or sort by multiple columns, create a composite index.
- **Monitor and Optimize Indexes**: Use tools such as EXPLAIN to analyze query performance and adjust indexes as needed.

Example Workflow to Create Indexes

1. Create a table:

```
CREATE TABLE employees (
    id INT PRIMARY KEY,
    first_name VARCHAR(50),
    last_name VARCHAR(50),
    department VARCHAR(50),
    salary INT
      );
```

2. Add indexes:

```
CREATE INDEX idx_last_name ON employees (last_name);
CREATE INDEX idx_department_salary ON employees (department,
salary);
```

3. Query indexed columns:

```
SELECT * FROM employees WHERE last_name = 'Smith';
SELECT * FROM employees WHERE department = 'Sales' AND salary > 
50000;
```

By creating and managing indexes effectively, you can significantly improve the performance of your MySQL database.

Show Indexes

In MySQL, you can view the indexes defined on a table using the **SHOW INDEX** statement. This command provides detailed information about the indexes, including their names, types, and the columns they are associated with.

Syntax to Display Indexes

```
SHOW INDEX FROM table_name;
```

Replace **table_name** with the name of the table for which you want to view the indexes.

Example to Create and Display Indexes

Suppose you have a table named **employees** with the following structure and indexes:

```
CREATE TABLE employees (
    id INT PRIMARY KEY,
    first_name VARCHAR(50),
    last_name VARCHAR(50),
    email VARCHAR(100) UNIQUE,
    department VARCHAR(50),
    salary INT,
    INDEX idx_last_name (last_name),
    INDEX idx_department_salary (department, salary)
);
```

To view the indexes on the **employees** table, run:

```
SHOW INDEX FROM employees;
```

Output:

The **SHOW INDEX** command returns a result set with the following columns:

Column Name	Description
Table	The name of the table.
Non_unique	Indicates if the index allows duplicate values (0 for unique, 1 for non-unique).

`Key_name`	The name of the index.
`Seq_in_index`	The position of the column in the index (for composite indexes).
`Column_name`	The name of the column included in the index.
`Collation`	How the column is sorted in the index (A for ascending, NULL for not sorted).
`Cardinality`	An estimate of the number of unique values in the index.
`Sub_part`	The number of characters indexed if only a prefix of the column is indexed.
`Packed`	Indicates if the index is packed (rarely used).
`Null`	Indicates if the column can contain NULL values (YES or '').
`Index_type`	The type of index (for example, BTREE, HASH, FULLTEXT, and so on).
`Comment`	Additional information about the index.
`Index_comment`	Any comment added to the index during creation.

Table 8.1: *The SHOW INDEX command returns the following information*

Example Output:

For the **`employees`** table, the output might look like this:

Table	Non_unique	Key_name	Seq_in_index	Column_name	Collation	Cardinality	Sub_part	Packed	Null	Index_type	Comment	Index_comment
employees	0	PRIMARY	1	id	A	5	NULL	NULL		BTREE		
employees	0	email	1	email	A	5	NULL	NULL	YES	BTREE		
employees	1	idx_last name	1	last_name	A	5	NULL	NULL	YES	BTREE		
employees	1	idx_department_salary	1	department	A	5	NULL	NULL	YES	BTREE		
employees	1	idx_department_salary	2	salary	A	5	NULL	NULL	YES	BTREE		

Table 8.2: *Displaying indexes and their information*

Explanation of the Output:

- **PRIMARY**: The primary key index on the **id** column. It is unique (**Non_unique = 0**).
- **email**: A unique index on the **email** column (**Non_unique = 0**).
- **idx_last_name**: A non-unique index on the **last_name** column (**Non_unique = 1**).
- **idx_department_salary**: A composite index on the **department** and **salary** columns. The **Seq_in_index** column shows the order of columns in the index.

Filtering Index Information

You can filter the output by specifying the database name or using the **WHERE** clause.

Example:

```
SHOW INDEX FROM employees WHERE Key_name = 'idx_last_name';
```

Alternative: Using information_schema:

You can also query the **information_schema.statistics** table to retrieve index information.

Example:

```
SELECT *
FROM information_schema.statistics
WHERE table_schema = 'your_database_name'
  AND table_name = 'employees';
```

By using **SHOW INDEX** or querying **information_schema**, you can easily inspect and manage the indexes on your MySQL tables.

Drop Indexes

In MySQL, you can drop (remove) an index from a table using the **DROP INDEX** statement. This is useful when an index is no longer needed or if you want to replace it with a different index. The following is a guide on how to drop indexes in MySQL:

Syntax to Drop an Index

```
DROP INDEX index_name ON table_name;
```

Above:

- **index_name**: The name of the index you want to drop.

- **`table_name`:** The name of the table from which the index will be dropped.

Steps to Drop an Index

1. **Identify the Index Name**:
   a. Use the **`SHOW INDEX`** command to list all indexes on a table and identify the name of the index you want to drop.
   b. Example:
   ```
   SHOW INDEX FROM employees;
   ```
2. **Drop the Index**:
   a. Use the **`DROP INDEX`** statement to remove the index.

Examples of Dropping Indexes

1. Dropping a Single-Column Index:

Suppose you have an index named **`idx_last_name`** on the **`employees`** table. To drop it:

```
DROP INDEX idx_last_name ON employees;
```

2. Dropping a Composite Index:

If you have a composite index (an index on multiple columns), you can drop it in the same way. For example, to drop an index named **`idx_department_salary`**:

```
DROP INDEX idx_department_salary ON employees;
```

3. Dropping a Unique Index:

Unique indexes can also be dropped using the same syntax. For example, to drop a unique index named **`idx_email`**:

```
DROP INDEX idx_email ON employees;
```

4. Dropping a Primary Key Index:

The primary key index is a special type of index. To drop it, you must use the **`ALTER TABLE`** statement:

```
ALTER TABLE employees DROP PRIMARY KEY;
```

Important Notes:

- **Permissions:**
  - You must have the **`ALTER`** privilege on the table to drop an index.

- **Impact on Performance:**
  - Dropping an index can improve the performance of **INSERT, UPDATE,** and **DELETE** operations because the index no longer needs to be maintained.
  - However, dropping an index may slow down **SELECT** queries that rely on the index for faster data retrieval.
- **Recreating an Index:**
  - If you drop an index by mistake, you can recreate it using the **CREATE INDEX** statement.

Example Workflow to Drop Indexes

1. **View Indexes**:

```
SHOW INDEX FROM employees;
```

Output:

Table	Non_unique	Key_name	Seq_in_index	Column_name
employees	0	PRIMARY	1	id
employees	1	idx_last_name	1	last_name
employees	1	idx_department_salary	1	department
employees	1	idx_department_salary	2	salary

***Table 8.3:** Displaying indexes*

2. **Drop an Index**:

```
DROP INDEX idx_last_name ON employees;
```

3. **Verify the Index is Dropped**:

```
SHOW INDEX FROM employees;
```

Output (after dropping **idx_last_name**):

Table	Non_unique	Key_name	Seq_in_index	Column_name
employees	0	PRIMARY	1	id
employees	1	idx_department_salary	1	department
employees	1	idx_department_salary	2	salary

***Table 8.4:** Displaying indexes after dropping an index*

Dropping Indexes in a Single Command

If you need to drop multiple indexes, you can execute multiple **DROP INDEX** statements in sequence.

Example:

```
DROP INDEX idx_last_name ON employees;
DROP INDEX idx_department_salary ON employees;
```

By following these steps, you can safely drop indexes in MySQL to optimize your database schema and performance.

Unique Index

In MySQL, a **unique index** ensures that all values in the indexed column(s) are unique. This means no two rows can have the same value(s) in the column(s) that are part of the unique index. Unique indexes are commonly used to enforce data integrity, such as preventing duplicate email addresses or usernames in a table.

Features of Unique Indexes

- **Uniqueness Constraint**:
  - A unique index prevents duplicate values in the indexed column(s).
  - If you attempt to insert or update a row with a duplicate value, MySQL will throw an error.
- **NULL Values**:
  - A unique index allows multiple **NULL** values in the indexed column(s), as **NULL** is considered an unknown value and is not equal to another **NULL**.
- **Performance**:
  - Unique indexes improve query performance for lookups, just like regular indexes.
  - They are particularly useful for columns frequently used in **WHERE** clauses or **JOIN** conditions.
- **Primary Key vs. Unique Index**:
  - A primary key is a special type of unique index that also enforces the **NOT NULL** constraint.
  - A table can have only one primary key but multiple unique indexes.

Creating a Unique Index

1. Creating a Unique Index When Defining a Table:

You can define a unique index directly in the **CREATE TABLE** statement.

Example:

```
CREATE TABLE users (
    id INT PRIMARY KEY,
    username VARCHAR(50) NOT NULL,
    email VARCHAR(100) NOT NULL,
    UNIQUE INDEX idx_email (email),      -- Unique index on the
email column
    UNIQUE INDEX idx_username (username) -- Unique index on the
username column
);
```

2. Adding a Unique Index to an Existing Table:

You can add a unique index to an existing table using the **CREATE UNIQUE INDEX** statement or the **ALTER TABLE** statement.

Syntax:

```
CREATE UNIQUE INDEX index_name ON table_name (column1, column2,
...);
```

Example:

```
CREATE UNIQUE INDEX idx_email ON users (email);
```

Alternatively, you can use **ALTER TABLE**:

```
ALTER TABLE users ADD UNIQUE INDEX idx_email (email);
```

Dropping a Unique Index

To drop a unique index, use the **DROP INDEX** statement.

Syntax:

```
DROP INDEX index_name ON table_name;
```

Example:

```
DROP INDEX idx_email ON users;
```

Handling Duplicate Values

If you try to insert or update a row with a duplicate value in a unique indexed column, MySQL will throw an error.

Example:

```
INSERT INTO users (id, username, email) VALUES (1, 'john_doe',
'john@example.com');
INSERT INTO users (id, username, email) VALUES (2, 'jane_doe',
'john@example.com'); -- Error: Duplicate entry 'john@example.com'
for key 'idx_email'
```

Composite Unique Index

A unique index can be created on multiple columns, ensuring that the combination of values in those columns is unique.

Example:

```
CREATE TABLE orders (
    order_id INT PRIMARY KEY,
    customer_id INT,
    product_id INT,
    UNIQUE INDEX idx_customer_product (customer_id, product_id)
);
```

In this example, the combination of **`customer_id`** and **`product_id`** must be unique.

Checking for Existing Unique Indexes

You can use the **`SHOW INDEX`** command to view the unique indexes on a table.

Example:

```
SHOW INDEX FROM users;
```

Output:

Table	Non_unique	Key_name	Seq_in_index	**Column_name**	**Collation**	**Cardinality**	**Null**	**Index_type**
users	0	PRIMARY	1	id	A	5		BTREE
users	0	idx_email	1	email	A	5		BTREE
users	0	idx_username	1	username	A	5		BTREE

Table 8.5: *Displaying indexes*

Here, `Non_unique = 0` indicates a unique index.

Best Practices for Unique Indexes

- **Use for Columns Requiring Uniqueness**: Apply unique indexes to columns such as email addresses, usernames, or any other field that must be unique.
- **Avoid Overusing Unique Indexes**: Only create unique indexes when necessary, as they add overhead to `INSERT` and `UPDATE` operations.
- **Combine with Other Indexes**: Use composite unique indexes for columns that need to be unique in combination (for example, `customer_id` and `product_id`).
- **Handle NULLs Carefully**: Remember that unique indexes allow multiple `NULL` values, so design your schema accordingly.

Example Workflow for unique index

1. **Create a Table with a Unique Index**:

```
CREATE TABLE employees (
    id INT PRIMARY KEY,
    employee_code VARCHAR(10) NOT NULL,
    email VARCHAR(100) NOT NULL,
    UNIQUE INDEX idx_employee_code (employee_code),
    UNIQUE INDEX idx_email (email)
);
```

2. **Insert Data:**

```
INSERT INTO employees (id, employee_code, email) VALUES (1,
'E001', 'john@example.com');
INSERT INTO employees (id, employee_code, email) VALUES (2,
'E002', 'jane@example.com');
```

3. **Attempt to insert duplicate data:**

```
INSERT INTO employees (id, employee_code, email) VALUES (3,
'E001', 'alice@example.com'); -- Error: Duplicate entry 'E001'
for key 'idx_employee_code'
```

4. **Drop the unique index:**

```
DROP INDEX idx_employee_code ON employees;
```

By using unique indexes, you can enforce data integrity and improve query performance in your MySQL database.

Clustered Index

In MySQL, a **clustered index** is a special type of index that determines the physical order of data in a table. Unlike non-clustered indexes (which store a separate copy of the indexed data), the clustered index directly affects how the rows of the table are stored on disk. Each table can have only one clustered index because the data rows themselves can only be sorted in one order.

Key Concepts of Clustered Indexes

- **Primary Key as Clustered Index:**
    - In MySQL, the primary key automatically becomes the clustered index.
    - If no primary key is defined, MySQL will look for the first **`UNIQUE NOT`** NULL index to use as the clustered index.
    - If neither exists, MySQL creates an internal hidden clustered index (using a hidden **`ROWID`** column).
- **Data Storage:**
    - The data rows are stored in the order of the clustered index.
    - This makes lookups using the clustered index very fast because the data is physically stored in the same order as the index.
- **Only One Clustered Index per Table:**
    - Since the data rows can only be stored in one physical order, a table can have only one clustered index.
- **Performance:**
    - Clustered indexes are highly efficient for range queries and sorting operations because the data is already stored in order.

How Clustered Indexes Work

- When you define a primary key, MySQL automatically creates a clustered index on that column.
- The data rows are stored in the order of the primary key.
- When you query the table using the primary key, MySQL can quickly locate the data because it knows the physical order of the rows.

Creating a Clustered Index

In MySQL, the clustered index is automatically created when you define a primary key. You cannot explicitly create a clustered index using a CREATE INDEX statement.

Example:

```
CREATE TABLE employees (
    id INT PRIMARY KEY,            -- Clustered index is
automatically created on `id`
    name VARCHAR(50),
    department VARCHAR(50),
    salary INT
);
```

In this example:

- The id column is the primary key.
- MySQL creates a clustered index on the id column, and the data rows are stored in the order of id.

Clustered Index with Composite Primary Key

If the primary key consists of multiple columns (composite primary key), the clustered index is created on the combination of those columns.

Example:

```
CREATE TABLE orders (
    order_id INT,
    customer_id INT,
    order_date DATE,
    PRIMARY KEY (order_id, customer_id)  -- Clustered index on
(order_id, customer_id)
);
```

In this example:

- The clustered index is created on the combination of **`order_id`** and **`customer_id`**.
- The data rows are stored in the order of **`order_id`** and **`customer_id`**.

Clustered Index Without a Primary Key

If a table does not have a primary key, MySQL will use the first **`UNIQUE NOT NULL`** index as the clustered index. If no such index exists, MySQL creates an internal hidden clustered index.

Example:

```
CREATE TABLE customers (
    customer_id INT UNIQUE NOT NULL,  -- Clustered index is
created on `customer_id`
```

```
    name VARCHAR(50),
    email VARCHAR(100)
);
```

Advantages of Clustered Indexes

- **Fast Data Retrieval**: Queries that use the clustered index (for example, primary key lookups) are very fast because the data is stored in the same order as the index.
- **Efficient Range Queries**: Range queries (for example, **BETWEEN**, >, <) are efficient because the data is physically stored in order.
- **Automatic Sorting**: Data is automatically sorted based on the clustered index, which can improve performance for sorting operations.

Disadvantages of Clustered Indexes

- **Only One per Table**: Since there can only be one clustered index, you must choose the primary key carefully.
- **Insert/Update/Delete Overhead**: Inserting, updating, or deleting rows can be slower because the data must be physically reordered to maintain the clustered index.
- **Fragmentation**: Over time, the physical order of data can become fragmented, requiring periodic maintenance (for example, **OPTIMIZE TABLE**).

Viewing Clustered Index Information

You can use the SHOW INDEX command to view the clustered index (primary key) of a table.

Example:

```
SHOW INDEX FROM employees;
```

Output:

Table	Non_unique	Key_name	Seq_in_index	Column_name	Index_type
employees	0	PRIMARY	1	id	BTREE

Table 8.6: *Displaying clustered index information*

The **Key_name** column shows **PRIMARY**, indicating the clustered index.

Best Practices for Clustered Indexes

- **Choose the Primary Key wisely**: The primary key should be unique, narrow (small), and static (rarely changing).

- **Use Auto-Increment for Primary Keys**: Auto-incrementing integers (**`INT`** or **`BIGINT`**) are ideal for primary keys because they are narrow, unique, and sequential.
- **Avoid Frequently Changing Primary Keys**: Changing the primary key value can lead to significant overhead because the data must be physically reordered.
- **Monitor Fragmentation**: Use **`OPTIMIZE TABLE`** periodically to defragment the table and maintain performance.

Example Workflow for Clustered Index

1. **Create a Table with a Clustered Index**:

```
CREATE TABLE students (
    student_id INT PRIMARY KEY AUTO_INCREMENT,  -- Clustered
index on `student_id`
    name VARCHAR(50),
    grade CHAR(1)
);
```

2. **Insert Data**

```
INSERT INTO students (name, grade) VALUES ('Alice', 'A');
INSERT INTO students (name, grade) VALUES ('Bob', 'B');
INSERT INTO students (name, grade) VALUES ('Charlie', 'C');
```

3. **Query using the Clustered Index:**

```
SELECT * FROM students WHERE student_id = 2;  -- Fast lookup
using the clustered index
```

4. **View Clustered Index Information:**

```
SHOW INDEX FROM students;
```

By understanding and using clustered indexes effectively, you can optimize the performance and organization of your MySQL tables.

Practical Exercise

Here is a practical exercise that builds on the previous **Employee Management System** and incorporates the MySQL topics of this lesson. This exercise will guide you through creating, displaying, and dropping indexes, as well as working with **Unique Indexes** and **Clustered Indexes**.

Exercise: Working with Indexes in MySQL

Step 1: Use the Existing Database

Use the **employee_management_joins** database created in the previous exercise.

```
USE employee_management_joins;
```

Step 2: Create Indexes

Create indexes on the employees and departments tables:

a. Create a **non-clustered index** on the **name** column of the **employees** table.

b. Create a **unique index** on the **email** column of the **employees** table (add the **email** column if it does not exist).

c. Create a **clustered index** on the **department_id** column of the **departments** table (**Note**: *In MySQL, the primary key is automatically a clustered index, so this step will demonstrate how MySQL handles clustered indexes*).

Here is the query:

```
-- Add email column if it doesn't exist
ALTER TABLE employees ADD COLUMN email VARCHAR(100);

-- Create non-clustered index on name
CREATE INDEX idx_employee_name ON employees(name);

-- Create unique index on email
CREATE UNIQUE INDEX idx_unique_email ON employees(email);

-- Clustered index is automatically created on the primary key
(department_id in departments table)
-- No additional action is needed for clustered indexes in MySQL.
```

Step 3: Show Indexes

Display the indexes for the **employees** and **departments** tables.

```
-- Show indexes for employees table
SHOW INDEX FROM employees;

-- Show indexes for departments table
SHOW INDEX FROM departments;
```

Step 4: Insert Records to Test Indexes

Insert records into the **employees** table to test the unique index on the **email** column.

```
-- Insert valid records
INSERT INTO employees (name, department_id, salary, email) VALUES
('Grace Lee', 2, 65000.00, 'grace.lee@example.com'),
('Henry Brown', 1, 52000.00, 'henry.brown@example.com');

-- Attempt to insert a duplicate email (should fail due to unique
index)
INSERT INTO employees (name, department_id, salary, email) VALUES
('Ivy Davis', 3, 58000.00, 'grace.lee@example.com'); -- This will
fail
```

Step 5: Drop Indexes

Drop the indexes created earlier:

a. Drop the non-clustered index on the **name** column.

b. Drop the unique index on the **email** column.

The following is the query:

```
-- Drop non-clustered index on name
DROP INDEX idx_employee_name ON employees;

-- Drop unique index on email
DROP INDEX idx_unique_email ON employees;
```

Step 6: Verify Indexes

Verify that the indexes have been dropped by displaying the indexes for the **employees** table.

```
SHOW INDEX FROM employees;
```

Step 7: Clustered Index in MySQL

In MySQL, the primary key is automatically a clustered index. To demonstrate this:

Retrieve the table definition of the departments table to see the clustered index (primary key).

```
SHOW CREATE TABLE departments;
```

Final Queries

```
USE employee_management_joins;

-- Add email column if it doesn't exist
ALTER TABLE employees ADD COLUMN email VARCHAR(100);

-- Create non-clustered index on name
CREATE INDEX idx_employee_name ON employees(name);

-- Create unique index on email
CREATE UNIQUE INDEX idx_unique_email ON employees(email);

-- Clustered index is automatically created on the primary key
(department_id in departments table)
-- No additional action is needed for clustered indexes in MySQL.

-- Show indexes for employees table
SHOW INDEX FROM employees;

-- Show indexes for departments table
SHOW INDEX FROM departments;

-- Insert valid records
INSERT INTO employees (name, department_id, salary, email) VALUES
('Grace Lee', 2, 65000.00, 'grace.lee@example.com'),
('Henry Brown', 1, 52000.00, 'henry.brown@example.com');

-- Attempt to insert a duplicate email (should fail due to unique
index)
INSERT INTO employees (name, department_id, salary, email) VALUES
('Ivy Davis', 3, 58000.00, 'grace.lee@example.com'); -- This will
fail

-- Drop non-clustered index on name
DROP INDEX idx_employee_name ON employees;

-- Drop unique index on email
DROP INDEX idx_unique_email ON employees;

SHOW INDEX FROM employees;

SHOW CREATE TABLE departments;
```

Expected Output

After completing the exercise, you should have:

- Created a **non-clustered index** on the name column of the **`employees`** table.
- Created a **unique index** on the email column of the **`employees`** table.
- Displayed the indexes for the employees and departments tables using SHOW INDEX.
- Tested the unique index by attempting to insert duplicate emails.
- Dropped the non-clustered and unique indexes.
- Verified that the indexes were dropped.
- Observed that the primary key in MySQL is automatically a **clustered index**.

This exercise covers all the topics of this lesson and provides hands-on practice with MySQL indexes.

Conclusion

We are now familiar with indexes in MySQL. Indexes in MySQL are essential for optimizing query performance, especially in large datasets. They allow faster data retrieval by reducing the need for full table scans. However, they come with trade-offs, such as increased storage and slower write operations. Properly using indexes, such as unique and clustered indexes, can significantly enhance database efficiency.

In the next chapter, we will learn how to create a new user in MySQL.

Points to Remember

- Indexes in MySQL are used to speed up data retrieval by reducing the need for full table scans.
- The **`CREATE INDEX`** statement is used to create an index on one or more columns of a table.
- The **`DROP INDEX`** statement is used to remove an existing index from a table.
- A unique index ensures that all values in the indexed column(s) are unique, preventing duplicates.
- A clustered index determines the physical order of data storage in a table. In MySQL, the primary key automatically creates a clustered index.
- A table can have only one clustered index because the data cannot be physically sorted in more than one way.
- Use the **`SHOW INDEX`** statement to display all indexes associated with a table.

Multiple Choice Questions

1. What is the primary purpose of an index in MySQL?
   a. To store data permanently
   b. To speed up data retrieval
   c. To delete data
   d. To create backups
2. Which statement is used to create an index in MySQL?
   a. ADD INDEX
   b. MAKE INDEX
   c. INDEX CREATE
   d. CREATE INDEX
3. What does a unique index ensure?
   a. Faster data retrieval
   b. No duplicate values in the indexed column
   c. Physical ordering of data
   d. Automatic backups
4. Which index determines the physical order of data in a table?
   a. Unique Index
   b. Non-Clustered Index
   c. Clustered Index
   d. Secondary Index
5. How do you remove an index in MySQL?
   a. DROP INDEX
   b. REMOVE INDEX
   c. DELETE INDEX
   d. ERASE INDEX

6. What is the default index created by a primary key in MySQL?
    a. Unique Index
    b. Full-Text Index
    c. Non-Clustered Index
    d. Clustered Index

Answer

1. b
2. d
3. b
4. c
5. a
6. d

Questions

1. What is the purpose of creating an index in MySQL?
2. How do you create an index on a single column in MySQL?
3. What is the difference between a unique index and a regular index?
4. How does a clustered index determine the physical storage of data in a table?
5. What happens if you try to insert duplicate values into a column with a unique index?
6. How do you remove an index from a table in MySQL?
7. What command is used to display all indexes on a table?
8. Why can a table have only one clustered index?

Key Terms

- **Index**: A database structure that improves the speed of data retrieval operations on a table.
- **Clustered Index**: An index that determines the physical order of data storage in a table.

- **Unique Index**: An index that ensures all values in the indexed column(s) are unique.
- **Primary Key**: A column or set of columns that uniquely identifies each row in a table and automatically creates a clustered index in MySQL.
- **Overhead**: The additional computational or storage cost associated with maintaining indexes, which can slow down write operations.
- **Physical Order**: The arrangement of data on disk, determined by a clustered index.

CHAPTER 9
MySQL Users

Introduction

This chapter covers how to create a new user in MySQL. The default user in MySQL is root, but we will learn how to easily create a user in MySQL. Other topics, such as how to drop a user, reset the password, and so on, are also covered in this chapter. We will also cover what are privileges in MySQL, and how to grant, show, and revoke privileges easily.

Structure

In this chapter, we will discuss the following topics:

- Creating Users in MySQL
- Dropping Users in MySQL
- Showing Users in MySQL
- Resetting the Password in MySQL
- Granting Privileges in MySQL
- Showing Privileges in MySQL
- Revoking Privileges in MySQL
- Best Practices for Securing MySQL Users
- Practical Exercise

Creating Users in MySQL

To create users in MySQL, you can use the **`CREATE USER`** statement. This statement allows you to create a new user account with a specific username and host. You can also set a password for the user during creation.

Syntax for Creating a User

Here is the basic syntax:

```
CREATE USER 'username'@'host' IDENTIFIED BY 'password';
```

Here:

- **username**: The name of the user you want to create.
- **host**: The host from which the user can connect. Use '**%**' to allow connections from any host or '**localhost**' to allow connections only from the local machine.
- **password**: The password for the user.

Example 1: Creating a User with a Password

```
CREATE USER 'john'@'localhost' IDENTIFIED BY 'secure_password';
```

This creates a user named **john** who can only connect from the local machine with the password **secure_password**.

Example 2: Creating a User Allowing Connections from Any Host

```
CREATE USER 'jane'@'%' IDENTIFIED BY 'another_password';
```

This creates a user named **jane** who can connect from any host with the password **another_password**.

Granting Privileges

After creating a user, you typically need to grant them privileges to access databases or perform specific actions. Use the **GRANT** statement for this:

```
GRANT ALL PRIVILEGES ON database_name.* TO 'username'@'host';
FLUSH PRIVILEGES;
```

Here:

- Replace **database_name** with the name of the database the user should have access to.
- Replace **username** and **host** with the user and host you created.
- **FLUSH PRIVILEGES** ensures the changes take effect immediately.

Example: Grant Privileges to a User

```
GRANT ALL PRIVILEGES ON my_database.* TO 'john'@'localhost';
FLUSH PRIVILEGES;
```

This grants **john** full access to the **my_database** database.

Verifying the User has been Created

To verify that the user was created successfully, you can query the **`mysql.user`** table:

```
SELECT User, Host FROM mysql.user;
```

This will list all users and their associated hosts.

Notes:

- *Always use strong passwords for security.*
- *Avoid using wildcard hosts ('**%**') unless necessary, as it can expose your database to external threats.*
- *Regularly review and manage user privileges to maintain security.*

Dropping Users in MySQL

To drop (delete) users in MySQL, you can use the **`DROP USER`** statement. This removes the user account and their associated privileges from the MySQL server.

Syntax for Dropping a User

The following is the syntax to drop a user in MySQL:

```
DROP USER 'username'@'host';
```

Here:

- **`username`**: The name of the user you want to delete.
- **`host`**: The host from which the user is allowed to connect. This must match the host specified when the user was created.

Example 1: Drop a User with a Specific Host

```
DROP USER 'john'@'localhost';
```

This deletes the user **`john`** who is allowed to connect only from **`localhost`**.

Example 2: Drop a User Allowing Connections from Any Host

```
DROP USER 'jane'@'%';
```

This deletes the user **`jane`** who is allowed to connect from any host ('**%**').

Example 3: Drop Multiple Users at Once

You can drop multiple users in a single statement by separating them with commas:

```
DROP USER 'user1'@'localhost', 'user2'@'%';
```

This deletes both **user1** (allowed from **localhost**) and **user2** (allowed from any host).

Verifying the User Has Been Dropped

To confirm that the user has been deleted, you can query the **mysql.user** table:

```
SELECT User, Host FROM mysql.user;
```

This will list all existing users. Ensure the dropped user no longer appears in the list.

Notes:

- **Privileges**: *Dropping a user also removes all privileges assigned to that user.*
- **Active Sessions**: *If the user is currently connected, they will not be disconnected immediately. However, they will not be able to reconnect after being dropped.*
- **Permissions**: *You need the* ***CREATE USER*** *privilege or the* ***DELETE*** *privilege on the* ***mysql.user*** *table to drop users.*
- **Recreate a User**: *If you accidentally drop a user, you can recreate them using the* ***CREATE USER*** *statement and reassign privileges.*

Example: Dropping and Recreating a User

If you accidentally drop a user, you can recreate them as follows:

```
-- Drop the user
DROP USER 'john'@'localhost';

-- Recreate the user
CREATE USER 'john'@'localhost' IDENTIFIED BY 'new_password';

-- Grant privileges (if needed)
GRANT ALL PRIVILEGES ON my_database.* TO 'john'@'localhost';
FLUSH PRIVILEGES;
```

This ensures the user is recreated with the same privileges.

Showing Users in MySQL

In MySQL, there is no direct command such as **SHOW USERS** to list all users. Instead, you can query the **mysql.user** table, which stores information about all user accounts and their privileges.

Query to List All Users

```
SELECT User, Host FROM mysql.user;
```

This query retrieves the **User** and **Host** columns from the **mysql.user** table, showing all user accounts and the hosts from which they are allowed to connect.

Example Output

The output might look as follows:

```
+------------------+-----------+
| User             | Host      |
+------------------+-----------+
| root             | localhost |
| john             | localhost |
| jane             | %         |
| admin            | 192.168.1.% |
+------------------+-----------+
```

Here:

- **User**: The username.
- **Host**: The host from which the user is allowed to connect. **%** means the user can connect from any host.

Additional Information

If you want to see more details about users, such as their authentication method or password expiration status, you can query additional columns from the **mysql.user** table:

```
SELECT User, Host, plugin, password_expired FROM mysql.user;
```

Here:

- **plugin**: Shows the authentication plugin used (for example, **mysql_native_password**, **caching_sha2_password**).
- **password_expired**: Indicates whether the user's password has expired (**Y** for yes, **N** for no).

Notes:

- **Permissions**: *To query the* ***mysql.user*** *table, you need the* ***SELECT*** *privilege on the* ***mysql*** *database.*
- **Host Column**: *Pay attention to the* ***Host*** *column, as it determines where the user can connect from. For example,* ***localhost*** *means the user can only connect from the local machine, while* ***%*** *allows connections from any host.*
- **System Users**: *Be cautious when modifying or deleting system users such as* ***root*** *or* ***mysql.sys****, as they are essential for MySQL's operation.*

Example: List Users with More Details

```
SELECT User, Host, plugin, password_expired, account_locked
FROM mysql.user;
```

This query provides additional details about each user, such as their authentication plugin, password status, and whether the account is locked.

Alternative: Using SHOW GRANTS

If you want to see the privileges assigned to a specific user, you can use the **SHOW GRANTS** statement:

```
SHOW GRANTS FOR 'username'@'host';
```

For example:

```
SHOW GRANTS FOR 'john'@'localhost';
```

This will display the privileges granted to the user **john** from **localhost**.

Resetting the Password in MySQL

Resetting a password includes resetting a password for a **user** as well as for a **root** user.

Let us see the steps for **Windows** and **Linux** separately.

Resetting a Password in MySQL on Windows

Method 1: Using ALTER USER (Recommended)

1. Open the MySQL Command Line Client or any MySQL client (for example, MySQL Workbench).
2. Log in as a user with sufficient privileges (for example, **root**).
3. Run the following command to reset the password:

   ```
   ALTER USER 'username'@'host' IDENTIFIED BY 'new_password';
   ```

   Example:

   ```
   ALTER USER 'john'@'localhost' IDENTIFIED BY 'new_secure_
   password';
   ```

Method 2: Using SET PASSWORD

1. Open the MySQL Command Line Client or any MySQL client.
2. Log in as a user with sufficient privileges.

3. Run the following command:

   ```
   SET PASSWORD FOR 'username'@'host' = PASSWORD('new_password');
   ```

   Example:

   ```
   SET PASSWORD FOR 'jane'@'%' = PASSWORD('another_new_password');
   ```

Resetting the Root Password on Windows

If you have lost access to the **`root`** password, follow these steps:

1. **Stop the MySQL Server**:
   - Open the Command Prompt as Administrator.
   - Stop the MySQL service:

     ```
     net stop MySQL
     ```

   (Replace **MySQL** with the exact name of your MySQL service if it is different.)
2. **Start MySQL in Safe Mode**:
   - Navigate to the MySQL **`bin`** directory (for example, **`C:\Program Files\MySQL\MySQL Server 8.0\bin`**).
   - Run the following command to start MySQL without password verification:

     ```
     mysqld --skip-grant-tables
     ```
3. **Reset the Root Password**:
   - Open a new Command Prompt window.
   - Connect to MySQL without a password:

     ```
     mysql -u root
     ```
   - Reset the root password:

     ```
     ALTER USER 'root'@'localhost' IDENTIFIED BY 'new_root_
     password';
     ```
   - Exit MySQL:

     ```
     exit;
     ```
4. **Restart MySQL**:
   - Stop the MySQL process in the first Command Prompt window (press **Ctrl + C**).
   - Restart the MySQL service:

     ```
     net start MySQL
     ```

Resetting a Password in MySQL on Linux

Method 1: Using ALTER USER (Recommended)

1. Open the terminal.
2. Log in to MySQL as a user with sufficient privileges:
   ```
   mysql -u root -p
   ```
3. Run the following command to reset the password:
   ```
   ALTER USER 'username'@'host' IDENTIFIED BY 'new_password';
   ```
   Example:
   ```
   ALTER USER 'john'@'localhost' IDENTIFIED BY 'new_secure_
   password';
   ```

Method 2: Using SET PASSWORD

1. Open the terminal.
2. Log in to MySQL as a user with sufficient privileges:
   ```
   mysql -u root -p
   ```
3. Run the following command:
   ```
   SET PASSWORD FOR 'username'@'host' = PASSWORD('new_password');
   ```
   Example:
   ```
   SET PASSWORD FOR 'jane'@'%' = PASSWORD('another_new_password');
   ```

Resetting the Root Password on Linux

If you have lost access to the **root** password, follow these steps:

1. **Stop the MySQL Server**:
   ```
   sudo systemctl stop mysql
   ```
2. **Start MySQL in Safe Mode**:
   ```
   sudo mysqld_safe --skip-grant-tables &
   ```
3. **Reset the Root Password**: Connect to MySQL without a password:
   ```
   mysql -u root
   ```
   - Reset the root password:
     ```
     ALTER USER 'root'@'localhost' IDENTIFIED BY 'new_root_
     password';
     ```
   - Exit MySQL:
     ```
     exit;
     ```

4. **Restart MySQL**:
   - Stop the MySQL safe mode process:
     ```
     sudo killall mysqld
     ```
   - Restart the MySQL service:
     ```
     sudo systemctl start mysql
     ```

Summary:

- **Windows**: Use **net stop MySQL** and **net start MySQL** to manage the MySQL service.
- **Linux**: Use **sudo systemctl stop mysql** and **sudo systemctl start mysql** to manage the MySQL service.
- Both systems support **ALTER USER** and **SET PASSWORD** for resetting passwords.

Granting Privileges in MySQL

Granting privileges in MySQL is done using the **GRANT** statement. Privileges control what actions a user can perform on databases, tables, or other database objects. The following is a detailed guide on how to grant privileges in MySQL:

Syntax for Granting Privileges

```
GRANT privilege_type ON database_name.table_name TO
'username'@'host';
```

Here:

- **privilege_type**: The type of privilege to grant (for example, **SELECT, INSERT, ALL PRIVILEGES**).
- **database_name.table_name**: The database and table to which the privileges apply. Use ***.*** for all databases and tables.
- **username**: The user to whom the privileges are granted.
- **host**: The host from which the user can connect (for example, **localhost, %**).

Common Privileges

Here are some commonly used privileges:

- **ALL PRIVILEGES**: Grants all permissions.
- **SELECT**: Allows reading data.
- **INSERT**: Allows inserting data.
- **UPDATE**: Allows updating data.
- **DELETE**: Allows deleting data.

- **CREATE**: Allows creating databases/tables.
- **DROP**: Allows dropping databases/tables.
- **ALTER**: Allows altering tables.
- **GRANT OPTION**: Allows the user to grant privileges to others.

Examples of Granting Privileges

Example 1: Grant All Privileges on a Specific Database

```
GRANT ALL PRIVILEGES ON my_database.* TO 'john'@'localhost';
```

This grants **john** full access to all tables in the **my_database** database when connecting from **localhost**.

Example 2: Grant Specific Privileges on a Table

```
GRANT SELECT, INSERT, UPDATE ON my_database.my_table TO
'jane'@'%';
```

This grants **jane** the ability to **SELECT**, **INSERT**, and **UPDATE** data in the **my_table** table of the **my_database** database from any host (**%**).

Example 3: Grant All Privileges on All Databases

```
GRANT ALL PRIVILEGES ON *.* TO 'admin'@'localhost';
```

This grants **admin** full access to all databases and tables when connecting from **localhost**.

Example 4: Grant Privileges with Grant Option

```
GRANT ALL PRIVILEGES ON my_database.* TO 'manager'@'localhost'
WITH GRANT OPTION;
```

This grants **manager** full access to **my_database** and allows them to grant privileges to other users.

Flushing Privileges

After granting privileges, you must flush the privileges to ensure the changes take effect:

```
FLUSH PRIVILEGES;
```

Viewing Granted Privileges

To see the privileges granted to a specific user, use the **SHOW GRANTS** statement:

```
SHOW GRANTS FOR 'username'@'host';
```

Example

```
SHOW GRANTS FOR 'john'@'localhost';
```

This displays all privileges granted to **john** on **localhost**.

Revoking Privileges

If you need to revoke privileges, use the **REVOKE** statement. For example:

```
REVOKE ALL PRIVILEGES ON my_database.* FROM 'john'@'localhost';
```

This removes all privileges for **john** on the **my_database** database.

Best Practices for Priviliges

Here are the best practices for granting privileges in MySQL:

- **Least Privilege Principle**: Grant only the minimum privileges necessary for a user to perform their tasks.
- **Avoid Wildcard Hosts**: Use **localhost** or specific IPs instead of **%** unless necessary.
- **Regularly Review Privileges**: Periodically check and clean up unused or excessive privileges.

Example Workflow

1. Create a user:
   ```
   CREATE USER 'new_user'@'localhost' IDENTIFIED BY 'password';
   ```
2. Grant privileges:
   ```
   GRANT SELECT, INSERT ON my_database.* TO 'new_user'@'localhost';
   ```
3. Flush privileges:
   ```
   FLUSH PRIVILEGES;
   ```
4. Verify privileges:
   ```
   SHOW GRANTS FOR 'new_user'@'localhost';
   ```

Showing Privileges in MySQL

To show the privileges granted to a user in MySQL, you can use the **SHOW GRANTS** statement. This command displays the privileges assigned to a specific user including global, database, and table-level privileges.

Syntax for Showing Privileges

```
SHOW GRANTS FOR 'username'@'host';
```

Here:

- **username:** The name of the user.
- **host**: The host from which the user is allowed to connect (for example, localhost, %).

Example 1: Show Privileges for a Specific User

```
SHOW GRANTS FOR 'john'@'localhost';
```

Sample Output

```
+--------------------------------------------------+
| Grants for john@localhost                        |
+--------------------------------------------------+
| GRANT USAGE ON *.* TO 'john'@'localhost'         |
| GRANT SELECT, INSERT ON my_database.* TO 'john'@'localhost' |
+--------------------------------------------------+
```

The first line (**GRANT USAGE ON *.***) indicates that the user has no global privileges.

The second line shows that **john** has **SELECT** and **INSERT** privileges on all tables in the **my_database** database.

Example 2: Show Privileges for the Current User

If you want to see the privileges for the currently logged-in user, you can use:

```
SHOW GRANTS;
```

Sample Output

```
+--------------------------------------------------+
| Grants for root@localhost                        |
+--------------------------------------------------+
| GRANT ALL PRIVILEGES ON *.* TO 'root'@'localhost' WITH GRANT OPTION |
+--------------------------------------------------+
```

This shows that the **root** user has all privileges on all databases and tables, along with the ability to grant privileges to others.

Example 3: Show Privileges for a User with Wildcard Host

If the user can connect from any host (**%**), use:

```
SHOW GRANTS FOR 'jane'@'%';
```

Sample Output

```
+-----------------------------------------------------+
| Grants for jane@%                                   |
+-----------------------------------------------------+
| GRANT USAGE ON *.* TO 'jane'@'%'                    |
| GRANT SELECT ON my_database.my_table TO 'jane'@'%'  |
+-----------------------------------------------------+
```

This shows that **jane** has **SELECT** privileges on the **my_table** table in the **my_database** database from any host.

Viewing Privileges from the MySQL Database

You can also query the **mysql** database directly to see privileges. The relevant tables are:

- **mysql.user**: Global privileges.
- **mysql.db**: Database-level privileges.
- **mysql.tables_priv**: Table-level privileges.
- **mysql.columns_priv**: Column-level privileges.

Example: Check Database-Level Privileges

```
SELECT * FROM mysql.db WHERE User = 'john' AND Host = 'localhost';
```

Example: Check Table-Level Privileges

```
SELECT * FROM mysql.tables_priv WHERE User = 'jane' AND Host = '%';
```

Notes:

- ***Permissions***: *To use **SHOW GRANTS**, you need the **SELECT** privilege on the **mysql** database or the **SHOW GRANTS** privilege.*
- ***Wildcard Hosts***: *If a user can connect from multiple hosts, you may need to check privileges for each host separately.*
- ***Global versus Specific Privileges***: *Global privileges (*.*) apply to all databases, while specific privileges (for example, **my_database.***) apply only to the specified database or table.*

Example Workflow

1. Create a user and grant privileges:
   ```
   CREATE USER 'test_user'@'localhost' IDENTIFIED BY 'password';
   GRANT SELECT, INSERT ON my_database.* TO 'test_user'@'localhost';
   FLUSH PRIVILEGES;
   ```

2. Show privileges:

   ```
   SHOW GRANTS FOR 'test_user'@'localhost';
   ```

3. Output:

```
+--------------------------------------------------+
| Grants for test_user@localhost                   |
+--------------------------------------------------+
| GRANT USAGE ON *.* TO 'test_user'@'localhost'     |
| GRANT SELECT, INSERT ON my_database.* TO 'test_user'@'localhost' |
+--------------------------------------------------+
```

Revoking Privileges in MySQL

To revoke privileges from a user in MySQL, you use the **REVOKE** statement. This command removes specific privileges previously granted to a user. The following is a detailed guide on how to revoke privileges in MySQL:

Syntax for Revoking Privileges

```
REVOKE privilege_type ON database_name.table_name FROM
'username'@'host';
```

Here:

- **privilege_type**: The type of privilege to revoke (for example, **SELECT, INSERT, ALL PRIVILEGES**).
- **database_name.table_name**: The database and table from which to revoke privileges. Use ***.*** for all databases and tables.
- **username**: The user from whom the privileges are revoked.
- **host**: The host from which the user is allowed to connect (for example, **localhost**, **%**).

Common Privileges to Revoke

Here are some commonly revoked privileges:

- **ALL PRIVILEGES:** Revokes all permissions.
- **SELECT**: Revokes the ability to read data.
- **INSERT**: Revokes the ability to insert data.
- **UPDATE**: Revokes the ability to update data.
- **DELETE**: Revokes the ability to delete data.
- **CREATE**: Revokes the ability to create databases/tables.

- **DROP:** Revokes the ability to drop databases/tables.
- **ALTER:** Revokes the ability to alter tables.
- **GRANT OPTION:** Revokes the ability to grant privileges to others.

Examples of Revoking Privileges

Example 1: Revoke All Privileges on a Specific Database

```
REVOKE ALL PRIVILEGES ON my_database.* FROM 'john'@'localhost';
```

This revokes all privileges for **john** on all tables in the **my_database** database when connecting from **localhost**.

Example 2: Revoke Specific Privileges on a Table

```
REVOKE SELECT, INSERT, UPDATE ON my_database.my_table FROM
'jane'@'%';
```

This revokes the **SELECT**, **INSERT**, and **UPDATE** privileges for jane on the **my_table** table in the **my_database** database from any host (**%**).

Example 3: Revoke All Privileges on All Databases

```
REVOKE ALL PRIVILEGES ON *.* FROM 'admin'@'localhost';
```

This revokes all privileges for **admin** on all databases and tables when connecting from **localhost**.

Example 4: Revoke Grant Option

```
REVOKE GRANT OPTION ON my_database.* FROM 'manager'@'localhost';
```

This revokes the ability for **manager** to grant privileges to other users on the **my_database** database.

Flushing Privileges

After revoking privileges, you must flush the privileges to ensure the changes take effect:

```
FLUSH PRIVILEGES;
```

Verifying Revoked Privileges

To verify that the privileges have been revoked, use the **SHOW GRANTS** statement:

```
SHOW GRANTS FOR 'username'@'host';
```

Example

```
SHOW GRANTS FOR 'john'@'localhost';
```

This displays all privileges granted to **john** on **localhost**. If the privileges were successfully revoked, they will no longer appear in the output.

Example Workflow

1. Grant privileges to a user:

```
GRANT SELECT, INSERT ON my_database.* TO 'john'@'localhost';
FLUSH PRIVILEGES;
```

2. Verify the granted privileges:

```
SHOW GRANTS FOR 'john'@'localhost';
```

Output:

```
+--------------------------------------------------+
| Grants for john@localhost                        |
+--------------------------------------------------+
| GRANT USAGE ON *.* TO 'john'@'localhost'         |
| GRANT SELECT, INSERT ON my_database.* TO 'john'@'localhost' |
+--------------------------------------------------+
```

3. Revoke the **INSERT** privilege:

```
REVOKE INSERT ON my_database.* FROM 'john'@'localhost';
FLUSH PRIVILEGES;
```

4. Verify the revoked privileges:

```
SHOW GRANTS FOR 'john'@'localhost';
```

Output:

```
+--------------------------------------------------+
| Grants for john@localhost                        |
+--------------------------------------------------+
| GRANT USAGE ON *.* TO 'john'@'localhost'         |
| GRANT SELECT ON my_database.* TO 'john'@'localhost' |
+--------------------------------------------------+
```

Notes:

- ***Revoking All Privileges***: *If you revoke all privileges, the user will still have the* **USAGE** *privilege, which allows them to connect to the MySQL server but perform no actions.*
- ***Revoking Grant Option***: *If you revoke the* ***GRANT OPTION****, the user can no longer grant privileges to others but retains their existing privileges.*
- ***Revoking Specific Privileges***: *You can revoke specific privileges without affecting other privileges the user may have.*

Best Practices for Securing MySQL Users

Here are some best practices to secure users in MySQL:

Securing MySQL users is critical to prevent unauthorized access, data breaches, and privilege escalation. The following are key best practices:

Follow the Principle of Least Privilege (PoLP)

- **Grant only necessary permissions** (for example, `SELECT` instead of ALL `PRIVILEGES`).
- Avoid using `GRANT ALL ON *.*` unless required.

```
GRANT SELECT, INSERT ON dbname.* TO 'user'@'localhost';
```

Use Strong Passwords & Authentication

- Enforce **complex passwords** (12+ chars, mixed case, numbers, symbols).
- Use MySQL's caching_sha2_password (default in MySQL 8+) instead of older `mysql_native_password`.

```
CREATE USER 'secureuser'@'%' IDENTIFIED WITH caching_sha2_
password BY 'Str0ngP@ss!';
```

Restrict User Access by Host

- Limit logins to specific IPs/hostnames (avoid 'user'@'%' for remote access).

```
CREATE USER 'admin'@'192.168.1.100'; -- Only from this IP
```

Regularly Audit Users & Privileges

- List all users and their permissions:

```
SELECT User, Host FROM mysql.user;
SHOW GRANTS FOR 'user'@'host';
```

- Remove unused accounts:

```
DROP USER 'olduser'@'%';
```

Secure Default Users

- Delete anonymous accounts:

```
DROP USER ''@'localhost'; -- Default in some installations
```

Use SSL/TLS for Remote Connections

- Require encrypted connections:

```
CREATE USER 'secureuser'@'%' REQUIRE SSL;
```

- Verify SSL status:

```
SHOW STATUS LIKE 'Ssl_cipher';
```

Enable Logging and Monitoring

- Track failed login attempts and privilege changes via:

  ```
  SET GLOBAL general_log = 'ON';
  ```

- Use tools such as **MySQL Enterprise Audit** or **Percona Audit Plugin**.

Practical Exercise

Here is a practical exercise that builds on the previous **Employee Management System** and incorporates the MySQL topics of this lesson. This exercise will guide you through creating and managing users, resetting passwords, and granting/revoking privileges in MySQL.

Exercise: Managing Users and Privileges in MySQL

Step 1: Use the Existing Database

Use the **employee_management_joins** database created in the previous exercise. If it does not exist, recreate it.

```
CREATE DATABASE IF NOT EXISTS employee_management_joins;
USE employee_management_joins;
```

Step 2: Create Users

Create three users:

- **hr_manager** with the password **hr123**.
- **it_manager** with the password **it123**.
- **finance_manager** with the password **finance123**.

The following is the query:

```
CREATE USER 'hr_manager'@'localhost' IDENTIFIED BY 'hr123';
CREATE USER 'it_manager'@'localhost' IDENTIFIED BY 'it123';
CREATE USER 'finance_manager'@'localhost' IDENTIFIED BY
'finance123';
```

Step 3: Show Users

Display the list of users in the MySQL server:

```
SELECT user, host FROM mysql.user;
```

Step 4: Grant Privileges

Grant specific privileges to each user:

- Grant **SELECT**, **INSERT**, and **UPDATE** privileges on the employees' table to **hr_manager**.
- Grant **SELECT**, **INSERT**, **UPDATE**, and **DELETE** privileges on the employees' table to **it_manager**.
- Grant **SELECT** privilege on the employees' table to **finance_manager**.

Here is the query:

```
-- Grant privileges to hr_manager
GRANT SELECT, INSERT, UPDATE ON employee_management_joins.
employees TO 'hr_manager'@'localhost';

-- Grant privileges to it_manager
GRANT SELECT, INSERT, UPDATE, DELETE ON employee_management_
joins.employees TO 'it_manager'@'localhost';

-- Grant privileges to finance_manager
GRANT SELECT ON employee_management_joins.employees TO 'finance_
manager'@'localhost';
```

Step 5: Show Privileges

Display the privileges granted to each user.

```
-- Show privileges for hr_manager
SHOW GRANTS FOR 'hr_manager'@'localhost';

-- Show privileges for it_manager
SHOW GRANTS FOR 'it_manager'@'localhost';

-- Show privileges for finance_manager
SHOW GRANTS FOR 'finance_manager'@'localhost';
```

Step 6: Reset Password

Reset the password for the **finance_manager** user to **newfinance123**.

```
ALTER USER 'finance_manager'@'localhost' IDENTIFIED BY
'newfinance123';
```

Step 7: Revoke Privileges

Revoke the **DELETE** privilege from the **it_manager** user.

```
REVOKE DELETE ON employee_management_joins.employees FROM 'it_
manager'@'localhost';
```

Step 8: Verify Privileges

Verify that the **DELETE** privilege has been revoked from the **it_manager** user.

```
SHOW GRANTS FOR 'it_manager'@'localhost';
```

Step 9: Drop Users

Drop the **finance_manager** user.

```
DROP USER 'finance_manager'@'localhost';
```

Step 10: Verify Users

Verify that the **finance_manager** user has been dropped by displaying the list of users.

```
SELECT user, host FROM mysql.user;
```

Final Queries

```
USE employee_management_joins;

CREATE USER 'hr_manager'@'localhost' IDENTIFIED BY 'hr123';
CREATE USER 'it_manager'@'localhost' IDENTIFIED BY 'it123';
CREATE USER 'finance_manager'@'localhost' IDENTIFIED BY 'fi-
nance123';

SELECT user, host FROM mysql.user;

-- Grant privileges to hr_manager
GRANT SELECT, INSERT, UPDATE ON employee_management_joins.
employees TO 'hr_manager'@'localhost';

-- Grant privileges to it_manager
GRANT SELECT, INSERT, UPDATE, DELETE ON employee_management_
joins.employees TO 'it_manager'@'localhost';

-- Grant privileges to finance_manager
GRANT SELECT ON employee_management_joins.employees TO 'finance
manager'@'localhost';

-- Show privileges for hr_manager
SHOW GRANTS FOR 'hr_manager'@'localhost';

-- Show privileges for it_manager
SHOW GRANTS FOR 'it_manager'@'localhost';

-- Show privileges for finance_manager
SHOW GRANTS FOR 'finance_manager'@'localhost';
```

```
ALTER USER 'finance_manager'@'localhost' IDENTIFIED BY
'newfinance123';

REVOKE DELETE ON employee_management_joins.employees FROM 'it_
manager'@'localhost';

SHOW GRANTS FOR 'it_manager'@'localhost';

DROP USER 'finance_manager'@'localhost';

SELECT user, host FROM mysql.user;
```

Expected Output

After completing the exercise, you should have:

- Created three users: **hr_manager**, **it_manager**, and **finance_manager**.
- Displayed the list of users using **SELECT** user, host FROM mysql.user.
- Granted specific privileges to each user using the **GRANT** statement.
- Displayed the privileges granted to each user using **SHOW GRANTS**.
- Reset the password for the **finance_manager** user.
- Revoked the **DELETE** privilege from the **it_manager** user.
- Verified the revocation of privileges using **SHOW GRANTS**.
- Dropped the **finance_manager** user.
- Verified the deletion of the user by displaying the list of users.

This exercise covers all the topics of this lesson and provides hands-on practice with MySQL user management and privileges.

Conclusion

We are now familiar with how to manage users in MySQL. Managing users and privileges in MySQL is essential for database security and access control. By creating, dropping, and modifying users, administrators can ensure that only authorized individuals access the database. Granting and revoking privileges allows fine-grained control over user actions. Proper user management helps maintain data integrity and security in MySQL databases.

In the next chapter, we will learn some advanced topics such as Triggers, Views, Transactions, and so on in MySQL.

Points to Remember

- Use **`CREATE USER`** to add new users and **`DROP USER`** to remove them.
- Always specify the host (localhost or %) when creating or managing users.
- Use **`ALTER USER`** to reset passwords securely.
- Grant only necessary privileges to users to follow the principle of least privilege.
- Use **`SHOW GRANTS`** to verify user privileges.
- Revoke privileges using **`REVOKE`** when they are no longer needed.
- Regularly audit user accounts and privileges for security.

Multiple Choice Questions

1. Which command is used to create a new user in MySQL?
   a. `MAKE USER`
   b. `CREATE NEW USER`
   c. `NEW USER`
   d. `CREATE USER`
2. Which table stores user information in MySQL?
   a. `mysql.users`
   b. `mysql.user`
   c. `mysql.data`
   d. `mysql.accounts`
3. How do you reset a user's password in MySQL?
   a. `CHANGE PASSWORD`
   b. `UPDATE USER`
   c. `ALTER USER`
   d. `MODIFY USER`
4. What does the GRANT command do?
   a. Assigns privileges to a user
   b. Deletes a user

   c. Displays user information

   d. Resets a user's password

5. Which command displays privileges for a user?

   a. `SHOW PRIVILEGES`

   b. `DISPLAY GRANTS`

   c. `SHOW GRANTS`

   d. `VIEW PRIVILEGES`

Answers

1. d
2. b
3. c
4. a
5. c

Questions

1. What is the syntax to create a new user in MySQL?
2. How do you delete a user from MySQL?
3. Which table stores user information in MySQL?
4. How can you reset a user's password in MySQL?
5. What is the purpose of the GRANT statement?
6. How do you check the privileges assigned to a user?
7. What happens if you revoke all privileges from a user?
8. Why is it important to specify the host when creating a user?

Key Terms

- **User**: An account with access to the MySQL server.
- **Host**: The location from which a user can connect (for example, localhost or %).
- **Privilege**: A permission to perform specific actions on a database or table.
- `GRANT`: A command to assign privileges to a user.
- `REVOKE`: A command to remove privileges from a user.
- `ALTER USER`: A command to modify user properties, such as passwords.
- `mysql.user`: A system table that stores user information.
- `SHOW GRANTS`: A command to display privileges for a user.

CHAPTER 10
MySQL Advanced

Introduction

This chapter covers the advanced topics of MySQL, including triggers. A trigger is a database object that is associated with a table. With that, other topics, such as transactions, partitioning, full-text search, and others are covered. We will also discuss the concept of stored procedure in MySQL with examples.

Structure

In this chapter, we will discuss the following topics:

- Triggers in MySQL
- Views in MySQL
- Regular Expressions in MySQL
- Full-Text Search in MySQL
- Transactions in MySQL
- Partitioning in MySQL
- Stored Procedures in MySQL
- Practical Exercise

Triggers

In MySQL, a **trigger** is a database object that is associated with a table and automatically executes or fires when a specific event occurs on that table. Triggers are used to enforce business rules, maintain data integrity, or automate certain tasks when data is inserted, updated, or deleted. Let us understand the concepts of Triggers, with their syntax and best practices.

Key Concepts of Triggers in MySQL

The following are some key concepts of triggers that will help you understand the events, the scope of triggers, and more:

- **Trigger Events**: Triggers are associated with one of the following events:
    - **`INSERT`**: Fires when a new row is inserted into the table.
    - **`UPDATE`**: Fires when a row in the table is updated.
    - **`DELETE`**: Fires when a row is deleted from the table.
- **Trigger Timing**: Triggers can be set to execute either:
    - **`BEFORE`**: The trigger runs before the event (for example, before an insert, update, or delete).
    - **`AFTER`**: The trigger runs after the event.
- **Trigger Scope**: Triggers are associated with a specific table and are activated only when the specified event occurs on that table.
- **`OLD` and `NEW` Keywords**: In triggers, you can access the data being modified using:
    - **`OLD`**: Refers to the existing row (before the change) in **`UPDATE`** and **`DELETE`** triggers.
    - **`NEW`**: Refers to the new row (after the change) in **`INSERT`** and **`UPDATE`** triggers.

Syntax for Creating a Trigger

The following is the syntax for creating a trigger in MySQL:

```
CREATE TRIGGER trigger_name
{BEFORE | AFTER} {INSERT | UPDATE | DELETE}
ON table_name
FOR EACH ROW
BEGIN
    -- Trigger logic here
END;
```

Example Triggers

Let us see some examples of triggers in MySQL.

- **`BEFORE INSERT` Trigger**: Ensures that a new employee's salary is not negative before inserting it into the **`employees`** table.

```
CREATE TRIGGER before_employee_insert
BEFORE INSERT ON employees
FOR EACH ROW
BEGIN
    IF NEW.salary < 0 THEN
        SET NEW.salary = 0;
    END IF;
END;
```

- **AFTER UPDATE Trigger**: Logs changes to the **employees** table in an **audit_log** table.

```
CREATE TRIGGER after_employee_update
AFTER UPDATE ON employees
FOR EACH ROW
BEGIN
    INSERT INTO audit_log (employee_id, old_salary, new_salary,
change_date)
    VALUES (OLD.employee_id, OLD.salary, NEW.salary, NOW());
END;
```

- **BEFORE DELETE Trigger**:

  Prevents deletion of rows from the **orders** table if the order status is '**shipped**'.

```
CREATE TRIGGER before_order_delete
BEFORE DELETE ON orders
FOR EACH ROW
BEGIN
    IF OLD.status = 'shipped' THEN
        SIGNAL SQLSTATE '45000' SET MESSAGE_TEXT = 'Cannot delete
shipped orders';
    END IF;
END;
```

Managing Triggers

Let us see how to manage triggers in MySQL:

- **View Triggers**: To list all triggers in a database:

```
SHOW TRIGGERS;
```

- **Drop a Trigger**:

  To delete a trigger:

```
DROP TRIGGER IF EXISTS trigger_name;
```

- **Modify a Trigger**: MySQL does not support directly modifying a trigger. You must drop and recreate it.

Advantages of Triggers

Here are the advantages of triggers in MySQL:

- Triggers can validate data before it is inserted or updated, ensuring consistency.
- Triggers can log changes to a separate audit table for compliance and debugging.
- Triggers can update related tables automatically when a change occurs.
- Instead of handling logic in the application, triggers centralize database-related rules.
- Triggers can enforce security checks before allowing data modifications.
- Triggers can interact with other databases or tables, enabling complex workflows.
- Triggers can initiate actions based on database events, such as sending notifications.

Limitations of Triggers

Here are the limitations of triggers in MySQL:

- Triggers can increase the complexity of the database and make debugging harder.
- Overusing triggers can lead to performance issues.
- Triggers are not always portable across different database systems.

Best Practices

The following are some best practices for triggers in MySQL:

- Use triggers sparingly and only when necessary.
- Keep trigger logic simple and efficient.
- Document triggers clearly to avoid confusion.
- Test triggers thoroughly to ensure they behave as expected.

Triggers are powerful tools in MySQL, but they should be used judiciously to maintain database performance and clarity.

Views

In MySQL, a **view** is a virtual table that is based on the result set of a SQL query. Views do not store data themselves but instead display data from one or more underlying tables. They are useful for simplifying complex queries, enhancing security, and providing a consistent interface to users.

Key Concepts of Views in MySQL

The following are the key concepts of views in MySQL:

- **Virtual Table**: A view does not physically store data. It dynamically retrieves data from the underlying tables whenever it is queried.
- **Simplified Querying**: Views can encapsulate complex queries, making it easier for users to retrieve data without writing lengthy SQL statements.
- **Security**: Views can restrict access to specific columns or rows of a table, providing a layer of security.
- **Updatable Views**: Some views can be updated (insert, update, delete), but this depends on the complexity of the view and the underlying query.

Syntax for Creating a View

The following is the syntax for creating a view in MySQL:

```
CREATE VIEW view_name AS
SELECT column1, column2, ...
FROM table_name
WHERE condition;
```

Example Views

Let us see some examples of creating views in MySQL:

- **Simple View**: Create a view that shows only the name and salary columns from the **employees** table.

  ```
  CREATE VIEW employee_names_salaries AS
  SELECT name, salary
  FROM employees;
  ```

  Query the view. Let us use **`SELECT *`** to display the view:

  ```
  SELECT * FROM employee_names_salaries;
  ```

- **Complex View:** Create a view that joins thc **orders** and **customers** tables to show order details along with customer names.

  ```
  CREATE VIEW order_details AS
  SELECT o.order_id, o.order_date, c.customer_name, o.total_amount
  FROM orders o
  JOIN customers c ON o.customer_id = c.customer_id;
  ```

  Query the View. Let us use **SELECT *** to display the view:

  ```
  SELECT * FROM order_details;
  ```

- **Conditional View:** Create a view that shows only active employees (for example, those with status = 'active').

  ```
  CREATE VIEW active_employees AS
  SELECT employee_id, name, department
  FROM employees
  WHERE status = 'active';
  ```

  Query the View. Let us use **SELECT *** to display the view:

  ```
  SELECT * FROM active_employees;
  ```

Managing Views

Let us see how to manage views in MySQL:

- **View Existing Views**: To list all views in a database:

  ```
  SHOW FULL TABLES WHERE TABLE_TYPE LIKE 'VIEW';
  ```

- **View Definition**: To see the SQL query used to create a view:

  ```
  SHOW CREATE VIEW view_name;
  ```

- **Drop a View**: To delete a view:

  ```
  DROP VIEW IF EXISTS view_name;
  ```

- **Update a View:** To modify a view, you must drop and recreate it:

  ```
  CREATE OR REPLACE VIEW view name AS
  SELECT new_column_list
  FROM table_name
  WHERE new_condition;
  ```

Updatable Views

A view is updatable if it meets the following conditions:

- The view is based on a single table.
- The view does not use aggregate functions, **GROUP BY**, or **DISTINCT**.
- The view does not use subqueries in the **SELECT** statement.

Example of an updatable view:

```
CREATE VIEW updatable_employee_view AS
SELECT employee_id, name, salary
FROM employees
WHERE department = 'Sales';
```

You can perform **INSERT, UPDATE,** or **DELETE** operations on this view, and the changes will be reflected in the underlying **employees** table.

Advantages of Views

Here are the advantages of views in MySQL:

- Views simplify complex queries by encapsulating multi-table joins and calculations
- Enhances security by restricting access to specific columns/rows
- Provides data abstraction to protect applications from schema changes
- Improves maintainability by centralizing query logic
- Reduces code duplication through reusable query definitions
- Enables computed columns without storing redundant data
- Offers logical data organization by combining related information
- Maintains backward compatibility during database restructuring
- Allows customized data presentation for different user roles

Limitations of Views

Here are the limitations of views in MySQL:

- **Performance**: Views can be slower than direct table queries, especially for complex queries.
- **Updatability**: Not all views are updatable.
- **Dependencies**: Views depend on the underlying tables. If the table structure changes, the view may break.

Best Practices

The following are the best practices of views in MySQL:

- Use views to simplify complex queries and improve readability.
- Avoid nesting views too deeply, as this can impact performance.
- Use views for security purposes to restrict access to sensitive data.

- Document views clearly to ensure they are understood and maintained properly.

Views are a powerful feature in MySQL that can help streamline database operations and improve data management.

Regular Expressions

In MySQL, **Regular Expressions (regex)** are used for pattern matching within strings. They allow you to perform complex searches and manipulations on text data. MySQL provides the REGEXP operator to work with regular expressions.

Key Concepts of Regular Expressions in MySQL

The following are the key concepts of regular expressions in MySQL:

- **REGEXP Operator:**
  - The REGEXP operator is used to match a string against a regular expression pattern.
  - It returns 1 if the pattern matches, otherwise 0.
- **Case Sensitivity:**
  - By default, REGEXP is case-insensitive in MySQL. To perform a case-sensitive match, use the REGEXP BINARY operator.
- **Common Regex Metacharacters**:
  - .: Matches any single character.
  - *: Matches zero or more occurrences of the preceding element.
  - +: Matches one or more occurrences of the preceding element.
  - ?: Matches zero or one occurrence of the preceding element.
  - ^: Matches the start of a string.
  - $: Matches the end of a string.
  - []: Matches any single character within the brackets.
  - [^]: Matches any single character not within the brackets.
  - |: Acts as an OR operator.
  - \`()\`: Groups patterns together.

Syntax of REGEXP in MySQL

The following is the syntax. The regular expression pattern goes in place of **`pattern`**:

```
SELECT column_name
FROM table_name
WHERE column_name REGEXP 'pattern';
```

Examples of Regular Expressions in MySQL

Here are some examples of regular expressions in MySQL:

- **Match a Specific Pattern**:

  Find all names that start with J:

  ```
  SELECT name
  FROM employees
  WHERE name REGEXP '^J';
  ```

- **Match Any Character**:

  Find all names that contain an:

  ```
  SELECT name
  FROM employees
  WHERE name REGEXP 'an';
  ```

- **Match Multiple Patterns**:

  Find all names that start with J or A:

  ```
  SELECT name
  FROM employees
  WHERE name REGEXP '^J|^A';
  ```

- **Match a Range of Characters:**

  Find all names that start with a letter between A and D:

  ```
  SELECT name
  FROM employees
  WHERE name REGEXP '^[A-D]';
  ```

- **Match a Specific Number of Characters**:

  Find all names that are exactly 5 characters long:

  ```
  SELECT name
  FROM employees
  WHERE name REGEXP '^.{5}$';
  ```

- **Match Digits:**

  Find all strings that contain at least one digit:

```
SELECT text
FROM logs
WHERE text REGEXP '[0-9]';
```

- **Case-Sensitive Match**:

  Find all names that start with j (case-sensitive):

```
SELECT name
FROM employees
WHERE name REGEXP BINARY '^j';
```

Common Regex Patterns in MySQL

The following are some regex patterns in MySQL:

Pattern	Description
'^abc'	Strings that start with abc.
'xyz$'	Strings that end with xyz.
'a.b'	Strings containing a, any character, and b.
'a*'	Strings containing zero or more as.
'a+'	Strings containing one or more as.
'a?'	Strings containing zero or one a.
'[abc]'	Strings containing a, b, or c.
'[^abc]'	Strings not containing a, b, or c.
'a{2,4}'	Strings containing a between 2 and 4 times.

Table 10.1: *Regex patterns in MySQL*

Combining REGEXP with Other MySQL Functions

We can also combine regular expressions in MySQL with other functions. Let us see some examples:

- **Filter and Sort**: Find all names containing an and sort them alphabetically:

```
SELECT name
FROM employees
WHERE name REGEXP 'an'
ORDER BY name;
```

- **Count Matches**: Count the number of names that start with J:

```
SELECT COUNT(*)
FROM employees
WHERE name REGEXP '^J';
```

- **Replace Matches**: Use **REGEXP** with **REGEXP_REPLACE** (available in MySQL 8.0+):

```
SELECT REGEXP_REPLACE(name, 'an', 'XX')
FROM employees;
```

Advantages of REGEXP in MySQL

The following are the advantages of regular expressions in MySQL:

- Enables powerful pattern matching beyond simple LIKE operations
- Provides flexible text search capabilities with complex matching rules
- Supports sophisticated string validation directly in SQL queries
- Reduces application code by handling pattern matching at database level
- Improves query precision with advanced wildcard and character class options
- Enables extraction of specific text patterns from string data
- Supports multiple matching conditions in a single expression
- Offers efficient data filtering for text-heavy columns
- Allows validation of email/phone/ID formats directly in queries
- Simplifies search operations with concise regex syntax

Limitations of REGEXP in MySQL

The following are the limitations of regular expressions in MySQL:

- MySQL's regex support is not as extensive as some other databases or programming languages.
- Complex regex patterns may not be supported.
- Performance can degrade with very large datasets or complex patterns.

Best Practices

Here are some best practices for regular expressions in MySQL:

- Use REGEXP for simple to moderately complex pattern matching.
- Avoid overly complex regex patterns for better performance.
- Test your regex patterns thoroughly to ensure they match the intended data.

- Use indexes on columns for faster searches when possible.

Regular expressions in MySQL are a powerful tool for pattern matching and data validation. Use them to enhance your queries and manipulate text data effectively!

Full-Text Search

Full-Text Search in MySQL is a powerful feature that allows you to perform advanced text searches on columns with large amounts of text data. Unlike simple pattern matching with **LIKE** or **REGEXP**, full-text search is optimized for natural language queries and can handle complex search requirements, such as finding words or phrases, ranking results by relevance, and handling stopwords.

Key Concepts of Full-Text Search in MySQL

The following are the key concepts of full-text search in MySQL:

- **Supported Storage Engines**: Full-text search is supported only by the **InnoDB** and **MyISAM** storage engines.
- **Full-Text Index**: A full-text index is a special type of index used for full-text searches. It must be created on text-based columns (**CHAR**, **VARCHAR**, or **TEXT**).
- **Natural Language Search**:
    - Searches for words or phrases in a natural language format.
    - Returns results ranked by relevance.
- **Boolean Mode Search**: Allows you to use Boolean operators (+, -, >, <, (), ~, *, “”) to refine your search.
- **Stopwords**: Common words (for example, “the”, “and”, “is”) are ignored in full-text searches. MySQL provides a default list of stopwords, which can be customized.
- **Minimum Word Length**: By default, MySQL ignores words shorter than 4 characters. This can be configured using the **ft_min_word_len** (for MyISAM) or **innodb_ft_min_token_size** (for InnoDB) system variables.

Enabling Full-Text Search

To use full-text search, you must create a **full-text index** on the column(s) you want to search.

Syntax for Creating a Full-Text Index:

```
CREATE FULLTEXT INDEX index_name
ON table_name (column1, column2, ...);
```

Performing Full-Text Searches

Natural Language Search

Searches for words or phrases in a natural language format. Results are ranked by relevance. The following is the syntax:

```
SELECT *
FROM table_name
WHERE MATCH(column1, column2, ...) AGAINST('search_query');
```

Example query to search for articles containing the word "database":

```
SELECT *
FROM articles
WHERE MATCH(title, body) AGAINST('database');
```

Boolean Mode Search

Allows you to use Boolean operators to refine your search.

```
SELECT *
FROM table_name
WHERE MATCH(column1, column2, ...) AGAINST('search_query' IN
BOOLEAN MODE);
```

Boolean Operators:

The following boolean operators are also used in boolean mode search:

- +: The word must be present.
- -: The word must not be present.
- >: Increase the word's relevance.
- <: Decrease the word's relevance.
- ~: Negate the word's relevance.
- *: Wildcard (matches words starting with the prefix).
- "": Exact phrase match.

Examples:

Let us see some examples of boolean mode search in MySQL:

- Search for articles containing "**MySQL**" but not "**Oracle**":

```
SELECT *
FROM articles
WHERE MATCH(title, body) AGAINST('+MySQL -Oracle' IN BOOLEAN
MODE);
```

- Search for articles containing the exact phrase "**relational database**":

```
SELECT *
FROM articles
WHERE MATCH(title, body) AGAINST('"relational database"' IN
BOOLEAN MODE);
```

- Search for articles containing words starting with "**data**":

```
SELECT *
FROM articles
WHERE MATCH(title, body) AGAINST('data*' IN BOOLEAN MODE);
```

Relevance Ranking

Full-text search returns a relevance score for each row, which can be used to rank results.

```
SELECT *, MATCH(title, body) AGAINST('search_query') AS relevance
FROM articles
WHERE MATCH(title, body) AGAINST('search_query')
ORDER BY relevance DESC;
```

Example query to rank articles by relevance for the word "**database**":

```
SELECT *, MATCH(title, body) AGAINST('database') AS relevance
FROM articles
WHERE MATCH(title, body) AGAINST('database')
ORDER BY relevance DESC;
```

Configuring Full-Text Search

Let us see how to configure full-text search in MySQL:

- **Stopwords**: MySQL uses a default list of stopwords. You can customize this list by modifying the **ft_stopword_file** system variable or creating your own stopword list.
- **Minimum Word Length**: Adjust the minimum word length for indexing using:
    - **ft_min_word_len** (for MyISAM)
    - **innodb_ft_min_token_size** (for InnoDB)
- **Rebuilding Indexes:**

  After changing full-text search settings, you may need to rebuild the indexes:

  ```
  REPAIR TABLE table_name QUICK;
  ```

Limitations of Full-Text Search

Here are some limitations of full-text search in MySQL:

- **Performance**: Full-text search can be slower on very large datasets.
- **Index Size**: Full-text indexes can consume significant disk space.
- **Language Support**: Full-text search is optimized for English and may not work as well for other languages.
- **No Wildcards in Natural Language Mode**: Wildcards (*) are only supported in Boolean mode.

Best Practices

The following are some best practices for full-text search in MySQL:

- Use full-text search for large text columns where **LIKE** or **REGEXP** would be inefficient.
- Combine full-text search with Boolean operators for advanced queries.
- Regularly optimize and maintain full-text indexes for better performance.
- Test and tune full-text search settings (for example, stopwords, minimum word length) for your specific use case.

Full-text search in MySQL is a powerful tool for querying and analyzing text data. Use it to build advanced search functionality in your applications!

Transactions

Transactions in MySQL are a fundamental feature that ensures data integrity and consistency when performing multiple database operations. A transaction groups a set of SQL statements into a single unit of work, which is executed as a whole. If all operations succeed, the transaction is committed, and the changes are saved permanently. If any operation fails, the transaction is rolled back, and all changes are undone.

Key Concepts of Transactions in MySQL

The following are the key concepts of transactions in MySQL:

- **ACID Properties:**
    - **Atomicity**: Ensures that all operations within a transaction are treated as a single unit. Either all operations succeed, or none are applied.

  - **Consistency**: Ensures that the database remains in a valid state before and after the transaction.
  - **Isolation**: Ensures that concurrent transactions do not interfere with each other.
  - **Durability**: Ensures that once a transaction is committed, the changes are permanent and survive system failures.
- **Transaction Control Statements:**
  - `START TRANSACTION` or `BEGIN`: Starts a new transaction.
  - `COMMIT`: Saves the changes made during the transaction permanently.
  - `ROLLBACK`: Undoes all changes made during the transaction.
  - `SAVEPOINT`: Creates a point within a transaction to which you can roll back.
  - `SET` **autocommit**: Controls whether each SQL statement is automatically committed.
- **Storage Engines**:
  - Transactions are supported by the **InnoDB** storage engine. The **MyISAM** engine does not support transactions.

Advantages of Transactions in MySQL

The following are the advantages of Transactions:

- Ensures data integrity through ACID (Atomicity, Consistency, Isolation, Durability) properties
- Groups multiple SQL operations into a single all-or-nothing unit of work
- Prevents partial updates by either committing all changes or rolling back entirely
- Maintains database consistency even during system failures
- Provides isolation between concurrent database operations
- Enables proper error handling with rollback capability
- Supports complex business logic requiring multiple coordinated changes
- Allows savepoints for partial rollback within large transactions
- Prevents data corruption from interrupted operations
- Manages concurrent access to shared data safely

Limitations of Transactions in MySQL

The following are the limitations of Transactions:

- **Performance Overhead**: Transactions introduce latency due to locking and logging.
- **Deadlocks Possible**: Concurrent transactions may deadlock, requiring manual resolution.
- **Long Transactions Block Resources**: Holding locks too long degrades concurrency.
- **No Nested Transactions**: MySQL does not support transactions within transactions.
- **Limited Savepoints**: Savepoints cannot fully replace nested transactions.
- **Isolation Trade-offs:** Higher isolation levels (for example, SERIALIZABLE) reduce performance.
- **Memory Usage**: Large transactions consume significant undo log space.
- **No DDL in Transactions**: Some schema changes (ALTER TABLE) auto-commit.
- **Application Logic Dependency**: Proper rollback handling must be coded explicitly.
- **No Timeout by Default**: Stuck transactions may require manual termination.

Syntax for Using Transactions

The following is the syntax for using transactions in MySQL:

```
START TRANSACTION;

-- SQL statements
INSERT INTO table_name (column1, column2) VALUES (value1,
value2);
UPDATE table_name SET column1 = value1 WHERE condition;

-- Commit or Rollback
COMMIT; -- Save changes
-- OR
ROLLBACK; -- Undo changes
```

Example of a Transaction

The following are some examples of Transactions in MySQL:

- **Simple Transaction**: Transfer funds between two accounts.

```
START TRANSACTION;

UPDATE accounts SET balance = balance - 100 WHERE account_id = 1;
UPDATE accounts SET balance = balance + 100 WHERE account_id = 2;

COMMIT;
```

If any of the **UPDATE** statements fail, the transaction can be rolled back to ensure data consistency.

- **Transaction with Rollback**: Roll back the transaction if an error occurs.

```
START TRANSACTION;

INSERT INTO orders (order_id, customer_id, amount) VALUES (101,
1, 50);
UPDATE inventory SET quantity = quantity - 1 WHERE product_id =
10;

-- Check for errors
IF @@ERROR > 0 THEN
    ROLLBACK;
ELSE
    COMMIT;
END IF;
```

- **Transaction with Savepoint**:

  Use a savepoint to roll back to a specific point within the transaction.

```
START TRANSACTION;

INSERT INTO orders (order_id, customer_id, amount) VALUES (102,
2, 100);
SAVEPOINT savepoint1;

UPDATE inventory SET quantity = quantity - 1 WHERE product_id =
10;

-- Roll back to savepoint1 if needed
ROLLBACK TO savepoint1;

COMMIT;
```

Autocommit Mode

Let us see what **autocommit** mode is in MySQL:

- By default, MySQL operates in **autocommit** mode, where each SQL statement is treated as a transaction and automatically committed.

- To disable **autocommit** and manually control transactions:
```
SET autocommit = 0;
```
- To re-enable **autocommit**:
```
SET autocommit = 1;
```

Isolation Levels

MySQL supports different isolation levels to control the visibility of changes made by one transaction to other concurrent transactions. The isolation levels are:

- **READ UNCOMMITTED**:
  - Allows transactions to see uncommitted changes made by other transactions.
  - Lowest isolation level and is prone to dirty reads.
- **READ COMMITTED**:
  - Ensures that transactions only see committed changes.
  - Prevents dirty reads but allows non-repeatable reads and phantom reads.
- **REPEATABLE READ** (Default in MySQL):
  - Ensures that if a transaction reads the same data multiple times, it will see the same values.
  - Prevents dirty reads and non-repeatable reads but allows phantom reads.
- **SERIALIZABLE**:
  - Ensures complete isolation by locking the entire table.
  - Prevents dirty reads, non-repeatable reads, and phantom reads.

Setting the Isolation Level:

```
SET TRANSACTION ISOLATION LEVEL isolation_level;
```

Example to set the isolation level:

```
SET TRANSACTION ISOLATION LEVEL READ COMMITTED;
```

Best Practices for Using Transactions

Let us see some best practices for using transactions in MySQL:

- **Keep Transactions Short**: Long-running transactions can lock resources and degrade performance.
- **Handle Errors Gracefully**: Always check for errors and use **ROLLBACK** to undo changes if necessary.

- **Use Appropriate Isolation Levels**: Choose the isolation level that balances performance and consistency for your application.
- **Avoid Unnecessary Locks**: Minimize the scope of transactions to reduce contention and improve concurrency.
- **Test Thoroughly**: Ensure that transactions behave as expected under different scenarios, including failures.

Example: Complete Transaction Workflow

Here is an example showing the transaction workflow in MySQL:

```
START TRANSACTION;

-- Insert a new order
INSERT INTO orders (order_id, customer_id, amount) VALUES (103,
3, 200);

-- Update inventory
UPDATE inventory SET quantity = quantity - 1 WHERE product_id =
10;

-- Check for errors
IF @@ERROR > 0 THEN
    ROLLBACK;
    SELECT 'Transaction failed. Changes rolled back.';
ELSE
    COMMIT;
    SELECT 'Transaction succeeded. Changes committed.';
END IF;
```

Transactions are a critical feature in MySQL for maintaining data integrity and consistency. Use them wisely to ensure your database operations are reliable and robust!

Partitioning

Partitioning in MySQL is a technique used to divide large tables into smaller, more manageable pieces called **partitions**. Each partition can be stored and accessed independently, which can improve query performance, simplify data management, and optimize storage. Partitioning is especially useful for tables with large amounts of data, such as log tables or historical data.

Key Concepts of Partitioning in MySQL

The following are the key concepts of partitioning in MySQL:

- **Partition Types**: MySQL supports several types of partitioning:
    - **Range Partitioning**: Partitions are defined based on a range of values (for example, dates or numeric ranges).
    - **List Partitioning**: Partitions are defined based on a list of values (for example, specific categories or regions).
    - **Hash Partitioning**: Partitions are defined using a hash function applied to a column.
    - **Key Partitioning**: Similar to hash partitioning, but MySQL handles the hashing internally.
    - **Composite Partitioning**: Combines multiple partitioning strategies (for example, range and hash).
- **Partition Pruning**: MySQL automatically excludes partitions that do not match the query conditions, improving performance.
- **Storage Engine**: Partitioning is supported by the **InnoDB** and **MyISAM** storage engines.
- **Limitations**:
    - Not all MySQL features are compatible with partitioning (for example, full-text indexes, foreign keys).
    - Partitioning columns must be part of the primary key or unique index.

Advantages of Partitioning in MySQL

The following are the advantages of Partitioning:

- **Improved Query Performance**: Partition pruning allows MySQL to scan only relevant partitions, speeding up queries.
- **Easier Data Management**: Partitions can be individually maintained (backup, restore, or delete).
- **Efficient Storage**: Older data can be moved to slower/cheaper storage while keeping active data in faster storage.
- **Parallel I/O Operations**: Partitions enable better disk I/O distribution for large tables.
- **Faster Bulk Deletes**: Dropping entire partitions is quicker than deleting rows individually.

- **Better Index Utilization**: Smaller partition-level indexes improve cache efficiency.
- **Scalability for Large Tables**: Helps manage tables with millions/billions of rows.
- **Simplified Archiving**: Old data can be archived by detaching entire partitions.
- **Balanced Workloads**: Different partitions can be assigned to different storage devices.
- **Better Cache Performance**: Frequently accessed partitions stay in memory longer.

Limitations of Partitioning in MySQL

The following are the limitations of Partitioning:

- **Limited Indexing**: Full-text indexes and spatial indexes are not supported.
- **Overhead on High Partition Counts**: Too many partitions degrade performance.
- **No Parallel Query Execution**: Partitions are scanned sequentially, not in parallel.
- **Memory Usage**: Each open partition consumes file descriptors and memory.
- **Schema Changes Complexity**: Altering a partitioned table can be slow and restrictive.
- **No Transactional Guarantees Across Partitions**: Some operations may not be atomic.
- **JOIN Performance Issues**: Partitioned tables in joins may not optimize well.
- **Aggregation Overhead**: GROUP BY and ORDER BY may require full partition scans.
- **Subpartitioning Restrictions**: Only certain partitioning combinations are allowed.
- **Manual Maintenance Required**: Adding/dropping partitions must be managed explicitly.

Syntax for Creating a Partitioned Table

The following is the syntax for creating a partitioned table in MySQL:

```
CREATE TABLE table_name (
    column1 datatype,
    column2 datatype,
    ...
)
```

```
PARTITION BY partition_type (column_name)
(
    PARTITION partition_name1 VALUES LESS THAN (value1),
    PARTITION partition_name2 VALUES LESS THAN (value2),
    ...
);
```

Types of Partitioning with Examples

Here are the types of partitioning with examples in MySQL:

- Range Partitioning

  Divides data based on a range of values (for example, dates or numbers).

  Example:

  Partition the **sales** table by year:

```
CREATE TABLE sales (
    sale_id INT,
    sale_date DATE,
    amount DECIMAL(10, 2)
)
PARTITION BY RANGE (YEAR(sale_date)) (
    PARTITION p0 VALUES LESS THAN (2021),
    PARTITION p1 VALUES LESS THAN (2022),
    PARTITION p2 VALUES LESS THAN (2023),
    PARTITION p3 VALUES LESS THAN (2024),
    PARTITION p4 VALUES LESS THAN MAXVALUE
);
```

- **List Partitioning**

  Divides data based on a list of values (for example, categories or regions).

  Example:

  Partition the **customers** table by region:

```
CREATE TABLE customers (
    customer_id INT,
    name VARCHAR(100),
    region VARCHAR(50)
)
PARTITION BY LIST (region) (
    PARTITION p_east VALUES IN ('NY', 'NJ', 'CT'),
    PARTITION p_west VALUES IN ('CA', 'WA', 'OR'),
    PARTITION p_other VALUES IN (DEFAULT)
);
```

- **Hash Partitioning**

  Distributes data evenly across partitions using a hash function.

  Example:

  Partition the **users** table by hashing the **user_id**:

```
CREATE TABLE users (
    user_id INT,
    username VARCHAR(50),
    email VARCHAR(100)
)
PARTITION BY HASH(user_id)
PARTITIONS 4;
```

- **Key Partitioning**

  Similar to hash partitioning, but MySQL handles the hashing internally.

  Example:

  Partition the **logs** table by the **log_id** column:

```
CREATE TABLE logs (
    log_id INT,
    log_message TEXT,
    log_date DATETIME
)
PARTITION BY KEY(log_id)
PARTITIONS 5;
```

- **Composite Partitioning**

  Combines multiple partitioning strategies.

  Example:

  Partition the **sales** table by year and then by region:

```
CREATE TABLE sales (
    sale_id INT,
    sale_date DATE,
    region VARCHAR(50),
    amount DECIMAL(10, 2)
)
PARTITION BY RANGE (YEAR(sale_date))
SUBPARTITION BY LIST (region) (
    PARTITION p0 VALUES LESS THAN (2021) (
        SUBPARTITION s0_east VALUES IN ('NY', 'NJ'),
        SUBPARTITION s0_west VALUES IN ('CA', 'WA')
    ),
```

```
        PARTITION p1 VALUES LESS THAN (2022) (
            SUBPARTITION s1_east VALUES IN ('NY', 'NJ'),
            SUBPARTITION s1_west VALUES IN ('CA', 'WA')
        )
    );
```

Managing Partitions

Let us see how to manage partitions in MySQL:

- **Add a Partition:**

  Add a new partition to a range-partitioned table:

  ```
  ALTER TABLE sales
  ADD PARTITION (PARTITION p5 VALUES LESS THAN (2025));
  ```

- **Drop a Partition**:

  Remove a partition and its data:

  ```
  ALTER TABLE sales
  DROP PARTITION p0;
  ```

- **Rebuild Partitions**:

  Rebuild partitions to optimize storage:

  ```
  ALTER TABLE sales
  REBUILD PARTITION p1, p2;
  ```

- **Truncate a Partition**:

  Remove data from a partition without dropping it:

  ```
  ALTER TABLE sales
  TRUNCATE PARTITION p1;
  ```

- **Check Partition Information**:

  View partition details for a table:

  ```
  SELECT *
  FROM INFORMATION_SCHEMA.PARTITIONS
  WHERE TABLE_NAME = 'sales';
  ```

Best Practices for Partitioning

The following are some best practices for partitioning in MySQL:

- **Choose the Right Partitioning Strategy**: Use range partitioning for time-series data, list partitioning for categorical data, and hash/key partitioning for even distribution.

- **Avoid Over-Partitioning**: Too many partitions can degrade performance due to increased overhead.
- **Use Partition Pruning**: Design queries to take advantage of partition pruning for better performance.
- **Monitor and Maintain Partitions**: Regularly check and optimize partitions to ensure they remain efficient.
- **Test Thoroughly**: Test partitioning strategies with realistic data and workloads to ensure they meet performance and management goals.

Example: Partitioning a Large Log Table

This query creates a partitioned table in MySQL called **server_logs**. Partitioning is a technique that divides a table's data into smaller, manageable parts, allowing for improved performance when working with large datasets.

The table is partitioned based on the year extracted from the **`log_date`** column using the **`YEAR()`** function. This means rows will be distributed into partitions according to the year.

```
CREATE TABLE server_logs (
    log_id INT AUTO_INCREMENT,
    log_date DATETIME,
    log_message TEXT,
    PRIMARY KEY (log_id, log_date)
)
PARTITION BY RANGE (YEAR(log_date)) (
    PARTITION p0 VALUES LESS THAN (2021),
    PARTITION p1 VALUES LESS THAN (2022),
    PARTITION p2 VALUES LESS THAN (2023),
    PARTITION p3 VALUES LESS THAN (2024),
    PARTITION p4 VALUES LESS THAN MAXVALUE
);
```

The table's partitioning structure makes it efficient to query logs based on the year, as MySQL can focus on specific partitions rather than scanning the entire table. This is especially useful for performance optimization when the dataset contains a large number of rows.

Query to fetch logs from 2022 (uses partition pruning):

```
SELECT *
FROM server_logs
WHERE YEAR(log_date) = 2022;
```

Partitioning is a powerful feature in MySQL for managing large datasets. Use it to improve query performance, simplify data maintenance, and optimize storage!

Stored Procedures in MySQL

Stored procedures in MySQL are a powerful feature that allows you to encapsulate a sequence of SQL statements into a single callable unit. They are stored in the database and can be invoked with a single call, which can simplify complex operations, improve performance, and enhance security.

Features of Stored Procedures

The following are the features of stored procedures in MySQL:

- **Encapsulation**: Group multiple SQL statements into a single procedure.
- **Reusability**: Once created, stored procedures can be reused across multiple applications.
- **Performance**: Stored procedures are precompiled, which can improve execution speed.
- **Security**: They can restrict direct access to tables and provide controlled access through the procedure.
- **Reduced Network Traffic**: Instead of sending multiple queries, you can send a single call to the procedure.

Let us now see how to create a stored procedure in MySQL with an example.

Creating a Stored Procedure

To create a stored procedure, use the **CREATE PROCEDURE** statement.

```
DELIMITER //

CREATE PROCEDURE procedure_name(IN param1 INT, OUT param2
VARCHAR(255))
BEGIN
    -- SQL statements
    SELECT column_name INTO param2 FROM table_name WHERE id =
param1;
END //

DELIMITER ;
```

This stored procedure retrieves a specific value (**column_name**) from a table (**table_name**) based on a matching **id** provided as input (**param1**). The result is returned to the caller using the output parameter (**param2**).

Here:

- **DELIMITER**: Changes the statement delimiter temporarily to allow the procedure to be defined.
- **IN**: Input parameter (passed to the procedure).
- **OUT**: Output parameter (returned by the procedure).
- **BEGIN ... END**: Encloses the body of the procedure.

Example: Stored Procedure

Let us see how to create a stored procedure using the **CREATE PROCEDURE** statement:

```
DELIMITER //

CREATE PROCEDURE GetEmployeeName(IN emp_id INT, OUT emp_name
VARCHAR(255))
BEGIN
    SELECT name INTO emp_name FROM employees WHERE id = emp_id;
END //

DELIMITER ;
```

The above stored procedure is designed to retrieve the name of an employee from the **employees** table based on the employee ID (**emp_id**) provided as input. The resulting name is returned to the caller via the output parameter **emp_name**.

Calling a Stored Procedure

Use the **CALL** statement to execute a stored procedure.

```
CALL GetEmployeeName(1, @name);
SELECT @name;
```

Here, **@name** is a user-defined variable to store the output.

Modifying a Stored Procedure

To modify an existing procedure, use the **ALTER PROCEDURE** statement. However, MySQL does not support direct modification of the procedure body. Instead, you must drop and recreate the procedure.

```
DROP PROCEDURE IF EXISTS GetEmployeeName;

CREATE PROCEDURE GetEmployeeName(IN emp_id INT, OUT emp_name
VARCHAR(255))
BEGIN
```

```
    SELECT name INTO emp_name FROM employees WHERE id = emp_id;
END //
```

Deleting a Stored Procedure

Use the **DROP PROCEDURE** statement to delete a stored procedure.

```
DROP PROCEDURE IF EXISTS GetEmployeeName;
```

Advantages of Stored Procedures

The following are the advantages of stored procedures in MySQL:

- **Code Reusability**: Write it once and use it many times.
- **Improved Performance**: Precompiled execution plans.
- **Security**: Control access to data through procedures.
- **Maintainability**: Centralize business logic in the database.

Disadvantages of Stored Procedures

The following are the disadvantages of stored procedures in MySQL:

- **Debugging**: Debugging can be challenging.
- **Portability**: Stored procedures are database-specific, making migration harder.
- **Complexity**: It can become difficult to manage for large applications.

Best Practices for Creating a Stored Procedure

The following are the best practices for creating a stored procedure in MySQL:

- Use meaningful names for procedures and parameters.
- Document the purpose and logic of each procedure.
- Avoid overly complex procedures; break them into smaller units if necessary.
- Test thoroughly before deploying to production.

Stored procedures are a valuable tool in MySQL for managing complex database operations efficiently and securely.

Practical Exercise

Here is a practical exercise that builds on the previous **Employee Management System** and incorporates the MySQL topics of this lesson. This exercise will guide you through creating **Triggers** and **Views**, using **Regular Expressions**, performing **Full-Text Search**, and managing **Transactions**.

Exercise: Employee Management System

Step 1: Create a New Database

Let us create a new database **employee_management_system**:

```
CREATE DATABASE employee_management_system;
USE employee_management_system;
```

Step 2: Create Tables

We already created the following tables in the previous lessons:

- **departments**: Stores department details.
  - department_id (INT, Primary Key, Auto Increment)
  - department_name (VARCHAR(50), Unique, Not Null
- **employees**: Stores employee details.
  - id (INT, Primary Key, Auto Increment)
  - name (VARCHAR(50), Not Null
  - department_id (INT, Foreign Key referencing departments.department_id)
  - salary (DECIMAL(10, 2), Not Null
  - join_date (DATE, Not Null)

Here is the query to create both the tables:

```
CREATE TABLE departments (
    department_id INT PRIMARY KEY AUTO_INCREMENT,
    department_name VARCHAR(50) NOT NULL UNIQUE
);

CREATE TABLE employees (
    id INT PRIMARY KEY AUTO_INCREMENT,
    name VARCHAR(50) NOT NULL,
    department_id INT,
    salary DECIMAL(10, 2) NOT NULL,
    join_date DATE NOT NULL,
    FOREIGN KEY (department_id) REFERENCES departments
(department_id)
);
```

Step 3: Insert Records

Insert records into the departments and employees tables:

```
-- Insert departments
INSERT INTO departments (department_name) VALUES
('HR'),
('IT'),
('Finance'),
('Marketing');

-- Insert employees
INSERT INTO employees (name, department_id, salary, join_date)
VALUES
('John Doe', 1, 50000.00, '2022-01-15'),
('Jane Smith', 2, 60000.00, '2022-03-22'),
('Alice Johnson', 3, 55000.00, '2022-07-30'),
('Bob Brown', 2, 62000.00, '2023-02-10'),
('Charlie Davis', 1, 48000.00, '2023-05-05'),
('Eva Green', NULL, 58000.00, '2024-01-10');
```

Step 4: Triggers

Create a trigger that automatically updates the **join_date** to the current date if it is not provided during an insert:

```
DELIMITER //
CREATE TRIGGER before_employee_insert
BEFORE INSERT ON employees
FOR EACH ROW
BEGIN
    IF NEW.join_date IS NULL THEN
        SET NEW.join_date = CURDATE();
    END IF;
END //
DELIMITER ;
```

Step 5: Views

Create a view that displays employee details along with their department names:

```
CREATE VIEW employee_details AS
SELECT e.id, e.name, e.salary, e.join_date, d.department_name
FROM employees e
LEFT JOIN departments d ON e.department_id = d.department_id;
```

Step 6: Regular Expressions

Use regular expressions to retrieve employees whose names start with J:

```
SELECT * FROM employees
WHERE name REGEXP '^J';
```

Step 7: Full-Text Search

Add a **FULLTEXT** index to the name column and perform a full-text search for employees with names containing John or Jane:

```
-- Add FULLTEXT index
ALTER TABLE employees ADD FULLTEXT(name);

-- Perform full-text search
SELECT * FROM employees
WHERE MATCH(name) AGAINST('John Jane');
```

Step 8: Transactions

Use a transaction to update the salary of an employee and insert a new employee. Rollback the transaction if any error occurs:

```
START TRANSACTION;

-- Update salary
UPDATE employees SET salary = 65000.00 WHERE id = 1;

-- Insert new employee
INSERT INTO employees (name, department_id, salary, join_date)
VALUES
('Frank White', 3, 52000.00, '2023-02-15');

-- Commit or rollback
COMMIT;
-- ROLLBACK; -- Use this if there's an error
```

Step 9: Stored Procedures

Create a stored procedure that retrieves employees by department.

```
DELIMITER //
CREATE PROCEDURE GetEmployeesByDepartment(IN dept_id INT)
BEGIN
    SELECT * FROM employees
```

```
    WHERE department_id = dept_id;
END //
DELIMITER ;
```

Step 10: Test the Stored Procedure

Call the stored procedure to retrieve employees in the IT department (**department_id = 2**).

```
CALL GetEmployeesByDepartment(2);
```

Step 11: Verify Data

Retrieve all records from the **employees** table and the **employee_details** view to verify the results of your queries:

```
SELECT * FROM employees;
SELECT * FROM employee_details;
```

Final Queries

The following are the final queries covering the topics of this chapter:

```
CREATE DATABASE employee_management_system;

CREATE TABLE departments (
    department_id INT PRIMARY KEY AUTO_INCREMENT,
    department_name VARCHAR(50) NOT NULL UNIQUE
);

CREATE TABLE employees (
    id INT PRIMARY KEY AUTO_INCREMENT,
    name VARCHAR(50) NOT NULL,
    department_id INT,
    salary DECIMAL(10, 2) NOT NULL,
    join_date DATE NOT NULL,
    FOREIGN KEY (department_id) REFERENCES departments
(department_id)
);

-- Insert departments
INSERT INTO departments (department_name) VALUES
('HR'),
('IT'),
('Finance'),
('Marketing');

-- Insert employees
```

```
INSERT INTO employees (name, department_id, salary, join_date)
VALUES
('John Doe', 1, 50000.00, '2022-01-15'),
('Jane Smith', 2, 60000.00, '2022-03-22'),
('Alice Johnson', 3, 55000.00, '2022-07-30'),
('Bob Brown', 2, 62000.00, '2023-02-10'),
('Charlie Davis', 1, 48000.00, '2023-05-05'),
('Eva Green', NULL, 58000.00, '2024-01-10');

DELIMITER //
CREATE TRIGGER before_employee_insert
BEFORE INSERT ON employees
FOR EACH ROW
BEGIN
    IF NEW.join_date IS NULL THEN
        SET NEW.join_date = CURDATE();
    END IF;
END //
DELIMITER ;

CREATE VIEW employee_details AS
SELECT e.id, e.name, e.salary, e.join_date, d.department_name
FROM employees e
LEFT JOIN departments d ON e.department_id = d.department_id;

SELECT * FROM employees
WHERE name REGEXP '^J';

-- Add FULLTEXT index
ALTER TABLE employees ADD FULLTEXT(name);

-- Perform full-text search
SELECT * FROM employees
WHERE MATCH(name) AGAINST('John Jane');

START TRANSACTION;

-- Update salary
UPDATE employees SET salary = 65000.00 WHERE id = 1;

-- Insert new employee
INSERT INTO employees (name, department_id, salary, join_date)
VALUES
('Frank White', 3, 52000.00, '2023-02-15');

-- Commit or rollback
COMMIT;
```

```
-- ROLLBACK; -- Use this if there's an error

DELIMITER //
CREATE PROCEDURE GetEmployeesByDepartment(IN dept_id INT)
BEGIN
    SELECT * FROM employees
    WHERE department_id = dept_id;
END //
DELIMITER ;

CALL GetEmployeesByDepartment(2);

SELECT * FROM employees;
SELECT * FROM employee_details;
```

Expected Output

After completing the exercise, you should have:

- Created a trigger to automatically set the **`join_date`** if not provided.
- Created a view to display employee details along with their department names.
- Used regular expressions to filter employee names.
- Added a **`FULLTEXT`** index and performed a full-text search.
- Used transactions to ensure data consistency.
- Verified the results by querying the **`employees`** table and the **`employee_details`** view.
- Created a stored procedure to retrieve employees by department.
- Tested the stored procedure to retrieve employees in the IT department

This exercise covers the topics of this lesson and provides hands-on practice with advanced MySQL features.

Conclusion

We are now familiar with some advanced topics in MySQL. MySQL offers powerful features such as triggers, views, regex, full-text search, transactions, and partitioning to enhance database functionality. These tools help in maintaining data integrity, simplifying queries, and improving performance. By leveraging these features, developers can build robust and efficient database systems. Understanding these concepts is essential for effective database management.

In the next chapter, we will discuss some more topics, such as Having, Group By, backup, restore, and many more.

Points to Remember

- Triggers automate actions on specific events such as **INSERT**, **UPDATE**, or **DELETE**.
- Views are virtual tables that simplify complex queries and enhance security.
- Regular expressions enable pattern matching in queries using the **REGEXP** operator.
- Full-text search is ideal for searching large text fields efficiently.
- Transactions ensure data integrity by grouping operations into a single unit.
- Partitioning improves performance by dividing large tables into smaller parts.
- Always test triggers and transactions to avoid unintended side effects.
- Use meaningful names for stored procedures and parameters.

Multiple Choice Questions

1. What is the purpose of a trigger in MySQL?
   a. To create virtual tables
   b. To automate actions on specific events
   c. Partition large tables
   d. To perform full-text searches
2. Which operator is used for regular expressions in MySQL?
   a. `REGEXP`
   b. `MATCH`
   c. `REGEXPRESSION`
   d. `SEARCH`
3. What does the MATCH function do in MySQL?
   a. Executes a trigger
   b. Creates a view
   c. Performs a full-text search
   d. Starts a transaction

4. Which of the following is NOT an ACID property?
   a. Flexibility
   b. Consistency
   c. Isolation
   d. Atomicity
5. What is the benefit of partitioning in MySQL?
   a. Simplifies complex queries
   b. Improves performance by dividing large tables
   c. Automates database actions
   d. Enforces data integrity
6. What is the statement used to modify an existing procedure in MySQL?
   a. `MODIFY STORED PROCEDURE`
   b. `ALTER STORED PROCEDURE`
   c. `MODIFY PROCEDURE`
   d. `ALTER PROCEDURE`

Answers

1. b
2. a
3. c
4. a
5. b
6. d

Questions

1. What is the purpose of a trigger in MySQL?
2. How does a view differ from a table?
3. What is the syntax for using regular expressions in MySQL?

4. When would you use a full-text search instead of a simple LIKE query?
5. What are the ACID properties of transactions?
6. How does partitioning improve database performance?
7. Can a trigger be created for a SELECT statement? Why or why not?
8. What are the limitations of using views in MySQL?
9. How to create a procedure in MySQL?

Key Terms

- **Trigger**: A database object that executes automatically on specific events.
- **View**: A virtual table created by a query.
- **Regex**: A pattern-matching tool used in queries.
- **Full-Text Search**: A method for searching text fields efficiently.
- **Transaction**: A group of operations executed as a single unit.
- **Partitioning**: Dividing a table into smaller, manageable parts.
- **ACID**: Properties (Atomicity, Consistency, Isolation, Durability) of transactions.
- **Virtual Table**: A table that does not store data but displays results from a query.
- **Stored procedures:** Allows you to encapsulate a sequence of statements into a single callable unit.

CHAPTER 11
MySQL Miscellaneous

Introduction

This chapter covers some key topics, such as **GROUP BY** and the **HAVING** clause, and backing up and restoring databases. With that, the optimization of the database and tables is also covered. By mastering its core functionalities and staying updated with advancements, users can leverage MySQL effectively for various applications.

We have also covered common error codes users may face while installing or working with MySQL. With that, some performance tips and future MySQL trends are also covered.

Structure

In this chapter, we will discuss the following topics:

- **GROUP BY** Clause in MySQL
- **HAVING** Clause in MySQL
- Altering a Table in MySQL
- Backing Up and Restoring a Database in MySQL
- Exporting and Importing a MySQL Database
- Error Codes in MySQL
- Performance Tips in MySQL
- Future Trends in MySQL

GROUP BY Clause in MySQL

The **GROUP BY** clause in MySQL is used to group rows that have the same values in specified columns into aggregated data. It is often used with aggregate functions such as **COUNT, SUM, AVG, MAX,** and **MIN** to perform calculations on each group of rows.

Key Points of GROUP BY Clause

Here are some key points of the GROUP BY Clause in MySQL:

- The **GROUP BY** clause groups rows based on one or more columns.
- It is typically used with aggregate functions to perform calculations on each group.
- If you use **GROUP BY**, the result set will contain one row per group.
- Columns in the **SELECT** statement that are not part of an aggregate function must be included in the **GROUP BY** clause.

Syntax of GROUP BY Clause

The following is the syntax of the GROUP BY Clause in MySQL:

```
SELECT column1, column2, aggregate_function(column3)
FROM table_name
WHERE condition
GROUP BY column1, column2
ORDER BY column1, column2;
```

Here, GROUP BY is used to group rows based on unique combinations of **column1** and **column2**. For each group, an aggregate function (for example, **SUM**, **COUNT**) is applied to **column3** to compute a summary value. The WHERE clause filters rows before grouping, and the ORDER BY clause sorts the grouped results by **column1** and **column2**. This approach efficiently organizes and analyzes data in MySQL.

Advantages of GROUP BY Clause

The following are the advantages of the GROUP BY Clause in MySQL:

- **Data Aggregation**
  - Allows you to summarize data by grouping rows that have the same values
  - Enables use of aggregate functions such as COUNT(), SUM(), AVG(), MAX(), MIN()
- **Efficient Data Analysis**
  - Simplifies complex data analysis by organizing results into logical groups
  - Reduces the need for multiple queries to get summary information
- **Improved Reporting**
  - Creates meaningful summaries from large datasets
  - Generates reports with subtotals and grouped information

- **Data Organization**
  - Structures results in a more readable format by grouping related records
  - Makes it easier to identify patterns and trends in data
- **Performance Benefits**
  - Often more efficient than retrieving all rows and processing them in the application code
  - Works well with proper indexing on grouped columns
- **Combination with Other Clauses**
  - Works powerfully with HAVING to filter groups (unlike WHERE which filters rows)
  - Can be used with ORDER BY to sort grouped results
- **Flexible Grouping Options**
  - Can group by single or multiple columns
  - Supports expressions in the GROUP BY clause

Example of `GROUP BY` Clause

Suppose you have a table named **orders** with the following columns: **`order_id`**, **`customer_id`**, **`order_date`**, and **`amount`**.

Table: `orders`

order_id	customer_id	order_date	amount
1	101	2025-01-01	100
2	102	2025-01-02	200
3	101	2025-01-03	150
4	103	2025-01-04	300
5	102	2025-01-05	250

***Table 11.1:** Output displaying the records of the orders table*

Query:

Find the total amount spent by each customer.

```
SELECT customer_id, SUM(amount) AS total_amount
FROM orders
GROUP BY customer_id;
```

Result:

customer_id	total_amount
101	250
102	450
103	300

Table 11.2: *Output displaying total amount spent by each customer*

In this example:

- The **GROUP BY** clause groups the rows by **customer_id**.
- The **SUM(amount)** function calculates the total amount spent by each customer.

Example of GROUP BY with Multiple Columns

Find the total amount spent by each customer on each order date.

```
SELECT customer_id, order_date, SUM(amount) AS total_amount
FROM orders
GROUP BY customer_id, order_date;
```

Result:

customer_id	order_date	total_amount
101	2025-01-01	100
101	2025-01-03	150
102	2025-01-02	200
102	2025-01-05	250
103	2025-01-04	300

Table 11.3: *Output displaying total amount spent by each customer on each order dare*

In this example:

- The **GROUP BY** clause groups the rows by both **customer_id** and **order_date**.
- The **SUM(amount)** function calculates the total amount spent by each customer on each order date.

Example of using GROUP BY with HAVING

Find customers who have spent more than $200 in total.

```
SELECT customer_id, SUM(amount) AS total_amount
FROM orders
GROUP BY customer_id
HAVING total_amount > 200;
```

This query calculates the total order amount for each customer in the `orders` table by grouping data based on `customer_id` and using the `SUM` function. The `HAVING` clause then filters the results, ensuring only those customers whose total amount exceeds **200** are included. The output displays the customer_id and their corresponding total amount. This is useful for analyzing customer spending habits.

Result:

customer_id	total_amount
102	450
103	300

Table 11.4: *Output displaying customers who spent more than a specific amount*

In this example:

- The `GROUP BY` clause groups the rows by `customer_id`.
- The **SUM(amount)** function calculates the total amount spent by each customer.
- The `HAVING` clause filters out customers whose total amount is not greater than 200.

Notes:

- *Columns in the **SELECT** statement that are not part of an aggregate function must be included in the **GROUP BY** clause.*
- *The **GROUP BY** clause can be used with multiple columns.*
- *The **GROUP BY** clause is often used with the **ORDER BY** clause to sort the results.*

Example of GROUP BY with ORDER BY

Find the total amount spent by each customer and sort the results by `total_amount` in descending order.

```
SELECT customer_id, SUM(amount) AS total_amount
FROM orders
GROUP BY customer_id
ORDER BY total_amount DESC;
```

Result:

customer_id	total_amount
102	450
103	300
101	250

Table 11.5: *Output displaying sorting the total amount spent by each customer*

The output displays the total amount sorted in descending order.

In this example:

- The **GROUP BY** clause groups the rows by **customer_id**.
- The **SUM(amount)** function calculates the total amount spent by each customer.
- The **ORDER BY** clause sorts the results by **total_amount** in descending order.

This is how the **GROUP BY** clause is used in MySQL to group rows and perform aggregate calculations on each group.

HAVING Clause in MySQL

The **HAVING** clause is used in combination with the **GROUP BY** clause to filter groups of rows based on a specified condition. It is used to filter records after the **GROUP BY** clause has been applied. It is often used in conjunction with aggregate functions such as **COUNT**, **SUM**, **AVG**, **MAX**, or MIN to filter groups of rows based on a specified condition.

Key Points of the HAVING Clause

The following are the important points of the **HAVING** Clause in MySQL:

- The **HAVING** clause is used to filter groups of rows.
- It is applied after the **GROUP BY** clause.
- It can be used with aggregate functions.
- Unlike the **WHERE** clause, which filters rows before grouping, the **HAVING** clause filters after grouping.

Syntax of HAVING Clause

The following is the syntax of the **HAVING** clause in MySQL:

```
SELECT column1, column2, aggregate_function(column3)
FROM table_name
WHERE condition
GROUP BY column1, column2
HAVING condition;
```

Advantages of HAVING Clause

The following are the advantages of the **HAVING** Clause in MySQL.

- **Group-Level Filtering**
  - Filters groups after aggregation (unlike **WHERE** which filters rows before grouping)

    - Enables conditional selection of entire groups based on aggregate values
- **Works with Aggregate Functions**
    - Allows filtering using results of `COUNT()`, SUM(), AVG(), MAX(), MIN(), and so on.
    - Example: HAVING SUM(sales) > 1000 or HAVING AVG(score) > 75
- **Complement to GROUP BY**
    - Essential for refining grouped results after aggregation
    - Works in conjunction with GROUP BY to provide precise control over grouped data
- **Complex Condition Support**
    - Supports multiple conditions with AND/OR operators
    - Can include both aggregate and non-aggregate conditions
- **Business Intelligence Applications**
    - Ideal for identifying groups that meet specific performance thresholds
    - Useful for finding outliers or exceptional cases in grouped data
- **Improved Query Efficiency**
    - More efficient than filtering aggregated results in application code
    - Reduces network traffic by filtering at the database level

Example of HAVING Clause

Suppose you have a table named **orders** with the following columns: **`order_id`**, **`customer_id`**, **`order_date`**, and **`amount`**.

Table: `orders`

order_id	customer_id	order_date	amount
1	101	2025-01-01	100
2	102	2025-01-02	200
3	101	2025-01-03	150
4	103	2025-01-04	300
5	102	2025-01-05	250

Table 11.6: *Orders table output*

Query:

Find customers who have spent more than $300 in total.

```
SELECT customer_id, SUM(amount) AS total_amount
FROM orders
GROUP BY customer_id
HAVING total_amount > 300;
```

Result:

customer_id	**total_amount**
102	450
103	300

Table 11.7: *Orders table output displaying customers who spent over a specific amount*

In this example:

- The **`GROUP BY`** clause groups the rows by **`customer_id`**.
- The **`SUM(amount)`** function calculates the total amount spent by each customer.
- The **`HAVING`** clause filters out customers whose total amount is not greater than 300.

Notes:

- *The **`HAVING`** clause can only be used with **`SELECT`** statements that include a **`GROUP BY`** clause.*
- *If you use the **`HAVING`** clause without a **`GROUP BY`** clause, it will treat the entire result set as a single group.*
- *The **`HAVING`** clause can include conditions with aggregate functions, whereas the **`WHERE`** clause cannot.*

Comparison of `HAVING` with `WHERE`

Let us see how the HAVING clause is different from the **`WHERE`** clause in MySQL:

- **`WHERE`**: Filters rows before any grouping is done.
- **`HAVING`**: Filters groups after the **`GROUP BY`** clause has been applied.

Example with `WHERE` and `HAVING`

Find customers who have placed more than one order and have spent more than $200 in total.

```
SELECT customer_id, COUNT(order_id) AS order_count, SUM(amount)
AS total_amount
```

```
FROM orders
WHERE order_date >= '2025-01-01'
GROUP BY customer_id
HAVING order_count > 1 AND total_amount > 200;
```

In this query:

- The **WHERE** clause filters orders placed on or after ‹2025-01-01›.
- The **GROUP BY** clause groups the results by **customer_id.**
- The **HAVING** clause filters groups where the customer has placed more than one order and the total amount spent is greater than $200.

This is how the **HAVING** clause is used in MySQL to filter grouped data based on aggregate conditions.

Altering a Table in MySQL

To alter a table in MySQL, you can use the **ALTER TABLE** statement. This statement allows you to modify the structure of an existing table, such as adding, deleting, or modifying columns, changing data types, renaming columns or the table itself, and more.

Here are some common use cases for **ALTER TABLE**:

Adding a New Column

To add a new column to a table:

```
ALTER TABLE table_name
ADD COLUMN column_name data_type [constraints];
```

Example:

```
ALTER TABLE employees
ADD COLUMN email VARCHAR(100);
```

Modifying an Existing Column

To change the data type or constraints of an existing column:

```
ALTER TABLE table_name
MODIFY COLUMN column_name new_data_type [constraints];
```

Example:

```
ALTER TABLE employees
 MODIFY COLUMN email VARCHAR(150) NOT NULL;
```

Renaming a Column

To rename an existing column:

```
ALTER TABLE table_name
RENAME COLUMN old_column_name TO new_column_name;
```

Example:

```
ALTER TABLE employees
RENAME COLUMN email TO work_email;
```

Dropping a Column

To remove a column from a table:

```
ALTER TABLE table_name
DROP COLUMN column_name;
```

Example:

```
ALTER TABLE employees
DROP COLUMN work_email;
```

Adding a Constraint

To add a constraint (for example, **PRIMARY KEY**, **FOREIGN KEY**, **UNIQUE**, **CHECK**):

```
ALTER TABLE table_name
ADD CONSTRAINT constraint_name constraint_type (column_name);
```

Example:

```
ALTER TABLE employees
ADD CONSTRAINT pk_employee_id PRIMARY KEY (employee_id);
```

Dropping a Constraint

To remove a constraint:

```
ALTER TABLE table_name
DROP CONSTRAINT constraint_name;
```

Example:

```
ALTER TABLE employees
DROP CONSTRAINT pk_employee_id;
```

Renaming a Table

To rename the table itself:

```
ALTER TABLE old_table_name
RENAME TO new_table_name;
```

Example:

```
ALTER TABLE employees
RENAME TO staff;
```

Changing Column Data Type

To change the data type of a column:

```
ALTER TABLE table_name
CHANGE COLUMN column_name new_column_name new_data_type;
```

Example:

```
ALTER TABLE employees
CHANGE COLUMN phone_number phone_number BIGINT;
```

Adding an Index

To add an index to a column:

```
ALTER TABLE table_name
ADD INDEX index_name (column_name);
```

Example:

```
ALTER TABLE employees
ADD INDEX idx_email (email);
```

Dropping an Index

To remove an index:

```
ALTER TABLE table_name
DROP INDEX index_name;
```

Example:

```
ALTER TABLE employees
DROP INDEX idx_email;
```

Notes:

- *Always back up your data before making structural changes to a table.*

- *Some operations (for example, modifying large tables) can be time-consuming and may lock the table.*
- *Use* ***DESCRIBE table_name****; to view the structure of a table before and after making changes.*

Backing Up and Restoring a Database in MySQL

Backing up and restoring a MySQL database on **Windows** is straightforward. The following are the detailed steps for both tasks using **Command Prompt**, **MySQL Workbench**, and **phpMyAdmin** (if you are using a local server stack such as XAMPP or WAMP).

Backing Up a MySQL Database on Windows

Using mysqldump (Command Prompt)

The **mysqldump** is a command-line tool that creates an SQL file containing the database structure and data. The steps include:

1. Open the **Command Prompt**: Press *Win* + R, type cmd, and hit *Enter*.
2. Navigate to the MySQL bin directory (if it is not added to your system PATH):

   ```
   cd C:\Program Files\MySQL\MySQL Server 8.0\bin
   ```

3. Run the **mysqldump** command to back up your database:

   ```
   mysqldump -u [username] -p[password] [database_name] > C:\path\
   to\backup_file.sql
   ```

   Example:

   ```
   mysqldump -u root -p mydatabase > C:\backup\mydatabase_backup.sql
   ```

   Here:

   - Replace [username], [password], and [database_name] with your MySQL credentials and database name.
   - Replace C:\path\to\backup_file.sql with the desired backup file path.
4. If you want to compress the backup, use a tool such as **7-Zip** or **WinRAR** to compress the .sql file.

Using MySQL Workbench (GUI Tool)

MySQL Workbench provides a graphical interface for backing up databases. The steps include:

1. Open **`MySQL Workbench`**.
2. Connect to your MySQL server.
3. Go to **`Server`** > **`Data Export`**.
4. Select the database(s) or tables you want to back up.
5. Choose the export options (for example, dump structure and data).
6. Specify the output file location (for example, C:\backup\mydatabase_backup.sql).
7. Click **`Start Export`**.

Restoring a MySQL Database on Windows

Using mysql Command (Command Prompt):

1. Open the **Command Prompt**.
2. Navigate to the MySQL bin directory (if necessary):
   ```
   cd C:\Program Files\MySQL\MySQL Server 8.0\bin
   ```
3. Run the **`mysql`** command to restore the database:
   ```
   mysql -u [username] -p[password] [database_name] < C:\path\to\backup_file.sql
   ```
   Example:
   ```
   mysql -u root -p mydatabase < C:\backup\mydatabase_backup.sql
   ```
   Here,
   - Replace [username], [password], and [database_name] with your MySQL credentials and database name.
   - Replace C:\path\to\backup_file.sql with the path to your backup file.

Using MySQL Workbench (GUI Tool):

1. Open **`MySQL Workbench`**.
2. Connect to your MySQL server.
3. Go to **`Server`** > **`Data Import`**.

4. Choose **Import from Self-Contained File** and select your backup file (for example, C:\backup\mydatabase_backup.sql).
5. Select the target database (or create a new one).
6. Click **Start Import**.

Best Practices for Backup and Restore

The following are the best practices for backup and restore in MySQL:

- **Test Your Backups:** Periodically test your backups by restoring them to ensure they work.
- **Store Backups Securely:** Keep backup files in a secure location, preferably on a different drive or in cloud storage.
- **Use Compression:** Compress large backup files to save disk space.
- **Backup Regularly:** Schedule regular backups based on how often your data changes.

Exporting and Importing a MySQL Database

Exporting and importing databases in MySQL are common tasks for migrating data, creating backups, or sharing data between environments. The following are the steps and commands to export and import databases in MySQL:

Exporting a Database on Windows

Using mysqldump (Command Prompt)

The **mysqldump** is available on Windows as part of the MySQL installation.

1. Open the **Command Prompt** (press *Win* + R, type **cmd**, and hit *Enter*).
2. Navigate to the MySQL bin directory (if it is not added to your system PATH). For example:

   ```
   cd C:\Program Files\MySQL\MySQL Server 8.0\bin
   ```
3. Run the **mysqldump** command to export your database:

   ```
   mysqldump -u [username] -p[password] [database_name] > C:\path\to\output_file.sql
   ```

   Example:

   ```
   mysqldump -u root -p mydatabase > C:\backup\mydatabase_export.sql
   ```

Here:

- Replace [username], [password], and [database_name] with your MySQL credentials and database name.
- Replace C:\path\to\output_file.sql with the desired output file path.

4. If you want to compress the export file, you can use a tool such as **7-Zip** or **WinRAR** to compress the .sql file after exporting.

Using MySQL Workbench (GUI Tool)

MySQL Workbench is a user-friendly GUI tool for managing MySQL databases on Windows. The steps include:

1. Open **`MySQL Workbench`**.
2. Connect to your MySQL server.
3. Go to **`Server`** > **`Data Export`**.
4. Select the database(s) or tables you want to export.
5. Choose the export options (for example, dump structure and data).
6. Specify the output file location (for example, C:\backup\mydatabase_export.sql).
7. Click **`Start Export`**.

Importing a Database on Windows

Using mysql Command (Command Prompt):

1. Open the **`Command Prompt`**.
2. Navigate to the MySQL bin directory (if necessary):

```
cd C:\Program Files\MySQL\MySQL Server 8.0\bin
```

Run the mysql command to import the database:

```
mysql -u [username] -p[password] [database_name] < C:\path\to\
input_file.sql
```

Example:

```
mysql -u root -p mydatabase < C:\backup\mydatabase_export.sql
```

Here:

- Replace [username], [password], and [database_name] with your MySQL credentials and database name.

- Replace C:\path\to\input_file.sql with the path to your SQL file.

Using MySQL Workbench (GUI Tool):

1. Open `MySQL Workbench`.
2. Connect to your MySQL server.
3. Go to `Server` > `Data Import`.
4. Choose `Import from Self-Contained File` and select your SQL file (for example, C:\backup\mydatabase_export.sql).
5. Select the target database (or create a new one).
6. Click `Start Import`.

Best Practices for Exporting and Importing a Database on Windows

The following are some of the best practices for exporting and importing a database on Windows:

- **Use Absolute Paths:** Always specify full paths for input/output files in commands.
- **Check MySQL Service:** Ensure the MySQL service is running before performing import/export operations.
- **Backup Before Importing:** Always back up your database before importing data to avoid accidental data loss.
- **Use MySQL Workbench for Ease:** If you are not comfortable with the command line, MySQL Workbench is a great alternative.

Error Codes in MySQL

MySQL uses various error codes to indicate different types of issues that can occur during database operations. These error codes are numerical and are accompanied by an error message that provides more details about the issue. The following is a list of some common MySQL error codes along with their meanings:

Common MySQL Error Codes

While installing and working on MySQL, you may get any of the following errors. Let us discuss the causes:

- `1005 (ER_CANT_CREATE_TABLE)`

 - **Message**: Can't create table %s (errno: %d)
 - **Cause**: Usually occurs when there is an issue with foreign key constraints or storage engine problems.

- **`1045 (ER_ACCESS_DENIED_ERROR)`**
 - **Message**: Access denied for user %s@%s (using password: %s)
 - **Cause**: Incorrect username or password, or the user does not have the necessary privileges.
- **`1054 (ER_BAD_FIELD_ERROR)`**
 - **Message**: Unknown column %s in %s
 - **Cause**: The specified column does not exist in the table.
- **`1062 (ER_DUP_ENTRY)`**
 - **Message**: Duplicate entry %s for key %s
 - **Cause**: Attempt to insert a duplicate value in a column that has a unique constraint.
- **`1064 (ER_PARSE_ERROR)`**
 - **Message**: You have an error in your SQL syntax; check the manual that corresponds to your MySQL server version for the right syntax to use near %s
 - **Cause**: Syntax error in the SQL query.
- **`1146 (ER_NO_SUCH_TABLE)`**
 - **Message**: Table %s.%s does not exist
 - **Cause**: The specified table does not exist in the database.
- **`1215 (ER_CANNOT_ADD_FOREIGN)`**
 - **Message**: Cannot add a foreign key constraint
 - **Cause**: Issues with foreign key constraints, such as mismatched data types or missing indexes.
- **`1216 (ER_NO_REFERENCED_ROW)`**
 - **`Message:`** Cannot add or update a child row: a foreign key constraint fails
 - **Cause**: Attempt to insert or update a row in a child table with a foreign key value that does not exist in the parent table.
- **`1217 (ER_ROW_IS_REFERENCED)`**
 - **Message**: Cannot delete or update a parent row: a foreign key constraint fails

  - **Cause**: Attempt to delete or update a row in a parent table that is referenced by a foreign key in a child table.
- `1451 (ER_ROW_IS_REFERENCED_2)`
  - **Message**: Cannot delete or update a parent row: a foreign key constraint fails (%s)
  - **Cause**: This is Similar to error 1217 but with more specific details.
- `2002 (CR_CONNECTION_ERROR)`
  - **Message**: Can't connect to local MySQL server through socket %s (%d)
  - **Cause**: The MySQL server is not running, or the socket file is not accessible.
- `2003 (CR_CONN_HOST_ERROR)`
  - **Message**: Can't connect to MySQL server on %s (%d)
  - **Cause**: The MySQL server is not reachable on the specified host and port.
- `2013 (CR_SERVER_LOST)`
  - **Message**: Lost connection to MySQL server during query
  - **Cause**: The connection to the MySQL server was lost while executing a query.
- `1049 (ER_BAD_DB_ERROR)`
  - **Message**: Unknown database %s
  - **Cause**: The specified database does not exist.
- `1051 (ER_BAD_TABLE_ERROR)`
  - **Message**: Unknown table %s
  - **Cause**: The specified table does not exist.

Handling MySQL Errors

Let us see how to handle the most common errors in MySQL:

- **Check the Error Message**: The error message usually provides detailed information about what went wrong.
- **Review SQL Syntax**: For syntax errors, carefully review the SQL query.
- **Check Privileges**: Ensure that the user has the necessary privileges to perform the operation.
- **Verify Data Integrity**: For foreign key errors, ensure that the data in the parent and child tables is consistent.

To fix the most common MySQL errors, we have created a playlist on YouTube. It covers over 10 fixes related to MySQL issues and errors. Here is the playlist link:

`https://www.youtube.com/playlist?list=PLSwH4ViBDl2RrLZg3yZ5EX-G1LUXAr9l2s`

Performance Tips in MySQL

Optimizing MySQL performance is crucial for ensuring that your database can handle large volumes of data and high numbers of queries efficiently. Here are some performance tips for MySQL:

- **Indexing:**
  - **Use Indexes Wisely**: Indexes can significantly speed up query performance, but they can also slow down write operations (**`INSERT`**, **`UPDATE`**, **`DELETE`**). Use indexes on columns that are frequently used in **`WHERE`** clauses, **`JOIN`** conditions, and **`ORDER BY`** clauses.
  - **Avoid Over-Indexing**: Too many indexes can degrade performance. Only create indexes that are necessary.
  - **Composite Indexes**: Use composite indexes for queries that filter on multiple columns.
- **Query Optimization:**
  - **Optimize Queries**: Use the **`EXPLAIN`** statement to analyze and optimize your queries. Look for full table scans and try to eliminate them.
  - **Avoid `SELECT`**: Only select the columns you need. Selecting all columns can increase the amount of data transferred and processed.
  - **Use `LIMIT`**: When you only need a subset of rows, use the LIMIT clause to reduce the number of rows processed.
- **Optimizing Joins and Subqueries:**
  - Prefer **JOINs** over subqueries where possible, as MySQL often optimizes JOINs better.
  - Use **`INNER JOIN`** instead of **`OUTER JOIN (LEFT/RIGHT JOIN)`** if possible, as they are generally faster.
  - **Avoid correlated subqueries** (subqueries that reference outer query columns), as they execute row-by-row and can be slow.
- **Efficient Use of Transactions:**
  - **Keep transactions short** to reduce locking and improve concurrency.
  - **Batch `INSERT/UPDATE/DELETE`** operations in a single transaction instead of multiple small transactions.

  - **Avoid long-running transactions** that hold locks and block other queries.
- **Optimizing Sorting and Grouping:**
  - Use `ORDER BY` on indexed columns to avoid expensive filesorts.
  - **Limit `GROUP BY`** to necessary columns–adding unnecessary columns increases sorting overhead.
  - **Consider using `GROUP BY` with `ORDER BY NULL`** if sorting is not needed (reduces sorting overhead).
- **Schema Design**
  - **Normalize Your Database**: Normalization reduces redundancy and improves data integrity. However, be cautious of over-normalization, which can lead to complex queries and joins.
  - **Use Appropriate Data Types**: Choose the smallest data type that can comfortably handle your data. For example, use INT instead of BIGINT if you don't need the extra range.
  - **Partitioning**: For large tables, consider partitioning to improve query performance and manageability.
- **Configuration Tuning:**
  - **Buffer Pool Size**: Adjust the **`innodb_buffer_pool_size`** to allocate more memory for caching data and indexes. This is one of the most important settings for InnoDB performance.
  - **Query Cache**: Be cautious with the query cache. In some cases, it can cause contention and slow down performance. Consider disabling it (`query_cache_type = 0`) if it does not provide a significant benefit.
  - **Connection Pooling**: Use connection pooling to reduce the overhead of establishing and closing connections.
- **Hardware and Infrastructure:**
  - **SSD Storage**: Use SSDs instead of HDDs for faster read/write operations.
  - **Sufficient RAM**: Ensure that your server has enough RAM to handle your workload, especially for the InnoDB buffer pool.
  - **Network Latency**: Minimize network latency by hosting your database server close to your application server.
- **Caching:**
  - **Application-Level Caching**: Use caching mechanisms such as Memcached or Redis to cache frequently accessed data.
  - **MySQL Query Cache**: While the query cache can be beneficial for read-heavy workloads, it can also cause contention. Evaluate its impact on your specific workload.

- **Maintenance:**
  - **Regular Maintenance**: Perform regular maintenance tasks such as **`OPTIMIZE TABLE`**, **`ANALYZE TABLE`**, and **`CHECK TABLE`** to keep your database in good shape.
  - **Backup and Recovery**: Implement a robust backup and recovery strategy to protect your data and ensure quick recovery in case of failure.
- **Monitoring and Profiling:**
  - **Monitor Performance**: Use tools such as MySQL Workbench, Percona Toolkit, or pt-query-digest to monitor and analyze database performance.
  - **Slow Query Log**: Enable the slow query log to identify and optimize slow-running queries.

Future Trends in MySQL

Predicting future trends in MySQL or any technology involves a degree of speculation, but based on current developments and industry directions, we can make educated guesses about what might be prominent in MySQL by 2026. Here are some potential trends:

- **Enhanced Cloud Integration**
  - **Managed Services**: Increased adoption of managed MySQL services such as Amazon RDS, Google Cloud SQL, and Azure Database for MySQL. These services offer scalability, high availability, and automated backups.
  - **Serverless Databases**: Growth in serverless database offerings where the database automatically scales based on demand, reducing the need for manual intervention.
- **Improved Performance and Scalability**
  - **Advanced Indexing**: Development of more sophisticated indexing techniques to handle larger datasets and more complex queries efficiently.
  - **Partitioning and Sharding**: Enhanced support for partitioning and sharding to improve the performance and manageability of large databases.
- **Machine Learning and AI Integration**
  - **Predictive Analytics**: Integration of machine learning models directly within MySQL for predictive analytics and real-time decision-making.
  - **Automated Tuning**: AI-driven tools for automated database tuning, performance optimization, and anomaly detection.
- **Enhanced Security Features**
  - **Advanced Encryption**: Improved encryption methods for data at rest and in transit, including support for quantum-resistant algorithms.

- **Fine-Grained Access Control**: More granular access control mechanisms to ensure data security and compliance with regulations such as GDPR and CCPA.

- **Real-Time Data Processing**
  - **Streaming Data**: Better support for real-time data processing and streaming data integration, allowing MySQL to handle time-series data and IoT applications more effectively.
  - **In-Memory Databases**: Increased use of in-memory databases for real-time analytics and high-speed transactions.
- **Polyglot Persistence**
  - **Multi-Model Support**: Enhanced support for different data models (document, graph, key-value) within the same database, allowing for more flexible data management.
  - **Interoperability**: Improved interoperability with other databases and data storage systems, facilitating polyglot persistence strategies.
- **Open Sourcc and Community Contributions**
  - **Community-Driven Innovations**: Continued strong community involvement leading to rapid innovation and feature development.
  - **Open Source Ecosystem**: Growth of the open-source ecosystem around MySQL, including plugins, extensions, and third-party tools.
- **Improved Developer Experience**
  - **Better Tooling**: Enhanced development tools and IDE integrations to improve productivity and ease of use.
  - **APIs and SDKs**: More robust APIs and SDKs for various programming languages, making it easier to integrate MySQL with different applications.
- **Sustainability and Green Computing**
  - **Energy-Efficient Operations**: Focus on reducing the environmental impact of database operations through energy-efficient hardware and optimized software.
  - **Sustainable Practices**: Adoption of sustainable practices in database management, including resource optimization and reduced carbon footprint.
- **Edge Computing**
  - **Edgc Databases**: Increased use of MySQL in edge computing scenarios, where data processing happens closer to the data source to reduce latency and bandwidth usage.

- **Distributed Architectures**: Enhanced support for distributed database architectures to support edge computing and decentralized applications.

Note: *For a free MySQL Tutorial with 40 lessons, refer to the following link from our YouTube Channel:*

`https://youtu.be/sgpDAiF-18o`

Conclusion

We are now familiar with some miscellaneous topics in MySQL. MySQL remains a powerful and versatile relational database management system, widely used for its ease of use and robust features. From filtering grouped data with the HAVING clause to optimizing performance and exploring future trends, MySQL continues to evolve to meet modern data management needs.

In the next chapter, we will create a capstone project that covers the essential MySQL topics we have covered in this book.

Points to Remember

- The **`HAVING`** clause filters grouped data, while the **`WHERE`** clause filters rows before grouping.
- The **`GROUP BY`** clause is used with aggregate functions to summarize data.
- Use **`ALTER TABLE`** to modify table structure, such as adding or dropping columns.
- The mysqldump is the standard tool for exporting and importing MySQL databases.
- Regularly back up your database to prevent data loss.
- Understand common MySQL error codes to troubleshoot issues effectively.
- Optimize MySQL performance by using indexes, avoiding **`SELECT *`**, and normalizing databases.

Multiple Choice Questions

1. What does the `HAVING` clause do?
   a. Filters rows before grouping
   b. Filters grouped data
   c. Sorts the result set
   d. Joins tables

2. Which clause is used with aggregate functions to summarize data?
    a. `WHERE`
    b. `ORDER BY`
    c. `JOIN`
    d. `GROUP BY`
3. What command is used to add a column to an existing table?
    a. `ADD COLUMN`
    b. `MODIFY TABLE`
    c. `ALTER TABLE`
    d. `UPDATE TABLE`
4. Which utility is used to export a MySQL database?
    a. Mysqlimport
    b. Mysqldump
    c. Mysqlbackup
    d. Mysqlrestore
5. What does MySQL error code 1045 indicate?
    a. Syntax error
    b. Access denied
    c. Foreign key constraint failure
    d. Table not found
6. Which of the following improves MySQL query performance?
    a. Normalizing the database
    b. Avoiding indexes
    c. Using `SELECT *`
    d. Fetching all columns

Answers

1. b
2. d
3. c
4. b
5. b
6. a

Questions

1. What is the difference between the HAVING and WHERE clauses?
2. How does the GROUP BY clause work with aggregate functions?
3. What are the steps to add a new column to an existing table in MySQL?
4. How can you export a MySQL database to a file?
5. What is the purpose of the mysqldump utility?
6. How do you troubleshoot a MySQL error with code 1064?
7. What are some best practices for improving MySQL performance?
8. What are the future trends in MySQL database management?

Key Terms

- **`HAVING` Clause:** Filters grouped data based on a condition.
- **`GROUP BY` Clause:** Groups rows with the same values into summary rows.
- **`ALTER TABLE`:** Modifies the structure of an existing table.
- **mysqldump:** A utility for exporting MySQL databases.
- **Backup:** A copy of the database to prevent data loss.
- **Error Code:** A numeric code indicating a specific MySQL error.
- **Index:** A database structure that improves query performance.
- **Normalization:** The process of organizing data to reduce redundancy.

Chapter 12
Capstone Project

Introduction

Let us create a comprehensive capstone project that covers these essential MySQL topics. We will go through each step again and see what the outputs would look like.

Structure

In this chapter, we will cover a capstone project. Let us first understand what the project implements.

Capstone Project: University Management System

The project provides a comprehensive guide to creating a **University Management System** using MySQL. It begins with the fundamental steps of creating a database and tables, followed by inserting records into these tables. It goes through various SQL operations, including creating tables, inserting records, using SELECT statements, and applying constraints such as PRIMARY KEY, FOREIGN KEY, UNIQUE, and NOT NULL. It also covers advanced SQL operations such as JOINs, Indexes, and TRIGGERS, demonstrating how these can be utilized to manage and query data effectively within the University Management System.

Later, we will dive into more complex SQL functions and operators such as the WHERE, AND, OR, NOT, and BETWEEN clauses, as well as built-in functions for strings, numbers, and dates. It also discusses aggregate functions, ORDER BY statements, and CASE statements. These examples are aimed at providing a robust understanding of how to perform various data manipulation and retrieval operations, ensuring the system can handle a wide range of queries and data processing tasks. We will emphasize the practical implementation of these concepts by showcasing real-time outputs of the queries.

Toward the end, we will explore user management within the MySQL environment, including creating and managing users, granting and revoking privileges, and using transactions for data integrity. We will also include examples of advanced features such as VIEWS, FULL-TEXT SEARCH, and STORED PROCEDURES, which are essential for efficient data retrieval and management. Overall, the project is an extensive system for anyone looking to build and manage a University Management System using MySQL, providing step-by-step guidance and practical examples to ensure thorough understanding and successful implementation.

Step 1: Create a Database

Creating a database is the first step in setting up your University Management System. A database is a structured collection of data that is stored electronically. By creating a database named **UniversityManagement**, you are establishing the foundation where all information related to the university, such as students, courses, enrollments, professors, and departments, will be stored. This is crucial for organizing and managing the data efficiently, ensuring easy access and manipulation as needed.

```
CREATE DATABASE UniversityManagement;
```

Output:

```
Query OK, 1 row affected (0.00 sec)
```

The database was created successfully.

Step 2: Create a Table

Tables are the building blocks of a database. In this step, we create a table named Students, which will hold information about the students enrolled in the university. Each column in the table represents an attribute of the students, such as their ID, first name, last name, date of birth, and major. The **AUTO_INCREMENT** feature ensures that each student gets a unique ID automatically, while the **PRIMARY KEY** constraint helps uniquely identify each record in the table.

```
CREATE TABLE Students (
    StudentID INT AUTO_INCREMENT PRIMARY KEY,
    FirstName VARCHAR(50) NOT NULL,
    LastName VARCHAR(50) NOT NULL,
    DateOfBirth DATE,
    Major VARCHAR(100)
);
```

Output:

```
Query OK, 0 rows affected (0.02 sec)
```

The table was created successfully.

Step 3: Insert Records

Inserting records into a table is essential for populating the database with actual data.

Here, we insert information about three students into the **Students** table. Each **INSERT INTO** statement adds a new record with specified values for first name, last name, date of birth, and major. This step is crucial for testing the database and ensuring that it can store and retrieve data accurately.

```
INSERT INTO Students (FirstName, LastName, DateOfBirth, Major)
VALUES ('John', 'Doe', '2000-01-15', 'Computer Science'),
       ('Jane', 'Smith', '1999-05-30', 'Mechanical Engineering'),
       ('Alice', 'Johnson', '2001-07-20', 'Electrical Engineering');
```

Output:

```
Query OK, 3 rows affected (0.01 sec)
Records: 3 Duplicates: 0 Warnings: 0
```

Three records were successfully inserted into the **Students** table.

Step 4: Add a Comment in MySQL

Comments are used to document the code and explain its purpose, making it easier for others (and yourself) to understand. They do not affect the execution of the SQL queries. Here, a comment is added to describe the **Students** table, which helps anyone reading the code to understand the structure and function of the table.

```
-- This is a comment to describe the Students table
```

Output:

```
No output, as it's a comment.
```

We have successfully added a comment above. Comments are not displayed in the output.

Step 5: SELECT Statement in MySQL

The **SELECT** statement is used to query and retrieve data from a table. In this step, we use the **SELECT** statement to fetch all records from the **Students** table. This is useful for viewing the data that has been inserted into the table and verifying that it is stored correctly.

```
SELECT * FROM Students;
```

Output:

StudentID	FirstName	LastName	DateOfBirth	Major
1	John	Doe	2000-01-15	Computer Science
2	Jane	Smith	1999-05-30	Mechanical Engineering
3	Alice	Johnson	2001-07-20	Electrical Engineering

Table 12.1: *Output displaying the records of the Students table*

We fetched all the records from the **Students** table.

Step 6: `SELECT DISTINCT` Statement in MySQL

The **SELECT DISTINCT** statement is used to retrieve unique values from a column. In this step, we use **SELECT DISTINCT** to fetch unique values of the **Major** column from the **Students** table. This helps identify the different majors that students are enrolled in, without duplicate entries.

```
SELECT DISTINCT Major FROM Students;
```

Output:

Major
Computer Science
Mechanical Engineering
Electrical Engineering

***Table 12.2:** Output displaying unique values from a column*

Step 7: `WHERE` Clause in MySQL

The **WHERE** clause is used to filter records based on specific conditions. In this step, we use the **WHERE** clause to fetch records from the **Students** table where the Major is **'Computer Science'**. This helps in retrieving only the relevant data based on the specified criteria.

```
SELECT * FROM Students WHERE Major = 'Computer Science';
```

Output:

StudentID	FirstName	LastName	DateOfBirth	Major
1	John	Doe	2000-01-15	Computer Science

***Table 12.3:** Output displaying records based on a specific condition*

Step 8: MySQL Data Types

Understanding and choosing the right data types for columns is essential for efficient data storage and retrieval. In this step, we used **INT** for **StudentID**, **VARCHAR** for **FirstName**, **LastName**, and **Major**, and **DATE** for **DateOfBirth**. **INT** is used for storing integer values, **VARCHAR** is used for variable-length character strings, and **DATE** is used for date values.

Explanation: We used **INT** for **StudentID**, **VARCHAR** for names and major, and **DATE** for date of birth.

Step 9: `LIMIT` Clause

The **LIMIT** clause is used to specify the number of records to retrieve. In this step, we use **LIMIT** to fetch only two records from the **Students** table. This is useful for limiting the amount of data returned by a query, especially when dealing with large datasets.

```
SELECT * FROM Students LIMIT 2;
```

Output:

StudentID	FirstName	LastName	DateOfBirth	Major
1	John	Doe	2000-01-15	Computer Science
2	Jane	Smith	1999-05-30	Mechanical Engineering

Table 12.4: *Output displaying only two records using the LIMIT clause*

Step 10: Alias

An alias is a temporary name given to a table or column. It is useful for making complex queries more readable and easier to understand. In this query:

- **FirstName** is aliased as **'First Name'**
- **LastName** is aliased as **'Last Name'**

The resulting output will display the columns with their aliased names.

```
SELECT FirstName AS 'First Name', LastName AS 'Last Name' FROM
Students;
```

Output:

First Name	Last Name
John	Doe
Jane	Smith
Alice	Johnson

Table 12.5: *Output displaying the usage of alias*

Step 11: Auto Increment

In MySQL, the **AUTO_INCREMENT** attribute is used to automatically assign a unique integer value to a column. This is typically used for primary key columns to ensure that each row has a unique identifier.

Explanation: **StudentID** is set to **AUTO_INCREMENT**.

Step 12: Not Null Constraint

The **NOT NULL** constraint ensures that a column cannot have NULL values. In this step, **FirstName** and **LastName** are set to **NOT NULL**, meaning every student must have a first and last name. This helps in maintaining data completeness and accuracy.

Explanation: **FirstName** and **LastName** are set to NOT NULL.

Step 13: Primary Key Constraint

The **PRIMARY KEY** constraint uniquely identifies each record in a table. In this step, **StudentID** is designated as the **PRIMARY KEY**, ensuring that each student can be uniquely identified by their **ID**. This is essential for establishing relationships between tables and performing efficient queries.

Explanation: **StudentID** is the **PRIMARY KEY**.

Step 14: Foreign Key Constraint

Foreign keys are used to establish relationships between tables. In this step, we create two tables, **Courses** and **Enrollments**, and use foreign keys to link **StudentID** and **CourseID** in the **Enrollments** table to the respective IDs in the **Students** and **Courses** tables. This helps in maintaining referential integrity and ensuring that data across tables is consistent.

```
CREATE TABLE Courses (
    CourseID INT AUTO_INCREMENT PRIMARY KEY,
    CourseName VARCHAR(100) NOT NULL
);

CREATE TABLE Enrollments (
    EnrollmentID INT AUTO_INCREMENT PRIMARY KEY,
    StudentID INT,
    CourseID INT,
    FOREIGN KEY (StudentID) REFERENCES Students(StudentID),
    FOREIGN KEY (CourseID) REFERENCES Courses(CourseID)
);
```

Output:

```
Query OK, 0 rows affected (0.04 sec)

Query OK, 0 rows affected (0.05 sec)
```

We have successfully linked the two tables above.

When a foreign key constraint is defined, MySQL automatically enforces rules:

- **Insert/Update**: If you try to insert an invalid **StudentID** or **CourseID** (one that does not exist in the referenced tables), MySQL rejects the operation.
- **Delete**: If you attempt to delete a student or course that is referenced in **Enrollments**, MySQL blocks it by default (unless ON DELETE CASCADE is used to automatically delete related enrollments).

Foreign keys help maintain data integrity and define clear relationships between tables, making the database more reliable and structured.

Step 15: Unique Constraint

The **UNIQUE** constraint ensures that all values in a column are unique. In this step, we create a **Professors** table with a **UNIQUE** constraint on the **Email** column, ensuring that no two professors can have the same email address. This is important for maintaining data integrity and avoiding duplicate entries.

```
CREATE TABLE Professors (
    ProfessorID INT AUTO_INCREMENT PRIMARY KEY,
    Email VARCHAR(100) UNIQUE
);
```

Output:

```
Query OK, 0 rows affected (0.03 sec)
```

We have set a UNIQUE constraint on the **Email** column above in a new table, **Professors.**

Step 16: Default Constraint

The **DEFAULT** constraint sets a default value for a column if no value is specified during insertion. In this step, we create a **Departments** table with a **DEFAULT** constraint on the **CreatedAt** column, setting its default value to the current timestamp. This ensures that the **CreatedAt** field is automatically populated with the current date and time when a new department is created.

```
CREATE TABLE Departments (
    DepartmentID INT AUTO_INCREMENT PRIMARY KEY,
    DepartmentName VARCHAR(100) NOT NULL,
    CreatedAt TIMESTAMP DEFAULT CURRENT_TIMESTAMP
);
```

Output:

```
Query OK, 0 rows affected (0.03 sec)
```

Above, we have set a default constraint on a specific column.

Step 17: CHECK Constraint

The **CHECK** constraint ensures that all values in a column satisfy a specific condition. In this step, we create a Grades table with a **CHECK** constraint on the **Grade** column, allowing only the values **'A'**, **'B'**, **'C'**, **'D'**, and **'F'**. This helps maintain data integrity by restricting invalid grade entries.

```
CREATE TABLE Grades (
    GradeID INT AUTO_INCREMENT PRIMARY KEY,
    Grade CHAR(1) CHECK (Grade IN ('A', 'B', 'C', 'D', 'F'))
);
```

Output:

```
Query OK, 0 rows affected (0.03 sec)
```

Step 18: AND Operator

The AND operator is used to combine multiple conditions in a WHERE clause. In this step, we use the AND operator to fetch records from the **Students** table where the Major is **'Computer Science'** and the **DateOfBirth** is before **'2001-01-01'**. This helps in retrieving data that meets both conditions.

```
SELECT * FROM Students WHERE Major = 'Computer Science' AND
DateOfBirth < '2001-01-01';
```

Output:

StudentID	FirstName	LastName	DateOfBirth	Major
1	John	Doe	2000-01-15	Computer Science

Table 12.6: *Output displaying the usage of AND operator*

Step 19: OR Operator

The OR operator is used to combine multiple conditions in a WHERE clause, where any of the conditions can be true. In this step, we use the OR operator to fetch records from the **Students** table where the **Major** is either **'Computer Science'** or **'Electrical Engineering'**. This helps in retrieving data that meets at least one of the conditions.

```
SELECT * FROM Students WHERE Major = 'Computer Science' OR Major
= 'Electrical Engineering';
```

Output:

StudentID	FirstName	LastName	DateOfBirth	Major
1	John	Doe	2000-01-15	Computer Science
3	Alice	Johnson	2001-07-20	Electrical Engineering

Table 12.7: *Output displaying the usage of OR operator*

Step 20: NOT Operator

The NOT operator is used to negate a condition in a **WHERE** clause. In this step, we use the NOT operator to fetch records from the **Students** table where the **Major** is not **'Mechanical Engineering'**. This helps in retrieving data that does not meet the specified condition.

```
SELECT * FROM Students WHERE NOT Major = 'Mechanical Engineering';
```

Output:

StudentID	FirstName	LastName	DateOfBirth	Major
1	John	Doe	2000-01-15	Computer Science
3	Alice	Johnson	2001-07-20	Electrical Engineering

Table 12.8: *Output displaying the usage of NOT operator*

Step 21: IN Operator

The **IN** operator is used to specify multiple values in a **WHERE** clause. In this step, we use the IN operator to fetch records from the **Students** table where the **Major** is either **'Computer Science'** or **'Electrical Engineering'**. This helps in simplifying the query when checking for multiple values.

```
SELECT * FROM Students WHERE Major IN ('Computer Science',
'Electrical Engineering');
```

Output:

StudentID	FirstName	LastName	DateOfBirth	Major
1	John	Doe	2000-01-15	Computer Science
3	Alice	Johnson	2001-07-20	Electrical Engineering

Table 12.9: *Output displaying the usage of IN operator*

Step 22: LIKE Operator

The **LIKE** operator is used for pattern matching in a **WHERE** clause. In this step, we use the **LIKE** operator to fetch records from the **Students** table where the **FirstName** starts with the letter '**J**'. This helps in retrieving data based on specific patterns.

```
SELECT * FROM Students WHERE FirstName LIKE 'J%';
```

Output:

StudentID	FirstName	LastName	DateOfBirth	Major
1	John	Doe	2000-01-15	Computer Science
2	Jane	Smith	1999-05-30	Mechanical Engineering

Table 12.10: *Output displaying the usage of LIKE operator*

Step 23: BETWEEN Operator

The **BETWEEN** operator is used to filter records within a range of values. In this step, we use the BETWEEN operator to fetch records from the **Students** table where the **DateOfBirth** is between **'2000-01-01'** and **'2001-12-31'**. This helps in retrieving data within a specific range.

```
SELECT * FROM Students WHERE DateOfBirth BETWEEN '2000-01-01' AND
'2001-12-31';
```

Output:

StudentID	FirstName	LastName	DateOfBirth	Major
1	John	Doe	2000-01-15	Computer Science
3	Alice	Johnson	2001-07-20	Electrical Engineering

Table 12.11: *Output displaying the usage of BETWEEN operator*

Step 24: String Built-in Functions

String functions are used to manipulate string values. In this step, we use the `UPPER` and **`LOWER`** functions to convert the **`FirstName`** to uppercase and the **`LastName`** to lowercase. This helps in formatting and standardizing string data.

```
SELECT UPPER(FirstName), LOWER(LastName) FROM Students;
```

Output:

UPPER(FirstName)	LOWER(LastName)
JOHN	doe
JANE	smith
ALICE	johnson

Table 12.12: *Output displaying the usage of UPPER() and LOWER() functions*

Step 25: Numeric Built-in Functions

Numeric functions are used to perform calculations on numeric data. In this step, we use the **`AVG`**, **`MAX`**, and **`MIN`** functions to calculate the average, maximum, and minimum values of the **`StudentID`** column. This helps in performing statistical analysis on numeric data.

```
SELECT AVG(StudentID), MAX(StudentID), MIN(StudentID) FROM
Students;
```

Output:

AVG(StudentID)	MAX(StudentID)	MIN(StudentID)
2.0	3	1

Table 12.13: *Output displaying the usage of numeric functions*

Step 26: Date Built-in Functions

Date functions are used to manipulate and retrieve information from date values. In this step, we use the **`YEAR`** function to extract the year part of the **`DateOfBirth`** column. This helps in analyzing and grouping data based on the year.

```
SELECT YEAR(DateOfBirth) AS BirthYear FROM Students;
```

Output:

BirthYear
2000
1999
2001

Table 12.14: *Output displaying the usage of date functions*

Step 27: Aggregate Functions

Aggregate functions are used to perform calculations on multiple values and return a single value. In this step, we use the **COUNT** and **AVG** functions to count the number of records and calculate the average value of the **StudentID** column. This helps in summarizing and analyzing data.

```
SELECT COUNT(*), AVG(StudentID) FROM Students;
```

Output:

COUNT(*)	AVG(StudentID)
3	2.0

Table 12.15: *Output displaying the usage of aggregate functions*

Step 28: ORDER BY Statement

The **ORDER BY** statement is used to sort the result set by one or more columns. In this step, we use the **ORDER BY** statement to sort the records in the **Students** table by the **LastName** column in ascending order. This helps in organizing and displaying data in a specific order.

```
SELECT * FROM Students ORDER BY LastName ASC;
```

Output:

StudentID	FirstName	LastName	DateOfBirth	Major
1	John	Doe	2000 01-15	Computer Science
3	Alice	Johnson	2001-07-20	Electrical Engineering
2	Jane	Smith	1999-05-30	Mechanical Engineering

Table 12.16: *Output displaying the usage of ORDER BY statement*

Step 29: Case Statement

The CASE statement is used to create conditional logic in SQL queries. In this step, we use the CASE statement to create a new column **ShortMajor** that abbreviates the **Major** values. This helps in simplifying and standardizing the display of major names.

```
SELECT StudentID, Major,
CASE
    WHEN Major = 'Computer Science' THEN 'CS'
    WHEN Major = 'Mechanical Engineering' THEN 'ME'
    ELSE 'EE'
END AS ShortMajor
FROM Students;
```

Output:

StudentID	Major	ShortMajor
1	Computer Science	CS
2	Mechanical Engineering	ME
3	Electrical Engineering	EE

Table 12.17: *Output displaying the usage of CASE statement*

This query retrieves student information from the **Students** table and transforms the **Major** field into abbreviated codes using a **CASE** expression.

The **CASE** statement works like a series of IF-THEN-ELSE conditions:

- When a student's major is **'Computer Science'**, it returns '**CS**'
- When a student's major is **'Mechanical Engineering'**, it returns '**ME**'
- For all other majors (the **ELSE** case), it returns '**EE**' (presumably standing for Electrical Engineering as a default).

Step 30: UPDATE Statement

The UPDATE statement is used to modify existing records in a table. In this step, we use the UPDATE statement to change the **Major** of the student with **StudentID 1** to **'Software Engineering'**. This helps in updating and maintaining accurate data.

```
UPDATE Students SET Major = 'Software Engineering' WHERE
StudentID = 1;
```

Output:

```
Query OK, 1 row affected (0.01 sec)
Rows matched: 1  Changed: 1  Warnings: 0
```

Step 31: INNER Joins

INNER JOIN is used to combine rows from two or more tables based on a related column between them. In this step, we use **INNER JOIN** to fetch the first names of students and the names of the courses they are enrolled in. This helps in retrieving related data from multiple tables.

```
SELECT Students.FirstName, Courses.CourseName
FROM Enrollments
INNER JOIN Students ON Enrollments.StudentID = Students.StudentID
INNER JOIN Courses ON Enrollments.CourseID = Courses.CourseID;
```

Output: No data to display since no records have been inserted into the **`Enrollments`** table yet.

The above query retrieves a list of student names along with the courses they are enrolled in by joining three tables together. The query:

- Uses **`INNER JOIN`**, so only returns records where matches exist in all tables
- Effectively "flattens" the relational data into a simple student-course list
- The order of joins does not matter in this case (MySQL optimizer handles it)

Here are the JOIN operations performed:

- **First `INNER JOIN`:**
  - Joins Enrollments with **`Students`** on matching **`StudentID`** values
  - This links each enrollment record to the corresponding student's details
- **Second INNER JOIN:**
  - Joins the result with **`Courses`** on matching **`CourseID`** values
  - This adds the course name information to each enrollment

Step 32: `LEFT` Join

`LEFT JOIN` is used to fetch all records from the left table and the matching records from the right table. If no match is found, **`NULL`** values are returned for columns from the right table. In this step, we use **`LEFT JOIN`** to fetch the first names of students and the names of the courses they are enrolled in, even if there are no matching records in the right table. This helps in retrieving all data from the left table along with any related data from the right table.

```
SELECT Students.FirstName, Courses.CourseName
FROM Students
LEFT JOIN Enrollments ON Students.StudentID = Enrollments.StudentID
LEFT JOIN Courses ON Enrollments.CourseID = Courses.CourseID;
```

Output: No data to display since no records have been inserted into the **`Enrollments`** table yet.

The above query retrieves a comprehensive list of all students and their enrolled courses, including students who are not enrolled in any courses.

The following are the JOIN Operations:

- **First `LEFT JOIN`:**
  - Keeps ALL records from the **`Students`** table
  - Adds matching records from **`Enrollments`** (if they exist)
  - If no enrollment, the **`Enrollments`** columns will be **`NULL`**
- **Second `LEFT JOIN`:**
  - Takes previous results (students + enrollments)
  - Adds matching course names (if enrollment exists)
  - If no enrollment, the Courses columns will be **`NULL`**

Step 33: `RIGHT` Join

`RIGHT JOIN` is used to fetch all records from the right table and the matching records from the left table. If no match is found, **`NULL`** values are returned for columns from the left table. In this step, we use **`RIGHT JOIN`** to fetch the first names of students and the names of the courses they are enrolled in, even if there are no matching records in the left table. This helps in retrieving all data from the right table along with any related data from the left table.

```
SELECT Students.FirstName, Courses.CourseName
FROM Students
RIGHT JOIN Enrollments ON Students.StudentID = Enrollments.StudentID
RIGHT JOIN Courses ON Enrollments.CourseID = Courses.CourseID;
```

Output: No data to display since no records have been inserted into the **`Enrollments`** table yet.

Step 34: `CROSS` Join

`CROSS JOIN` is used to return the Cartesian product of two tables, meaning every row from the first table is combined with every row from the second table. In this step, we use **`CROSS JOIN`** to fetch the first names of students and the names of the courses, producing all possible combinations of students and courses. This is useful for generating combinations of records for analysis or testing purposes.

```
SELECT Students.FirstName, Courses.CourseName
FROM Students
CROSS JOIN Courses;
```

Output: No data to display since no records have been inserted into the **`Courses`** table yet.

Step 35: `FULL` Join

`FULL JOIN` is used to fetch all records when there is a match in either left (**`Students`**) or right (**`Courses`**) table records. It returns **`NULL`** values for columns of the table where there is no match. Since MySQL does not support the **FULL JOIN** directly, we simulate it using a combination of **LEFT JOIN, UNION**, and **RIGHT JOIN**. In this step, we use this simulated **FULL JOIN** to fetch the first names of students and the names of the courses they are enrolled in.

```
SELECT Students.FirstName, Courses.CourseName
FROM Students
LEFT JOIN Enrollments ON Students.StudentID = Enrollments.
StudentID
LEFT JOIN Courses ON Enrollments.CourseID = Courses.CourseID
UNION
SELECT Students.FirstName, Courses.CourseName
FROM Students
RIGHT JOIN Enrollments ON Students.StudentID = Enrollments.
StudentID
RIGHT JOIN Courses ON Enrollments.CourseID = Courses.CourseID;
```

Output: No data to display since no records have been inserted into the **Enrollments** and **Courses** tables yet.

The above query combines two different perspectives of the student-course relationship using **UNION** to create a comprehensive report.

The 1st part before **UNION** retrieves all students and any courses they are enrolled in. If a student is not enrolled in any course, their name will still appear, but the course name will be **NULL**.

The 2nd part after **UNION** retrieves all courses and the students enrolled in them. If a course has no students enrolled, it will still appear, but the student name will be **NULL**.

Step 36: Create Indexes

Indexes are used to improve the speed of data retrieval operations on a table at the cost of additional storage space and maintenance during write operations. In this step, we create an index named **idx_major** on the **Major** column of the **Students** table. This helps in speeding up queries that filter or sort data based on the **Major** column.

```
CREATE INDEX idx_major ON Students(Major);
```

Output:

```
Query OK, 0 rows affected (0.02 sec)
```

Step 37: Show Indexes

The **SHOW INDEX** statement is used to display information about indexes on a table. In this step, we use **SHOW INDEX** to retrieve details about the indexes on the **Students** table. This helps in understanding the structure and usage of indexes in the table.

```
SHOW INDEXES FROM Students;
```

Output:

Table	Non_unique	Key_name	Seq_in_index	Column_name	Collation	Cardinality	Sub_part	Packed	Null	Index_type	Comment	Index_comment	Visible	Expression
Students	0	PRIMARY	1	StudentID	A	3	NULL	NULL		BTREE			YES	NULL
Students	1	idx_major	1	Major	A	3	NULL	NULL	YES	BTREE			YES	NULL

Table 12.18: *Output displaying the usage of the INDEX statement*

Step 38: Unique Index

A unique index ensures that the values in the indexed column(s) are unique. In this step, we create a unique index named **idx_email** on the **Email** column of the **Professors** table. This ensures that no two professors can have the same email address, maintaining data integrity and avoiding duplicate entries.

```
CREATE UNIQUE INDEX idx_email ON Professors(Email);
```

Output:

```
Query OK, 0 rows affected (0.02 sec)
Records: 0 Duplicates: 0 Warnings: 0
```

Step 39: Clustered Index

A clustered index determines the physical order of data in a table. MySQL automatically creates a clustered index on the **PRIMARY KEY**. This step explains that the **StudentID** column, which is the primary key of the **Students** table, automatically serves as the clustered index, ensuring that the data is physically stored in the order of **StudentID**.

Explanation: MySQL automatically creates a clustered index on the **PRIMARY KEY**.

Step 40: Create Users

Creating users in MySQL allows for better database security and access control. In this step, we create a new user named **dbuser** with the password '**password**'. This user can later be granted specific privileges to access and manipulate the database.

```
CREATE USER 'dbuser'@'localhost' IDENTIFIED BY 'password';
```

Output:

```
Query OK, 0 rows affected (0.02 sec)
```

Step 41: Show Users

The **SELECT** statement is used to display the list of users in the MySQL server. In this step, we use a query to fetch the usernames from the **mysql.user** table. This helps in verifying the creation and existence of database users.

```
SELECT User FROM mysql.user;
```

Output:

User
root
dbuser

***Table 12.19:** Output displaying the list of users*

Step 42: Grant Privileges

Granting privileges allows a user to perform specific actions on the database. In this step, we grant all privileges on the **UniversityManagement** database to the user **dbuser**. This allows **dbuser** to perform any action within the specified database, ensuring they have the necessary permissions.

```
GRANT ALL PRIVILEGES ON UniversityManagement.* TO 'dbuser'@'
localhost';
```

Output:

```
Query OK, 0 rows affected (0.01 sec)
```

Step 43: Show Privileges

The **SHOW GRANTS** statement is used to display the privileges granted to a user. In this step, we use the **SHOW GRANTS** statement to fetch the privileges of the user **dbuser**. This helps in verifying the permissions assigned to the user.

```
SHOW GRANTS FOR 'dbuser'@'localhost';
```

Output:

Grants for dbuser@localhost
GRANT USAGE ON . TO 'dbuser'@'localhost'
GRANT ALL PRIVILEGES ON UniversityManagement.* TO 'dbuser'@'localhost'

***Table 12.20:** Output displaying the grants for a user*

Step 44: Revoke Privileges

Revoking privileges removes specific permissions from a user. In this step, we revoke all privileges on the **UniversityManagement** database from the user **dbuser**. This ensures that the user no longer has the ability to perform actions within the specified database.

```
REVOKE ALL PRIVILEGES ON UniversityManagement.* FROM
'dbuser'@'localhost';
```

Output:

```
Query OK, 0 rows affected (0.01 sec)
```

Step 45: Triggers

Triggers are special procedures that are automatically executed in response to certain events on a table. In this step, we create a trigger named **before_insert_students** that automatically converts the **FirstName** of a student to uppercase before inserting a new record into the **Students** table. This helps in maintaining data consistency and ensuring that names are stored in a standardized format.

```
CREATE TRIGGER before_insert_students
BEFORE INSERT ON Students
FOR EACH ROW
SET NEW.FirstName = UPPER(NEW.FirstName);
```

Output:

```
Query OK, 0 rows affected (0.04 sec)
```

Step 46: Views

Views are virtual tables created by a query. They allow for simplified querying and abstraction of complex queries. In this step, we create a view named **CS_Students** that selects the first names and last names of students enrolled in the Computer Science major. This helps in creating a focused view of specific data for easier access and analysis.

```
CREATE VIEW CS_Students AS
SELECT FirstName, LastName
FROM Students
WHERE Major = 'Computer Science';
```

Output:

```
Query OK, 0 rows affected (0.01 sec)
```

Step 47: Regular Expressions

Regular expressions are used for pattern matching in string data. In this step, we use a regular expression to fetch records from the **Students** table where the **FirstName** starts with the letter '**A**'. This is useful for retrieving data that matches specific patterns.

```
SELECT * FROM Students WHERE FirstName REGEXP '^A';
```

Output:

StudentID	FirstName	LastName	DateOfBirth	Major
3	Alice	Johnson	2001-07-20	Electrical Engineering

Table 12.21: *Output displaying the uage of pattern matching*

Step 48: Full-Text Search

Full-text search allows for searching text-based data in a more flexible way than the LIKE operator. In this step, we create an **Articles** table and perform a full-text search to find articles that mention '**MySQL**'. This helps in performing advanced text searches within the content.

```
CREATE TABLE Articles (
    ArticleID INT AUTO_INCREMENT PRIMARY KEY,
    Title VARCHAR(200),
    Content TEXT,
    FULLTEXT(Title, Content)
);

INSERT INTO Articles (Title, Content) VALUES ('MySQL Tutorial',
'This is a tutorial on MySQL');

SELECT * FROM Articles WHERE MATCH (Title, Content) AGAINST
('MySQL');
```

Output:

ArticleID	Title	Content
1	MySQL Tutorial	This is a tutorial on MySQL

Table 12.22: *Output displaying how to search text based data*

Step 49: Transactions

Transactions are used to ensure that a series of SQL operations are executed as a single unit, maintaining data integrity. In this step, we use a transaction to update the Major of one student and delete another student. This ensures that either both operations are successful or neither is applied.

```
START TRANSACTION;
UPDATE Students SET Major = 'Data Science' WHERE StudentID = 2;
DELETE FROM Students WHERE StudentID = 3;
COMMIT;
```

Output:

```
Query OK, 1 row affected (0.01 sec)
Query OK, 1 row affected (0.01 sec)
```

Step 50: Having Clause

The **HAVING** clause is used to filter groups based on a specified condition, often used with **GROUP BY**. In this step, we use the **HAVING** clause to find majors with more than one student. This helps in filtering groups of data based on specific criteria.

```
SELECT Major, COUNT(*) as NumStudents
FROM Students
GROUP BY Major
HAVING COUNT(*) > 1;
```

Output: No data to display as no major has more than one student after the deletion in the transaction.

Step 51: Group By Clause

The **GROUP BY** clause is used to group rows that have the same values in specified columns into summary rows. In this step, we use **GROUP BY** to count the number of students in each major. This helps in summarizing and analyzing data based on groups.

```
SELECT Major, COUNT(*) as NumStudents
FROM Students
GROUP BY Major;
```

Output:

Major	NumStudents
Computer Science	1
Data Science	1

Table 12.23: *Output displaying the usage of GROUP BY Clause*

Step 52: Stored Procedures

Stored procedures are reusable code that can be executed with a single call. In this step, we create a stored procedure to retrieve all students from a specific major. This helps in encapsulating complex queries and reusing them efficiently.

Let's create a stored procedure to retrieve all students from a specific major:

```
DELIMITER //
CREATE PROCEDURE GetStudentsByMajor(IN majorName VARCHAR(100))
BEGIN
    SELECT * FROM Students WHERE Major = majorName;
END //
DELIMITER ;
```

You can call the stored procedure as follows:

```
CALL GetStudentsByMajor('Computer Science');
```

Output:

StudentID	FirstName	LastName	DateOfBirth	Major
1	John	Doe	2000-01-15	Computer Science

Table 12.24: *Output displaying the usage of* STORED PROCEDURES

This completes the capstone project, which covers a wide range of MySQL topics. Each step provides practical examples and outputs to ensure a thorough understanding of database management and SQL operations.

Conclusion

This project serves as a comprehensive and practical guide to building a robust University Management System using MySQL. It equips users with essential knowledge, starting from database creation and basic SQL operations to advanced functionalities such as constraints, joins, triggers, and complex query handling. By incorporating real-time examples and focusing on data manipulation, retrieval techniques, and user management, the system ensures reliability and efficiency.

The inclusion of advanced features such as transactions, views, and stored procedures further enhances its usability for dynamic data environments. This guide is an invaluable resource for mastering MySQL and implementing a well-rounded management system effectively.

Index

A

B

C

D

E

V

W